THE
HISTORY OF
THAILAND

ADVISORY BOARD

THE
HISTORY OF
THAILAND

Patit Paban Mishra

The Greenwood Histories of the Modern Nations
Frank W. Thackeray and John E. Findling, Series Editors

 GREENWOOD

AN IMPRINT OF ABC-CLIO, LLC
Santa Barbara, California • Denver, Colorado • Oxford, England

Copyright 2010 by Patit Paban Mishra

Library of Congress Cataloging-in-Publication Data

Mishra, Patit Paban.

  The history of Thailand / Patit Paban Mishra.
    p. cm. — (The Greenwood histories of the modern nations)
  Includes bibliographical references and index.
    ISBN 978-0-313-34091-8 (hard copy : alk. paper) — ISBN 978-1-57356-791-6 (ebook)
1. Thailand—History. I. Title.
DS571.M57   2010
959.3—dc22   2010020760

ISBN: 978-0-313-34091-8
EISBN: 978-1-57356-791-6

14 13 12 11 10   1 2 3 4 5

This book is also available on the World Wide Web as an eBook.
Visit www.abc-clio.com for details.

Greenwood
An Imprint of ABC-CLIO, LLC

ABC-CLIO, LLC
130 Cremona Drive, P.O. Box 1911
Santa Barbara, California 93116-1911

This book is printed on acid-free paper ∞

Manufactured in the United States of America

Contents

Series Foreword

The Greenwood Histories of the Modern Nations series is intended to provide students and interested laypeople with up-to-date, concise, and analytical histories of many of the nations of the contemporary world. Not since the 1960s has there been a systematic attempt to publish a series of national histories, and as series advisors, we believe that this series will prove to be a valuable contribution to our understanding of other countries in our increasingly interdependent world.

Some 40 years ago, at the end of the 1960s, the Cold War was an accepted reality of global politics. The process of decolonization was still in progress, the idea of a unified Europe with a single currency was unheard of, the United States was mired in a war in Vietnam, and the economic boom in Asia was still years in the future. Richard Nixon was president of the United States, Mao Tse-tung (not yet Mao Zedong) ruled China, Leonid Brezhnev guided the Soviet Union, and Harold Wilson was prime minister of the United Kingdom. Authoritarian dictators still controlled most of Latin America, the Middle East was reeling in the wake of the Six-Day War, and Shah Mohammad Reza Pahlavi was at the height of his power in Iran.

Since then, the Cold War has ended; the Soviet Union has vanished, leaving 15 independent republics in its wake; the advent of the computer age has radically transformed global communications; the rising demand for oil makes the Middle East still a dangerous flashpoint; and the rise of new economic powers such as the People's Republic of China and India threatens to bring about a new world order. All of these developments have had a dramatic impact on the recent history of every nation of the world.

For this series, which was launched in 1998, we first selected nations whose political, economic, and sociocultural affairs marked them as among the most important of our time. For each nation, we found an author who was recognized as a specialist in the history of that nation. These authors worked cooperatively with us and with Greenwood Press to produce volumes that reflected current research on their nations and that were interesting and informative to their readers. In the first decade of the series, more than 40 volumes were published, and as of 2008, some are moving into second editions.

The success of the series has encouraged us to broaden our scope to include additional nations, whose histories have had significant effects on their regions, if not on the entire world. In addition, geopolitical changes have elevated other nations into positions of greater importance in world affairs, and so we have chosen to include them in this series as well. The importance of a series such as this cannot be underestimated. As a superpower whose influence is felt all over the world, the United States can claim a "special" relationship with almost every other nation. Yet many Americans know very little about the histories of nations with which the United States relates. How did they get to be the way they are? What kind of political systems have evolved there? What kind of influence do they have on their own regions? What are the dominant political, religious, and cultural forces that move their leaders? These and many other questions are answered in the volumes of this series.

The authors who contribute to this series write comprehensive histories of their nations, dating back, in some instances, to prehistoric times. Each of them, however, has devoted a significant portion of their book to events of the past 40 years because the modern era has contributed the most to contemporary issues that have an impact on U.S. policy. Authors make every effort to be as up-to-date as possible so that readers can benefit from discussion and analysis of recent events.

In addition to the historical narrative, each volume contains an introductory chapter giving an overview of that country's geography, political institutions, economic structure, and cultural attributes. This is meant to give readers a snapshot of the nation as it exists in the contemporary world. Each history also includes supplementary information following the narrative, which may include a time line that represents a succinct chronology of the nation's historical evolution, biographical sketches of the nation's most important historical figures, and a glossary of important terms or concepts that are usually expressed in languages other than English. Finally, each author prepares a comprehensive bibliography for readers who wish to pursue the subject further.

Readers of these volumes will find them fascinating and well written. More importantly, they will come away with a better understanding of the contemporary world and the nations that compose it. As series advisors, we hope that this series will contribute to a heightened sense of global understanding as we move through the early years of the twenty-first century.

Frank W. Thackeray and John E. Findling
Indiana University Southeast

Preface

Thailand is a fascinating country with a very rich civilization. It was in Thailand that the world's first rice cultivator had the unique opportunity to plough the field. Even today it is the world's leading exporter of rice. Home to one of the earliest iron and bronze cultures, it may be regarded as a "cradle of civilization." Though not recognized as one of the world's pristine centers of civilizations like that of Egypt, Mesoamerica, Mesopotamia or China, it was one of those early centers of civilizing human development.

Remaining free from colonial rule, Thailand was one of those countries that was able to become special and unique in its own way. Today, Thailand is a mosaic of ethnic, linguistic, cultural, historical, and physical features. External influences from Indian, Chinese, Islamic, and European civilizations have left deep imprints on the indigenous culture of Thailand.

Although Thailand has received a transfusion of culture from other civilizations, it has added to that culture its own nuances and shades of meaning through centuries. As a result, the country has not lost its idiom. It has maintained its separate identity and independence in spite of invasion from neighboring regions and the expansion of colonialism in Southeast Asia. The name "Siam" was in vogue officially from 1855 to 1939 and again between 1946 and 1949. It is Siam that the world sees in performances of the musical *The King and I*. Since 1949 the region has been called Thailand. In the language of Thai, the official name of the country is *Ratchaanachak Thai* (Kingdom of Thailand).

This book is meant for high school and undergraduate students, as well as for general readers interested in learning about Thailand. It is divided into 11 chapters along with an introduction, chronology of events, biographical entries on key figures, a bibliography, glossary, and selected pictures and maps. Although the book is written in India, the author has spent long periods in Thailand at different times.

This personal experience has facilitated the research that went into writing the book, including consulting indigenous source materials, undertaking field work inside of Thailand, and for expressing the feelings most visitors have for this very beautiful country. The author has followed a chronological pattern in delineating the subject. Unlike a research work, it is not crammed with source citations. The author has tried his best to consult the latest materials available on the subject and write in an objective matter.

The author is indebted to his family members, Professor Andrew Waskey, Mr. Subaramya Nambiaruran and to Ms. Kaitlin Ciarmiello for their ungrudging help and cooperation.

Timeline of Historical Events

BEFORE COMMON ERA (B.C.E.)

500,000	Ordinary stone tools used
10,000	Domestication of plants as indicted by findings from Spirit Caves
10,000 to 7,000	Use of nuts, pepper, cucumber and beans as evident from findings of the Spirit Cave
5,000	Beginning of rice cultivation. The excavations at Non Nok Tha yield rice chaff
3600 to 1000	Settlement in Ban Chiang, a "cradle of civilization"
2500	Metal works of bronze and iron
2100	Settlement at Ban Non Wat
1500	Copper site of Non Pa Wai
1000	Ban Prasat pottery at Prasat Hin Phanom Wan

Third Century B.C.E.   The Buddhist missionary is sent by Indian King
                        Asoka (273–232 B.C.E.)

COMMON ERA (C.E.)

First Century C.E.   Strong evidence of Indo–Thai trading relationship

500   Mon Kingdom of Dvaravti in Thailand with capital
                        at Nakhon Pathom; advent of Buddhism; spread of
                        Indian culture

Mid-Sixth Century   Southern Thailand comes under domain of the
                        Kambuja Kingdom

Late Seventh Century   Establishment of Haripunjaya in Lamphun region of
                        northern Thailand; extension of political influence
                        of Sri Vijaya on Dvaravati; capital city is Chaiya, in
                        southern Thailand

802   The Khmer empire is established by King
                        Jayavarman (802–834) in Cambodia; Thailand comes
                        under its sway

1238   First independent Thai state called Sukhothai
                        founded by Sri Indraditya (r. 1238–1270); the
                        Sukhohthai period continues until 1350

1239   Rama Khamheng (1239–1298), Thailand's best-
                        known king and creator of Thai script, begins his
                        reign during the Golden Period

1254   Waves of Thai migrants move to Sukhothai from
                        Yunnan after Mongol conquest

1259   Lanna (Lan Na) Kingdom founded by Prince
                        Mengrai (1239–1317); it continues until 1558

1350   Rama Tibodi I (1312–1369) founds the Kingdom of
                        Ayudhya in central Thailand; the laws promulgated
                        by Rama Tibodi continue in principle for six centu-
                        ries; a combination of indigenous practices and
                        Indian legal concepts, this legal system exhibited
                        characteristics of the society of that time

1431   The Khmer capital Angkor is captured by Ayudhya
                        King Borommaracha II (r. 1424–1448)

1511	Arrival of Portuguese envoy Duarte Fernandez to carry on trade
1569	Fall of Ayudhya to the Burmese after a prolonged siege
1590–1605	Reign of King Naresuan, the Great; the Burmese are ousted from Ayudhya; trading agreement is formed with the Dutch
1656	King Narai the Great ascends the throne, ruling for 32 years, concluding a trading agreement with European powers and modernizing the Kingdom
1668	Arrival of Islamic missionaries
1685	The Jesuits establish a mission in Thailand
1697	Cambodia acknowledges Thai sovereignty
1767–1782	Reign of Phya Thaksin, liberator of Thailand after the Burmese devastation of Ayudhya in April 1767; a new capital at Thonburi; establishes a puppet ruler in Cambodia in 1771 and after five years takes over Chiang Mai; occupation of Vientiane; famous Emerald Buddha is returned in 1779
1782	Beginning of Chakri dynasty, which still exists today; new capital at Bangkok built by King Rama I; the sultans of Malay Peninsula like Kedah, Kelantan, and Trenggannu acknowledge the suzerainty of the Thai monarch; flowering of Thai literature; the *Ramakien* (Thai version of the Indian epic the *Ramayana*) is written
1785	Renewed attacks by the Burmese are repelled
1809–1824	Reign of Rama II
1822	First trade treaty with Britain
1833	Treaty of friendship and commerce with the United Sates; a British Indian mission demands Siam open up for more free trade
1851	Mongkut ascends the throne in 1851 as Rama IV; signing of unequal treaties with European powers

1868	Accession of Rama V, commonly known as Chulalongkorn; initiates an era of reforms of Thai society and economy
1874	Edict abolishing slavery; complete abolition after 31 years
1893	Franco–Siamese treaty of October 3, 1893, the French protectorate over Laos, Thailand gives up its claim on the territories of the left bank of the Mekong River covering most of the area of modern Laos
1896	First railroad opens from Bangkok to Ayudhya
1904	Anglo–French treaty is signed; Thailand gives up Champassak and three years afterward Sayaboury provinces to the French
1909	Anglo-Thai Convention of 1909; Thailand gives up its suzerain rights over the four southern states of the Malay Peninsula: Kedah, Perlis, Kelantan, and Trengganu; Britain recognizes the Thai control over the Muslim-dominated Pattani province
1910	Chulalongkorn dies on October 23, now observed as a national holiday; reign of King Rama VI, Vajiravudh, begins
1912	Abortive coup attempt
1916	Foundation of Chulalongkorn University
1917	Thailand joins the Allied cause in the First World War on July 22
1919	Thailand participates in Paris Peace Conference and becomes a member of the League of Nations
1925	Accession of King Prajadhipok (Rama VII)
1927	*Khana Rasdr* (People's Party) comes into existence
1929	Financial crisis in Thailand due to worldwide depression
1930	Communist Party of Siam is formed
1932	Revolution on June 24 converts the absolute monarchy to a constitutional one; a new constitution is

established on December 10; Monapahorn Nitithada (1884–1948) of the *Khana Rasdr* becomes the first prime minister

1934   Foundation of Thammasat University

1935   Reign of Rama VIII begins

1938   Appointment of Phibul Songkhran as premier; he holds the post until 1944 and again from 1948 to 1957

1939   World War II begins on September 3; Thailand declares neutrality

1941   Japan invades Thailand on December 8; pact with Japan; Thailand declares war against the Allies; Japan claims it will help in getting back Thai territories lost to Britain

1943   Pridi Panomyong forms an underground resistance movement against the Japanese; free Thai Movement in the United States is set up by ambassador Seni Pramoj

1946   Accession of King Bhumibol Adulyadej, Rama IX, Thailand's longest-reigning monarch

1948   Islamic insurgency in southern Thailand

1949   A new permanent constitution is created

1950   Thailand sends troops to Korea

1951   Communist Party of Thailand sends cadres to rural areas

1954   Thailand joins Southeast Asian Treaty Organization

1957   Army chief Sarit Thanarat (1909–1963) seizes power by a coup

1958   Thanom Kittikachorn becomes premier in January after elections; Sarit's second coup in October; his economic policies result in American and Japanese investment and the rise of a new wealthy class due to land speculation and sustained economic growth of 5 percent per year

1961	Thailand forms the Association of Southeast Asia (ASA) along with Malaysia and the Philippines
1962	Rusk–Thanat Agreement of 1962 is signed, representing American guarantee of Thai security
1963	Thanom A. Kittikhachon (1911–2004) is appointed premier by the king; close collaboration with the United States in Vietnam War
1964	Bombing of North Vietnam by the United States from Thai bases
1965	Communist insurgency in northeastern Thailand; Thai combat units in South Vietnam
1967	Formation of ASEAN (Association of Southeast Asian Nations)
1968	Promulgation of a new constitution with a Senate and a House of Representatives
1969	In the February 1969 elections, Thanom's United Thai People's Party secures 75 seats out of 219 in the lower house, giving them the largest representation among the thirteen parties
1971	Military rule imposed
1972	Agitation by the National Student Center of Thailand, increased communist insurgency in the northern provinces
1973	Student unrest and mass demonstrations leads to the end of Thanom's regime in October
1974	Promulgation of new constitution; increased social unrest and politicization of the nation along liberal and conservative lines; September demonstration in Bangkok by peasants, workers, monks, and students; tenth constitution is created in October
1975	The end of war in Vietnam; unification of Vietnam; proliferation of bars, massage parlors, and hotels for entertainment of American military personnel; the nation begins to face problems arising out of exodus of refugees from Laos and Vietnam; Seni Pramoj,

	leader of the Democratic Party, heads a coalition government; Seni's brother Kukrti succeeds him
1976	Massacre at Thammasat University by right-wing activists and police on October 6; return of military rule; General Thanin Kraivixien is installed as the premier; another military coup and General Kriangsak Chomanan becomes premier
1978	Diplomatic relations are restored with Vietnam
1979	China declares that it will no longer help the Thai communists
1980	General Prem Tinsulanonda's premiership begins; follows economic policy leading to Thailand's economic growth in the 1980s
1981	The abortive coup of "Young Turks" is led by General San Chipatima
1982	Offensive against drug lord Khun Sa, who escapes to Myanmar; threat from the communist insurgency in northeastern Thailand
1983	Parliamentary elections and formation of government by Prem
1984	Devaluation of Thai currency, baht, by 14.8 percent
1985	Thai–Vietnamese border clashes
1988	Chatichai Choonhavan becomes premier after elections
1989	Damage in Chumphon and Ranong provinces due to Typhoon Gay
1991	17th military coup since 1932; Anand Panyarachun, a civilian, becomes the premier
1992	Chuan Leekpai, leader of the Democratic Party, becomes Premier after the September elections
1994	Thai culture promotion year
1995	Constitution Drafting Assembly is formed; Banharn Silparcha of the Thai Nation Party is the new Premier

1996   New Aspiration Party under leadership of Chavalit
                       Yongchaiyudh emerges victorious after resignation
                       of Banharn

1997   Beginning of Economic Crisis

1998   Thaksin Shinawatra establishes *Thai Rak Thai* (Thai
                       love Thai) Party; controversial antidrug drive begins

2001   Thaksin Shinawatra (1949–) becomes prime minister

2003   Controversial "war against drugs" continues

2004   Thailand becomes world's leading exporter of rice;
                       eruption of violence in Muslim-dominated region
                       of southern Thailand kills more than 600 in two
                       years; December 26, 2004, tsunami hits Thailand's
                       southwest coast, killing thousands; Thailand is the
                       tenth largest supplier of foreign troops in Iraq

2005   Thailand becomes the world's seventh-leading
                       exporter of automobiles

2006   Security alliance of the United States of Thailand
                       along with Japan, South Korea, Australia, and the
                       Philippines; Prime Minister Thaksin resigns on
                       April 4 after protest demonstrations and afterward
                       ousted by a military coup on September 19 led by
                       General Sonthi Boonyaratglin (1946–)

2007   *Thai Rak Thai* Party banned in May; eruption of
                       violence in Yala province

2008   Coalition government of Samak Sundaravej, political
                       crisis in Thailand, and Abhisit Vejjajiva's ministry in
                       December

2009   The Thai army cracks down on antigovernment
                       protesters in the month of April

2010   The supporters of Thaksin called "Red Shirts" hold
                       demonstrations and clash with army which leads
                       to the death of 27 persons on April 10; the situation
                       calms down after Abhisit announces plans for hold-
                       ing elections

Thailand (Cartography by Bookcomp, Inc.)

1

Introduction to Thailand

HISTORY

The Southeast Asian country of Thailand ("Land of the Free") has a glorious history and rich culture. Its first permanent settlements date to about 40,000 years ago, as the archaeological excavations of recent decades have revealed. These and subsequent peoples practiced early forms of plant domestication, cultivated rice, and used metals such as bronze and iron to make tools.

The Chao Praya River Valley in Western Thailand became the nourishing ground of Thai civilization and history. The first Kingdoms that arose in Thailand were strongly influenced by Buddhism and Hinduism. Thai culture took form out of a unique blend of Indian customs and indigenous elements involving cultural interaction with India, rather than transplantation of Indian culture.

Though the exact origin of the Mon Kingdom of Dvaravati is unknown, its Buddhist character is well attested. The oldest known Mon-Buddhist inscription, near the central province of Nakhon Pathom, is dated to the sixth century C.E. Before those who would become the Thai people came to Thailand in large numbers by the beginning of the thirteenth century, different areas of

Thailand were under the Funan, Chenla, and Sri Vijaya Kingdoms. The neighboring Khmers also had established authority in central Thailand. Due to pressure from the Mongols, the ancestors of today's Thais were compelled to leave the Kingdom of Nan Chao, in what is now China's Yunnan area. The migration to the south was slow at first but increased significantly with the conquest of Nan Chao by the Mongols in 1253. The decline of Khmer power in the river areas of what was becoming Thailand weakened resistance to the migration among groups already present in the region.

In 1238, the Thais declared themselves independent after challenging Khmer suzerainty. Sri Indraditya (r. 1238–1270) set up the first Thai state, which the Thais called Sukhothai.

Rama Khamheng (1239–1298) was the most famous Thai king, his reign regarded as the golden era in the Kingdom's history. In the middle of the fourteenth century, Thai political power shifted from the Chao Praya Basin farther south to Ayudhya with the establishment of a new Kingdom in central Thailand. Within a span of 20 years, the Kingdom extended its territories to include the entire Chao Praya, part of Mon country in the west, and the Malay Peninsula in the south. The Khmer capital, Angkor, was captured by the Ayudhya king Borommaracha II (r. 1424–1448) in 1431, resulting in an influx of Khmer bureaucrats, artisans, and Brahmans (Hindu priestly class) to Ayudhya. The second half of the sixteenth century was notable for a disastrous war with Myanmar. During the second half of the eighteenth century, the Kingdom's decline was accompanied by the sacking of the beautiful 400 year-old city of Ayudhya. The city was not immediately rebuilt after the expulsion of the Burmese. Within a few decades, the Thai capital was established in Bangkok. The new period in Thai history known as the Bangkok period began with the establishment in 1782 of a new dynasty, the Chakri, which has reigned to the present day.

During the nineteenth century, Thailand remained free from colonial domination due to a policy of modernization, its leaders' astute diplomacy, and the geographical location of the country. Thai kings such as Rama V and Chulalongkorn gave territorial concessions to the British and French; however, the colonial powers only cooperated to keep Thailand a buffer zone. Thailand remained as an independent state, keeping her religious and cultural values intact. After the First World War, it joined the League of Nations. The rulers followed a foreign policy best suited to the country's independence. Internal political pressures, changes in class structure and political consciousness, and worldwide depression led to the revolution of 1932, after which a constitutional monarchy was established. Struggle between democratic forces and the military became a regular feature of Thai politics after the revolution.

In the Cold War period Thailand joined alliances with the United States and became the closest U.S. defense ally in Southeast Asia. Even without its alliance with the United States and other Western nations, Thailand very likely would still have had to grapple with the problem of communist insurgency. The nation recovered from the financial crisis of 1997, but the Islamic insurgency had made southern Thailand a zone of bloodshed and violence. Notwithstanding these difficulties, the country remained stable. But the struggle between the army and the clamor for democracy continues in Thailand.

PEOPLE AND POPULATION

The people belonging to the Thai ethnic group constitute about 80 percent of the population of Thailand. These Khon Thai migrated to Thailand in different historical periods but mostly, as noted, after the conquest of Nan Chao by the Mongols. The Thais form a part of a Tai ethnolinguistic people found in the neighboring countries of Thailand. Inside the country, the Thais are concentrated in central Thailand, constituting 36 percent of the population. The rest are Thai-Lao, northern Thai, and southern Thai people. The Chinese are the largest minority group, making up 15 percent of the population. Other groups include Malays, hill tribes, Burmese, Indians, and refugees from Indochinese countries. The mountains of northern Thailand are home to a number of diverse groups of different hill tribes such as the Akha, the Hmong (Meo), Karen, Lisu, Lahu, and Mien, numbering about half a million. Interethnic relationships in Thailand are known to be somewhat better than in other Southeast Asian nations. While not giving up their culture and language, sizable numbers of minorities have adopted Thai names and speak the Thai language. This makes it rather difficult to determine the ethnic character of a person from their name alone. Moreover, the Lao people, who number about 20 million and live in the northeastern region (more than the 6.5 million in Laos), are related to the Thais ethnically and can mix with the Thais easily. With a population of 67 million as per the estimate of the Thailand National Statistic Office, 2009 (urban population constitutes 31.6 percent of total population), Thailand has a low population density of 327 per square mile. The annual rate of population growth was 0.68 percent and birthrate 13.9 births per one thousand persons. About 68 percent of the people live in rural areas and the rest of the population is found in cities like Bangkok, Songhkla, Suratthani, Chiang Mai, Chiang Rai, Chantaburi, Nakhon Ratchasima, and Khon Khaen. Bangkok, with about 6.3 million inhabitants, has become overcrowded, with 10 percent of the country's urban population living in the capital. Migration is from rural areas to cities as well as to other Southeast Asian countries, Canada, and the United States.

ECONOMY

With a strong agricultural base, the multifaceted economy of Thailand has resulted in growth in industry and technology. One of the Asian tigers, the economic growth of Thailand in the decade following the mid-1980s was remarkable. But the depreciation of Thai currency (baht) to about 26 percent in September 1996 led to the collapse of stock and property markets. The International Monetary Fund secured for Thailand $17.2 billion in loans. There was a huge scaling down of expenditures in government and private sectors. Thailand endured the financial crisis after the government initiated a series of economic reforms in 1997. In human development, it showed tremendous progress. The Human Development Index rate is 73. With a Human Poverty Index Rate of 28, the population below poverty line is only 10 percent, although poverty is still significant in poorer regions and villages. The country has a very low unemployment rate of about 1.5 percent. With the gains made by the urban middle class, Thailand has become a large market for expensive cars and costly consumer goods. Its gross domestic product (GDP) grew by 5 percent in 2006. The inflation rate was 2.5 percent. External debt was only 32 percent of GDP, and foreign reserves amounted to U.S. $67 billion. An increase in exports—in particular rice, textiles, fishery products, jewelry, automobiles, and electrical appliances—and a fall in imports were major factors behind the GDP growth. Compared to 4.3 percent for the year 2005, the export volumes increased to 8.5 in 2006. The import growth fell from 9.3 percent in 2005 to 1.6 in 2006. Thailand imports commodities such as capital and intermediate goods, raw materials, and fuels.

HEALTH

In recent decades, Thailand has taken steps to provide better health care for its people. These include the government's passing of a series of measures such as the Medical Facilities Act of 1998, the Thai Health Promotion Foundation Act of 2001, and the National Health Security Act of 2002. The government has taken necessary measures to reduce poverty by an agenda of 30 baht health programs all over Thailand to reduce health-related poverty. In hospitals and primary health centers, this program has resulted in giving better service to the patients. The percentage of persons receiving access to medical facilities at the time of illness has risen from 49 percent in 1991 to 71.6 in 2004 due to the nation's universal health care plan. The country also was a pioneer in providing medication to persons infected by HIV/AIDS. A sustained public awareness program, along with official measures, resulted in containing the HIV-infected adult population below 2 percent. However, the health care system in Thailand is not uniform throughout the country despite the fact that health resources per capita are higher than those of other nations. Compared to those in rural areas, the city dwellers have better access to health services. The inequity is reflected in resource allocation between the capital and northeast region. In 2003, the bed/population and doctor/population ratios in Bangkok were 1:206 and 1:767 respectively. In the northeast, the ratios were 1:759 and 1:7,251 respectively. The infant mortality rate (IMR) was 1.85 times higher in nonmunicipal areas than in the municipalities.

EDUCATION

The literacy rate in Thailand is much higher than those in other Asian and African countries, around 92.6 percent. Until the middle of the nineteenth century, the Buddhist *wat* (temple) was the disseminator of education. Through a policy of modernization, the Thai rulers improved the country's educational system, and in the last half century has shown a significant expansion of secondary and higher education. The 1977 National Scheme of Education initiative achieved universal primary education. The National Education Law of 1999, mandating nine years of compulsory education from the age of six, allowed for 12 years of free education altogether. About 96 percent of students had finished sixth grade and 48 percent twelfth grade in 2004. The student enrollment in schools was about 8.8 million in the same year. Among the major institutions of higher learning in Thailand are Chulalongkorn University, Mahidol University, Thammasat University, Silpakorn University, and the Asian Institute of Technology. Thai students also went in substantial numbers to the United States, Australia, Japan, and European nations for higher education. The national male-to-female ratio for university graduates is roughly even.

GEOGRAPHY

With an area spanning 198,270 square miles, Thailand is the size of New Mexico and Arizona combined. It is the third largest nation in Southeast Asia. Myanmar lies to the west and northwest, Laos to the northeast, and Cambodia to the east. To the south, the Malay Peninsula is bordered to the west by the Andaman Sea and to the east by the Gulf of Thailand. Thailand enjoys a tropical climate with long hours of sunshine and high humidity. The three main seasons are hot (March–June), rainy (July–October), and dry/cool (November–February). In the hot season, the temperature reaches about 40 degrees Celsius (104 degrees Fahrenheit) in many parts and in the cool season it is 10 degrees Celsius (50 degrees Fahrenheit) in north Thailand. Climate is dependent on the Southeast Asian monsoons. In the cool season, northeast winds blow from land to sea. A high-pressure zone is created over Southeast Asia as the sea takes a much longer time to cool than land. The interregnum hot season follows before the advent of the southwesterly monsoon, during which winds blowing from the Indian Ocean meet the low-pressure area of the mainland, resulting in rain. The average annual rainfall is sixty inches. Southern Thailand, which is in the direct way of monsoon winds, receives around one hundred inches per year. Flashfloods occur in many regions of the country during the monsoons. In the mountainous region, the temperature is much cooler.

Thailand has a rich diversity of wildlife, with elephants, rhinoceros, tiger, leopards, wild ox, water buffalos, gibbons, and other mammals found in the forests. Roughly 50 percent of the country was covered by forests in 1960s, but by the end of twentieth century, it had depleted to 20 percent. The government designated some forests as protected areas for conservation and recreation. The production forests are for the export of logs and timber, whose export had increased from 50,000 cubic meters to 2 million cubic meters per year from 1991 to 2001. The deforestation has caused climatic changes and landslides. It also threatens the survival of 30 mammal species.

With a long coastline of 2,000 miles; 12-nautical-mile territorial sea and a 200-nautical-mile exclusive economic zone are claimed by Thailand. The holiday resorts on beaches in Thailand are famous worldwide and generate foreign exchange for the country. However, due to their location they can face devastating natural calamities. The dead from the tsunami of December 26, 2004, included many foreign tourists.

Thailand is famous for its gemstones, teak industry, rice, and rubber. Mined resources include tin, lead, gypsum, tungsten, and zinc. Unfortunately, the opium grown in its remote regions has attracted many smugglers and other criminals.

Thailand is divided into 75 provinces, each in turn subdivided into *amphoe* (county), *tambon* (district) and *muban* (village). The largest province is Nakhon Ratchasima in central Thailand, followed by Chiang Mai in the northwest. It is also categorized into five regional groups such as the North, Northeast (Isan), central, east, and southern regions. The special administrative area of Bangkok is the 76th province. Topographically, Thailand is divided into four main regions: North, Northeast, Central, and South. Each has a unique geographical feature. Northern Thailand is marked by mountains, fertile river valleys, and waterfalls. The highest mountain of Thailand, Doi Inthanon (8,417 feet) is situated in Chiang Mai province. The mountains along the Myanmar border go down through the Kra Isthmus to the southern border with Malaysia. In the North, the Ping, Wahng, Yom, and Nahn rivers flowing southward join to form the Chao Praya River in central Thailand. A part of the famous opium-growing region known as the Golden Triangle is situated here. The Northeast, or Isan, region, bordered by the Mekong River demarcating the

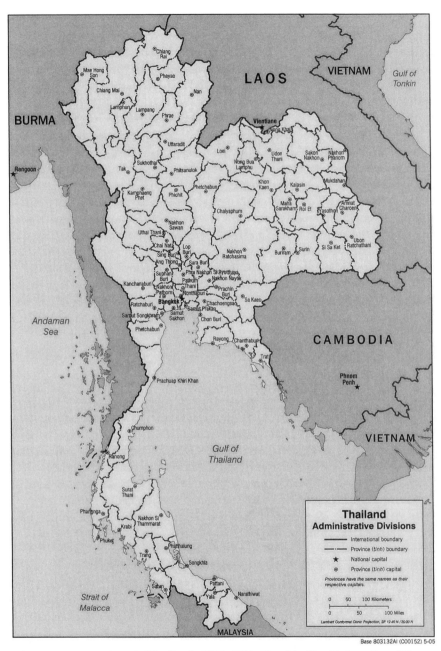

Administrative regions in Thailand, 2005. (CIA. Provided by University of Texas Libraries, http://www.lib.utexas.edu/maps)

Thai-Lao border and to the south by Cambodia, is composed of the Korat plateau, low hills, and shallow lakes. One of the poorest regions of Thailand, it is not productive agriculturally due to frequent floods. The Mun River rises in the Khao Yai National Park, moves east, and joins the Mekong River, where the controversial Pak Mun dam is situated. The Chi and Po are two other regions of this area. The famous Ban Chiang archaeological site testifying to the oldest Bronze Age civilization is located in northeastern Thailand. A large fertile plain sustained by the Chao Praya River is the dominant feature of central Thailand. Surrounded by mountains and plateaus, the central plain extends down to the Gulf of Thailand. The "Rice Bowl of Asia," much of Thailand's rice, other crops, and fruits are grown in the region. The Chao Praya and Mekong river systems sustain the agricultural economy of the country. The Chao Praya's networks of canals support waterborne life in addition to navigation. As the cradle of many civilizations in the past, central Thailand dominates the economic and political life of the nation. The capital city of Bangkok is situated at the southern edge of central Thailand.

The southern or peninsular Thailand extending through the Kra Isthmus to the Thai-Malaysian border is dominated by rain forests and long coastlines. It is the home of the commercial seaports of Thailand. Rice is cultivated and rubber is produced in the region. Tin mining, tourism, and coconut plantations are also sources of commercial activity.

SOCIAL CHARACTERISTICS

The Thai society presents a harmonious balance between tradition and modernity. Educated Thais may wear Western dress, listen to Pop music, or go out dancing in clubs. But they will not give up the traditional values that the society has handed down through the centuries. These include respect for elders, good manners, taking part in Thai festivals, a strong faith in Karma, and the belief in rebirth through reincarnation. Harmonious relationships in the workplace, cordial relations among employer and employees, and avoidance of conflict are important in Thai society. *Djai-yen* ("keep cool"), *sanook sanam* ("enjoy life and be happy"), *mai pen rai* ("never mind"), *kreng chai* ("not to hurt other's feeling"), and *phut prachot* ("masking the feeling") are some of the common Thai phrases that represent this philosophy of life. The famous Thai smile will be there while one is confronting difficult situations. A unique Thai identity has developed, influenced to a large extent by the precepts of Buddhism. Avoiding the extremities of life by following a Middle Path characterizes Thai life. A general Thai identity, or Ekkalak Thai, is to be found whether one is in a remote village or in cosmopolitan Bangkok. A Thai will be a modern person yet also traditional. This unique blending makes Thai society quite special.

In traditional Thai society, which is hierarchical, a family includes not only the husband and wife but also includes grandparents, parents, unmarried siblings, and widowed male and female relatives. Several generations usually live in the same house as it is the norm of Thai society to take care of aged parents. Age is an important factor for determining the status of a person and the loyalty, obedience, and respect that person is due. A child learns to show respect to parents and elders. In turn, the child is looked after by the seniors. The relationship is carried over afterward, when the child becomes an adult. Important decisions are undertaken with the permission of parents. The husband is considered to be the head of the family. Family members have to abide by the decisions of the patriarch, the most senior member of the family. Although he has considerable hold on family governance as the husband, the voice of the wife also counts. It is not uncommon in Thai society to see the importance of the youngest daughter, who eventually inherits the parental property and takes care of aged parents.

With the growth of urbanization, technological advancement, and better job opportunities, the family structure in Thailand is changing. Migration from rural areas to cities has resulted in the smaller nuclear family becoming the norm in many quarters of Thai society. These city dwellers prefer to have nuclear families with only a husband, wife, and children. When children grow older and marry, they prefer to have their own, separate homes. But tradition lingers on, and couples take care of their aged parents when there is need. Although individuals select their own life partners, families play an important role. The groom has to get the consent of the bride's parents, who sometimes get *sin sawt* ("bride money"). Polygamy was prevalent in the past among the aristocracy. Today it is rarely found, although instances exist where a wealthy man keeps another wife known as minor wife.

In spite of the cultural impact of the West, Thai etiquette has remained unchanged. With a smile, Thais greet one another by saying *Sawadi*, with palms joining and fingers outstretched. The palms are held at the breast height. When one greets a senior, the position of the palm goes up against the body and the bow is more exaggerated. The younger person is the first to greet the elder, and the latter reciprocates. The *wai*, or greeting, has a deeper meaning, originating from doctrines of Hinduism. It is believed that divinity resides in the human body and the greeting is a demonstration of respect to that divinity. Therefore human beings must be respected. The Thai avoid body contact. The head, the noblest part of the body, must not be touched, and pointing by the foot is a form of insult. Shoes should be removed before entering a home.

The modernization process, contact with the West, industrialization, expansion of education, involvement in the Vietnam War, and other factors have had a great impact on Thai society. Social mobility has become common.

The employment boom between 1985 and 1996 witnessed people flocking from rural areas to the cities. In industrial and service sectors, 55 percent of the labor force is employed out of 35.3 million workers, according to 2004 figures. The manufacturing share of the GDP has shown a tremendous growth; from 22 percent in 1980 to 35 percent in 2004. With avenues for growth opened, combined with foreign investment and technology, new previously unknown job opportunities have appeared.

The status of women has increased with the expansion of educational opportunities, and today a vast majority of women are employed in different sectors. Taking the husband's family name after marriage has not been required since 2003. But the status of women is degraded to an extent by the growth to 100 billion baht per year of the sex industry. Its origins may be traced to the proliferation of bars, massage parlors, and escort services at the time of the Vietnam War, when U.S. soldiers stationed in Vietnam came to Thailand for R&R, or rest and relaxation as it was called. After the war, the clientele changed from military personnel to male tourists from all over the world. But it should be kept in mind that not all tourists come to Thailand for sex alone. The 8 million tourists visiting the country per year are interested in its history, scenic beauty, magnificent monuments, and Thai hospitality.

Like any other country Thailand is beset with social problems. Environmental pollution, congestion in cities, AIDS, drug trafficking and human trafficking, extortion, corruption, terrorism in southern Thailand, the gap between rich and poor, and regional imbalances are among the society's major ills. There are, however, welcome signs as people accept civil instruction from the government, which is taking measures to eradicate the problems plaguing the Thai society.

Education has played an important role in raising public consciousness. The country's nongovernmental agencies are actively working to address and mitigate the problems. The Thai government is sufficiently aware of the country's problems and is taking steps with various pieces of legislation to keep social evils in check. In 1999, it enacted the Money Laundering Prevention and Suppression Act B.E. Thailand has attracted money launderers as a transit country for narcotics and a center for counterfeit goods, gambling dens, lotteries, and underground banking systems. The act stipulated seven predicate offenses including trafficking in women or children for sexual purposes, fraud, financial institution fraud, customs evasion, extortion, narcotics trafficking, and drug smuggling.

CULTURAL LIFE

The cultural life of Thailand is rich and vibrant. In spite of external influences, the country has retained its unique character. In various traditional spheres, Thai culture has excelled. Religion has been an important factor in shaping the destinies of the Thai people. About 90 percent of the population is Buddhist, with Muslims constituting about 6 million people, the largest minority group. In the three southern provinces of Patttani, Narathiwat, and Yala, Muslims are in the majority with about 76 percent of the population adhering to the Islamic faith. About one percent is Christian, and a small number of Confucians, Taoists, Hindus, and Sikhs are found spread throughout Thailand.

The history of Buddhism in Thailand has been closely interlinked with developments of the religion in India, Sri Lanka, and Southeast Asia. The Buddhist missionaries and traders played an important role in disseminating the message of Buddha. Although it has been argued that Buddhism had taken roots in Thailand from the time of Buddha himself, a clear picture of its entry emerges from the period of Mauryan king Asoka (273–236 B.C.E).

In the third or fourth century C.E. the Buddhist missionaries Theras Sona and Uttara came to Suvarnabhumi, with its capital at Nakon Pathom, to propagate Buddhism. A huge stupa, Pathom Chedi, was built to commemorate the event. The coming of Mahayana Buddhism in the seventh century C.E. to southern Thailand is the second stage of development of Buddhism in Thailand. The third phase of Buddhism, known as *Pukam* (Pagan) Theravada Buddhism, was introduced in the eleventh century C.E. It came from the Thaton capital of Mons, but some historians argue that it came from Nakon Pathom. Under the king Rama Kamhaeng (1239–1298), a fourth phase, known as *Lankavong*, began to predominate in Thailand. It came from Sri Lanka, which had become an important center of Theravada Buddhism in the twelfth century C.E. The coexistence of indigenous and nonindigenous elements in Thai Buddhism has been a hallmark throughout its history. The idea of *phi* (spirits), an animistic belief, is pervasive in Thailand, denoting spirits of town, spirits of house, caves, and other places. These spirits are concerned with mundane problems like health and prosperity. Small model houses are constructed to serve as homes for the spirits. The combination of *phi*, an indigenous concept, along with *thewada* (Devata or God) from Hindu–Buddhist cosmology, arose from the process of merging different religious traditions. Sometimes the higher spirits were also called deva, brahma, or other names. Along with animistic practices, Buddhism also interacted with Hindu cultural patterns that had been introduced. The rapprochement between Indian traditions and Thai Buddhism could be broadly divided into two categories, one operating in royalty and the other present in the social system, customs, arts, and other parts of the culture. The invoking of gods from the Hindu pantheon such as Siva, Vishnu, and Ganesha in different ceremonies is prevalent. It is common to find houses or buildings with the icon of the Hindu god Ganesha at the entrance. One can find in Bangkok the famous Erawan shrine dedicated to Lord Brahma, where the Thais congregate to worship and bow their heads in reverence. Consequently a single distinct tradition emerged in Thailand out of animistic beliefs, Hinduism, and Buddhism. The Thai people have shown tremendous capacity to harmonize different traditions and yet retain their own distinctive nature.

At the time of decline of the Indianized Kingdoms of Southeast Asia, Islam began to penetrate the region. The Arab traders played an active role in bringing the region under the spell of Islam. Islam is strongly installed in Thailand's southern provinces close to Malaysia. The Muslims of the region have been asking for greater autonomy for some time. The central plains of Thailand include Muslims of Persian, Pakistani, Indian, and Indonesian and Cham descent. Those Muslims in the northern provinces of Lampang, Chiang Mai, and Chiang Rai are from Myanmar and southern China. The cultural life of the Muslims differs from the general Thai population in language, manners, and customs. One can see in southern Thailand numerous mosques. There are some churches in Bangkok. Some Vietnamese refugees and tribes of northeastern Thailand profess Roman Catholicism. Although the Chinese have been integrated into the Thai society with Thai names, they have their own shrines and festivals. In the Chinatown area of Bangkok, one can taste the Chinese way of life and culture. The Chinese New Year festival is a big occasion in Thailand. Even in some Thai houses, one can find a Chinese shrine called *Tee-Ju-Iya*. Unlike the Chinese, the Hindus and Sikhs have not integrated fully into the society. The Hindu temples and Gurdwaras are there in the country, but the number is much less. An Indian woman with a sari or traditional *salwar kammez* could be easily recognized. The Sikhs retain long hair and wear turbans.

In Thai cultural life, festivals play an important role. Throughout the year, there are religious and secular festivals, which make Thai culture very colorful. The That Phanom Festival of the northeastern province of Nakhon Phanom in the month of January is a large gathering of the Thais. The Chiang Mai Flower Festival held in the month of February is observed in memory of Buddha's preaching to the monks. The Dove Festival, an occasion where singing doves are celebrated in Yala province, is held in the month of March. The Chakri Day on April 6 is observed in honor of Rama I (1737–1809). To mark the beginning of the Buddhist New Year, the Songkran Festival is observed throughout Thailand April 13–15. During this festival, in a symbol of cleansing and renewal, Thais throw water on each other. Offerings are made in the Buddhist *wats*, and the monks receive food as well as new garments. White powder is smeared on the face as a sign of protection from evil. The city of Chiang Mai is most famous for this festival, where the revelry of Songkran is enjoyed by Thais as well as by tourists coming from all over the world.

The coronation day and the Visakha Puja, in memory of Buddha's life are observed in the month of May.

The famous festival of the Royal Ploughing Ceremony began in the period of the Sukhothai dynasty, marking the beginning of the rice-growing season in May. It is observed annually with two ceremonies, a cultivating ceremony and a ploughing ceremony. The ceremonies are held at Sanam Luang, the Royal Grounds, with Brahmans (Hindu priests) chanting hymns. The Asalha Puja, held in July, commemorates Buddha's first sermon. The queen's birthday is celebrated on the twelfth of August, which is a public holiday. The Chinese Buddhists observe a nine-day celebration held in late September to early October, during which time they eat only vegetarian food. In November, the Loi Krathong festival comes, which is observed on a full-moon night. People flock to the *klong* (canal) or river and (*loi*) float *krathong* (small boats) with flowers, incense, and candles in the hope that good fortune will be brought to them. One can visualize a myriad of flickering lights on the water as night falls. Sometimes, fireworks displays and beauty contests are held. The festival has become one of the most important in the country. The fifth of December is a public holiday to commemorate the king's birthday and is celebrated with portraits of the king embellishing the buildings of cities and villages. December 10 is Constitution Day, a public holiday.

The official language of Thailand is Thai, from the Tai family of languages. It possesses 44 consonants and 32 vowels. Whereas 40 percent of the population speaks Thai, 50 percent use related Tai languages. Chinese, too, is used by some, while those who have higher education often speak English. Malay is spoken in some quarters of southern Thailand. The Thai alphabet was derived from the Indian Devanagari script, which originated during the reign of Sukhothai King Rama Khamheng in 1283. The Thai language has absorbed Khmer, Pali, and Sanskrit words. Some of the ancient place names of Thailand such as Sukhothai, Ayuthia, Haripunjaya; Lopburi, Dvaravati, and Sajjanalaya have origins in Sanskrit. The influence of India is marked on the names of the kings also: Indraditya, Rama, Ananda, Suryavamsa Mahadharmarajadhiraja, Cakrapat, Trailok, etc. Innumerable words in the Thai language originate in Sanskrit, including *Akas (Akas), Maha (Maha), Sthani (Sthan), Racha (Raja), Sabadi (Svasti), Pratehet (Prades), Narai (Narayana), Isaun (Isvara), Samkha (Samgha), Jatura (Catura), Radu (Rtu), Tepa (Deva), Thatu (Dhatu), Phram (Brahmana), Nakhon (Nagara), Sakhon (Sagara), Pinai (Vinaya)*, and many more. The language is spoken all over the country along with regional dialects.

Thailand's classical literature is based on tradition, legends, and history. The oldest known poem, the *Suphasit Phra Ruongs*, was written in the late 1200s. Thailand's first love story was *Lilit Phra Lo*. The reign of King Narai (r. 1656–1688) saw a flowering of Thai literature. Indian classical texts have had a strong influence on Thai literature and stories of Sakuntala, Madanabodha,

Savitri, and Ilorat became part of it. The stories from the *Ramayana* were incorporated into Thai literature, with Rama I authoring the Thai version of the ancient Sanskrit epic, the *Ramakien*, a work that would influence Thai literature, painting, dance, and drama. The *Ramakien* differed in many ways from the original *Ramayana* of Valmiki. For example, in the Thai version of the story, Hanumana is a romantic person falling in love with ladies, Ravana's daughter Vinayaki assumes the form of Sita; Dasaratha and Ravana are cousins. Sunthon Phu (1786–1855) is the celebrated author of the famous romantic adventure *Phra Aphai Mani* and the travelog nine *Nirats*. Thai literary works were in verse form until 1850. From the latter part of the nineteenth century, Thai literature addressed themes and plots about common people and their problems. Kings such as Rama II (r. 1809–1824), Rama V (r. 1867–1910), and Rama VI (r. 1910–1925), all themselves notable authors, exercised royal patronage of literature. In the modern period, Thai authors have written about social problems and the life of the common people. Phya Anuman Rajadhon (1888–1969) was an authority on Thai culture. Angkarn Kalayanaponge wrote about nature and environmental pollution. Some of the notable authors of the modern period are Boobpha Nimmanhaemindha, Malai Choopinit, Mai Muang Doem, Yakhop, Kukrit Pramoj, Krisna Asokesin, Seni Saowaphong, Suwanee Sukhontha, Vanich Charungkichanand, Saksiri Meesomsueb, and Pira Pira Sudham.

The art and architecture of Thailand were influenced by Indian and Khmer styles. While the concepts were borrowed, the choice of pattern and other details add an indigenous touch to artistic and architectural designs. The genius of Thai artists can be seen in the temples (*wat*), stupa (*pra*), monasteries (*vihara*), and halls (*bot*) found in the monuments of Sri Deva, Visnulok, Svargalok, Vajrapuri, Lopburi, Sukhothai, Ayuthia, and Bangkok. Historic sites and structures include the Emerald Buddha Temple, Grand Palace, Wat Suthat, Wat Arun, and Wat Benchamabophit. The tiered roof of Thai architecture was influenced by the *sikhara* of the Hindu temples. The superimposed roofs, glazed colored tiles, gilding, and decorative sculptures add magnificence. The scenes of the *Ramakien* also are found in temples of Thailand. On the bas-relief of Phimai temple, there are scenes depicting Rama's war with Ravana. The paintings on the outer gallery of Emerald Buddha Temple depict scenes from the *Ramakien* such as remorseful Sita in Lanka and the Rama-Ravana battle. Of course, today tall buildings, skyscrapers, apartments, and resorts are also found in Thailand.

Thai sculpture encompassed icons of Hindu gods and Buddha. Images of Vishnu have been found from the Si Thep (Sri Deva) area in the Chao Praya Basin dating to the end of sixth century C.E. The inscription of Rama Tibodi I (1312–1369) spoke of the installation of images of Siva, Vishnu, and Buddha. Large bronze statues of Siva and Vishnu were erected at Kampen Phet.

In Thailand Buddhism and Hinduism were often fused together and there was no differentiation. In Sukhothai, Wat Pra Pai Luang and Wat Sisawai were built for Brahmanical worship as evident from sculptures of Hindu gods and goddesses. The icons of Parvati, Hanumana, Ganesa, Indra, Brahma, and others are found in the *wats* in Thailand. Images of Buddha in various sitting, standing, and reclining positions have adorned numerous monuments. The serenity of the face, smoothness of the metals, simplicity of form, and perfect style have made these icons exquisite. The Buddha images vary from the gigantic seated Buddha of Wat Si Chum to tiny amulets.

Thai music and musical instruments were influenced by neighboring regions, but it was assimilated by evolving into a unique type. The *piphat* and *khruang sai* musical instruments are used in religious gatherings and theatres. Apart from these two, the Thais have developed instruments including the *phin, sang, pichanai, krachap pi, chakhe,* and *thon.* In festivals, marriages, and folk theater one can find use of flutes, stringed musical instruments, and gongs. The two types of folk music are called *luk thung* and *kantrum.* Due to the influence of Western music, new forms are being introduced like *luk grung* and *wong shadow.* The *String* was the first Thai pop band. Sometimes traditional music was mixed with the Western style.

The Thai classical dance form in Thailand shows influence from Cambodia and India with themes taken from the *Ramakien.* The Thai classical dance took Indian body movements, evolving into its own special style. The *khon, lakhon,* and *fawn Thai* are some varieties of classical dance. With its stories from the *Ramakien,* the masked dance drama called *khon* has become very popular. Folk dances include *wai khru, ram muay,* and *likay.* In the shadow plays known as *nang,* stories of Rama and Sita are enacted.

One can find beautiful paintings of Thailand on the walls of temples, palace interiors, cloth banners, and manuscripts. Murals of Bangkok's Wat Suthat and Thon Buri's Wat Suwannaram are fine examples depicting the episodes of Buddha's life, Jataka stories, and scenes from the *Ramakien.* The Western style has influenced contemporary Thai painters, whose works combine tradition and modernity.

Textiles, earthenware, silverware, and pottery comprise Thai crafts. Cotton and silk weaving of Thailand have a long tradition. Thai silk is famous all over the world. The northeastern region is famous for silverware, producing exquisite bowls and boxes. From the ancient Ban Chiang civilization, the art of shaping and baking clay has survived to the present day, with the discovery of pots, water jugs, flower vases, and animal figures. The celadon industry of Thailand was famous during the Sukhothai period, with products exported outside the country. Thailand is well known for its crafts like woodcarving, lacquer work, basketry, mother-of-pearl inlay, and metalwork. Thai cuisine has been influenced by Chinese stir frying techniques and noodles along with

Indian curry. But it has its own culinary style. Delicious spicy and hot Thai food with a wonderful blend of basic flavors is popular throughout the world. Rice is a staple food and a meal usually includes meat, salads, soup, noodles, curry, and rice. Fresh tropical fruits like mango, banana, rambutan, jackfruits, papaya, and other fruits serve as desserts. Iced coffee or tea and alcohol are taken as beverages. Some of the delicious and popular Thai dishes are *dtom kai jai* (chicken soup), *rad na* (rice noodles), *pad see ew* (fermented sausages with fried rice), *khanom chin namya* (boiled round rice noodles along with curry sauces and fresh vegetables), *massuman jai* (spicy curry with chicken) and *lahb moo* (spicy salad).

GOVERNMENT AND POLITICS

After the 1932 revolution, the Thai rulers became constitutional monarchs. The nation was governed by prime ministers, who were appointed by the king. They came to power because of democratic processes or military coups. The politics of Thailand witnessed democracy and military rule playing musical chairs. A party system would be in place, constitutions would be drafted, and elections would be held—all pointing to the advent of a democratic form of government. But then military intervention would turn democracy into a sham. This has been the fate of Thailand since 1932. During its three-quarters of a century of constitutional monarchy, the country has experienced 17 successful military coups. Alternate sharing of power between civilians and the military has put Thai politics into a permanent state of flux. Infighting among elites for greater shares in the political process opposed at times by the dominance of the bureaucracy has marked Thai politics with instability.

The authority of the central government is superior to that of provincial and municipal governments in the unitary state of Thailand. The central government is composed of three branches: executive, legislative, and judiciary. The king is head of state and the commander-in-chief of the armed forces. He appoints the prime minister. The latter is usually the leader of the dominant party or coalition parties supporting him. The prime minister heads the cabinet, which does not have more than 35 members. The legislative organ of the government is a bicameral legislature called Ratha Sapha (National Assembly) consisting of the Sapha Poothaen Rassadorn (House of Representatives) and the Woothi Sapha (Senate). The former has 500 members; 400 are elected directly from single-member constituencies and the rest elected proportionately through a party list. It has a four-year term limit. The Senate has 200 members elected for six years from the districts within the Thai provinces.

Thailand has a three-level court system. The Supreme Court is the apex body followed by Court of Appeal and Courts of First Instance. For the Muslims, there are the sharia courts. Military courts deal with cases involving military personnel. Citizens are guaranteed equal justice under the law. An Election Commission supervises the elections, and voters must be 18 years old. The Buddhist monks do not cast votes because it is forbidden by religious convention.

The Khana Rasdr (People's Party) came into existence in 1927 and formed the government after the 1932 revolution. The history of political parties in Thailand has not been a happy one, as they were banned frequently. From 1933 to 1945 and again from 1958 to 1968 political parties did not function. The military was taking an upper hand. Later, laws such as the 1981 Political Parties Act was enacted to revamp the party system. The measure called for a minimum number of members of Parliament and made it mandatory to contest one-fourth of all parliamentary seats. Critics of the Thai political parties—which include the Thai Rak Thai (Thai Love Thai), Phak Prachatipat (Democratic Party), Phak Chart Thai (Thai Nation Party), Phak Khwam Wang Mai (New Aspiration Party), and Phak Mahachon (Great People's Party)—suggest the parties often lack clear-cut ideologies while tending to cater only to the needs of an individual or a small group.

The dominance of the military continued until October 1973, when student involvement and mass demonstrations ended the military rule. There was a return to civilian government, although the top brass of the military continued to have some influence in the politics of the nation. (Although the present king, Bhumibol Adulyadej, does not enjoy any real power, his political acumen and popularity among the Thai masses has been a stabilizing factor in the country's politics.) The years 1991 and 1992 were turbulent in Thai politics. The seventeenth military coup occurred in 1991, with Anand Panyarachun (b. 1932), a civilian, becoming premier. Elections were held in March 1992 in which General Suchinda Kraprayoon (b. 1933) was selected as the new prime minister. But the coup leader Suchinda faced demonstrations in May that resulted in shootings by the military of unarmed protestors, which in turn led to Suchinda's resignation. Anand became the interim prime minister, a role he held until Chuan Leekpai (b. 1938), leader of the Democratic Party, was elected in September. After three years, the Constitution Drafting Assembly met. Banharn Silparcha of the Thai Nation Party became the new premier. There followed increased demands for political reforms as ministerial offices were used for personal gains and electoral system was abused by politicians.

A new liberal constitution came into effect in 1997. The prime minster holding the office for four years was to be elected by the political party having the most seats in the House of Representatives. The 1997 constitution established further principles to strengthen the party system.

Chuan headed a seven-party coalition after the November 1997 elections. His rule came under severe criticism as the government's policy was perceived as helping big companies and it faced many corruption scandals. With a populist agenda, the Thai Rak Thai was emerging as a major political force, and it won the 2001 elections with an absolute majority. With a large and unprecedented electoral mandate, it has initiated major reforms but has also faced challenges. An anti-drug campaign ended in April 2003 with 2,275 people having been killed. This was a campaign of police aggression and the dead were drug dealers. Looming large in southern Thailand was an Islamic insurgency that led to 500 deaths in 2004. The deadly tsunami of December 26, 2004, killed more than 5,300 people in coastal Thailand.

The Thai Rak Thai won the election of 2005 with outstanding results. Officially registered in July 1998, the party is under the leadership of telecommunications billionaire Thaksin Shinawatra (b. 1949), who built up the cadre by inducting persons with varied ideologies and by launching a popular campaign. Thaksin, the founder of Shinawatra Computer and Communications Group, has helped to make Thailand's communication system world-class. He was the deputy premier in 1995. His party secured an absolute majority in 2001 elections, winning 248 out of 500 seats of the House of Representatives. In the legislative elections of February 2006, it won 375 out of 500 seats.

The Thai Nation Party secured 41 seats in the 2001 elections and was a coalition partner in Thaksin's government. Banharn Silpa-Archa (b. 1932), its leader, was prime minister from July 1995 to December 1996. The leader of the New Aspiration Party, General Chavalit Yongchaiyudh (b. 1932), was commander-in-chief of the Royal Thai Army before entering politics. He was prime minister from November 1996 to November 1997 but resigned after the Asian financial crisis. He made an alliance with Thaksin's Party to contest the 2001 elections. Afterward the New Aspiration Party merged with Thai Rak Thai and Chavalit became deputy premier in Thaksin's cabinet.

Thaksin continued as premier after his party's spectacular victory in the February 2005 elections. For the first time, a single-party government governed the nation. However, charges of corruption and abuse of power were brought against Thaksin by the opposition and this dissolved the Parliament. In spite of the overwhelming support of the rural people, Thaksin had alienated the Bangkok elite by disregarding their views. In the 2005 general elections, the Democratic Party, which came into existence in 1945, was against military interference in politics, and took part in the "People Power" movement of 1992, received 18.3 percent of the popular vote and 96 out of 500 seats. Its leader, Chuang Leekpai, hails from the Trang province in South Thailand, and he was the Parliament Speaker in 1987. He led coalition governments from 1992 to 1995 and again from 1997 to 2001. Chuang is also responsible for the party's dominance in southern Thailand.

In the April 2006 elections, amid mass rallies against Thaksin, the Thai Rak Thai still won 57 percent of the vote. But the opposition boycott and protest vote forced him to resign. The Supreme Court invalidated the elections. Thaksin remained the caretaker premier. On September 19, 2006, while he was at the United Nations General Assembly, the military staged a coup.

The junta, calling itself the Council for Democratic Reform, dissolved Parliament and imposed martial law. Its leader, Sonthi Boonyaratkalin (b. 1946), a Muslim and commander-in-chief of the Royal Thai Army, was backed by retired army commander General Surayud Chulanont (b. 1943) and Privy Council president General Prem Tinsulanonda (b. 1920), advisers to the king. Surayud was appointed as prime minister in October 2006. A constitutional tribunal was instituted, which dissolved the Thai Rak Thai in May 2007 for election fraud and banned Thaksin from politics for five years. The complex political configurations, business considerations, power politics, and instances of personal ambition have left the Thai political scene somewhat murky and muddled. The junta promised restoration of a democratic process. In 2008, the People's Power Party formed the government after emerging victorious in the elections. The country witnessed political turmoil and again there was a new government of the Democratic Party led by Abhisit Vejjajiva (b. 1964) in December. His government faced demonstrations and mass rallies by the supporters of Thaksin called "Red Shirts." They paralyzed central Bangkok from March 2010. In a clash with the army, about 39 demonstrators were killed and 300 injured. The situation continued to be tense in spite of withdrawal of protest by the Red Shirts on May, 19, 2010.

2

From Prehistory to Pre-Thai Kingdoms

Recent archaeological discoveries have pushed back the prehistory of Thailand to a much earlier period than was initially recognized by researchers of previous generations. The country has been credited with the earliest rice cultivation in the world as well as an important Bronze Age culture. Permanent human habitation began in Thailand about 40,000 years ago. Its earliest inhabitants went through an evolutionary process. Archaeological evidence discovered in different regions of Thailand such as Ban Chiang, Spirit Caves, Non Nok Tha, Non Mak La, Non Muang Kao, Sab Champa Non Muang Kao, and Ban Lum Khao point toward a developed society, economy, and culture. The early peoples of Thailand domesticated plants and animals. They also made use of bronze and iron tools and lived in villages. As the earliest prehistory of Thailand unfolds itself to researchers, we gain glimpses from the findings of that archaeological sites that dot the country.

ARCHAEOLOGICAL SITES

Ordinary stone tools have been found dating back to 500,000 B.C.E. in north, northeast, and central Thailand. These implements of the Paleolithic period provide a picture of the early culture of prehistoric human life. The earliest settlement is dated about 40,000 years old at Lang Rong Rien in northern Thailand. The domestication of plants began around 10,000 B.C.E. as is indicated by the findings from the Spirit Caves, where archaeologists have determined that people used nuts, pepper, cucumber, and beans sometime between 10,000 and 7,000 B.C.E.

Humans were living near the waterways of Thailand's rivers from an early date. Neolithic settlements studied by archeologists have revealed that their culture included the use of tools and objects made of bone and shells. Rock paintings discovered belonging to this period depict domesticated animals, fish, wild animals, and people dancing.

The archaeological excavation made in the village of Ban Chiang in Udonthani province of Thailand brought worldwide attention to the fact that the early occupants of the country were thriving during the Bronze Age. The earliest known bronze culture of the world is located on the Korat plateau in northeastern Thailand. The area witnessed the production of bronze bracelets, bells, necklaces, and axes and spearheads around 3600 B.C.E. The prehistoric culture dating from around 3600 B.C.E. to 200 C.E. reveals the development from an agricultural community in the Neolithic period to the Bronze and Iron Ages. Archaeological excavations have yielded painted pottery, cord-marked pottery, animal bone, human skeletons, glass beads, bracelets, and other objects.

The discovery in the advancement in agriculture has been gleaned from the remains of plant seeds, such as rice. The people lived a simple life in villages. There was no urbanization and the rural inhabitants had no kings or political structure. Warfare was absent in the Ban Chiang culture. With knowledge of agriculture and metallurgy, these people's primary productions were pottery and bronze materials. So precocious were they that even the Chinese received their knowledge of bronze from the Ban Chiang people.

The Ban Chiang culture flourished near water sources where rice cultivation was the main source of livelihood. Hunting was done with spears, axes, and arrows. Domestication of the water buffalo allowed the Ban Chiang to use the draft animal for farming and other projects. The clay rollers found at the site point toward printed designs on the textiles. Archaeologists also found that they made stylistic ceramic vessels with painted designs. Ornaments were made of stone as well as glass beads. The people also used amulets of earthenware and bronze bangles.

In the graves, ornaments, utensils, and skeletons have been found that give a picture of the customs of the people. Belief in a life after death has been inferred by archaeologists by their manner of burial, which was internment with the personal belongings of the deceased for use in the next life. The findings at Ban Chiang demonstrate a developed knowledge in bronze and iron metallurgy. Neither Mesopotamia nor China no longer holds the credit of pioneer in this art. The Ban Chiang people were well adapted to the forests as well as to the wetlands. They also used trading networks with other regions. However, eventually deforestation and soil erosion forced the people to migrate to other regions, causing the Ban Chiang culture to an end.

The Non Muang Kao culture, or the Mound of the Ancient City, a large settlement in the Mun Valley located in northeast Thailand on the Korat Plateau, is another major archaeological site. It was occupied in the Bronze Age beginning in 500 B.C.E. and continued into the Iron Age. Ceramics found in the region date only to before 600 C.E. Ban Lum Khao, Noen-U-Loke, and Mon Muang Kao were important sites in the Mun River Valley. The sites had plastered floors, wooden posts, and ordinary graves. Glass beads, rings made of bronze and iron, and Phimai Black pottery vessels have been found in the graves. The pottery from graves contained traces of rice. There were also remains of animals like deer, dog, cattle, and pigs.

The 110 burial sites of Ban Lum Khao in the upper Mun Valley contained the bones of pigs and fish, bangles, shellfish, and vessels. In the cemetery, bones of infants, children, and adults were found. Burial was simple, neither wrapped nor in jars. This Bronze Age occupation beginning from 500 B.C.E. of the upper Mun River Valley also contained remains of fish, turtle, frogs, birds, wild water buffalo, pet dogs, and burnt fibers of bamboo. Ceramics were cord-marked ware and decorated black pottery. Excavators at the site of Ban Lum Khao found over 400 pottery vessels. They included round vessels, open bowls, and vessels with round bases. The site yielded bangles made of marine shell and marble. The Ban Lum Khao site has parallels in the cemeteries of Ban Prasat, Noen U-Loke and Non Nok Tha, which points toward similar a culture in the second half of first millennium B.C.E.

In the Khon Khaen province of Northeast Thailand, the archaeological site of Non Nok Tha is noted for evidence found there of rice cultivation and Bronze Age culture. Excavations yielded rice chaff belonging roughly to 5, 000 B.C.E. This was the earliest evidence of rice (*Orzya sativa*) cultivation for the whole world. Grain imprints were found in the pottery shards. The independent bronze culture emerged in the region around 2000 B.C.E. Apart from pottery shards and bronze materials, the site yielded iron objects, remains of skeletons after burials, and burial offerings. There was even evidence of a settlement of metalworkers. The cultural deposit of the site showed an evolutionary process passing through bronze and iron ages from the third millennium B.C.E. to the early centuries of the Common Era.

THE MON KINGDOMS

In the Bronze and Iron Ages, there was neither urban life nor any warfare. The simple village life gradually gave way to regional Kingdoms. The river valley in central and northern Thailand became the major centers of Thai history and civilization. Different ethnic groups like the Mons, Khmers, and others formed early Kingdoms having Hindu-Buddhist practices. These lasted until the emergence of Sukhothai in 1238, the first Thai Kingdom. The earliest states were contributions of the Mons, who hail Dwarvati as the first Mon Kingdom. The Mon people were living in lower Myanmar (Burma) and northern Thailand along the Chao Praya River Valley. Some historians believe that the Mons were descendants of immigrants from the southern Orissa and northern Andhra Pradesh region of India. The Mons were probably a mixture of all these people.

Animism with ancestor worship had been the primitive belief of the people until they were strongly influenced by Buddhism. The advent of Buddhism began from the period of Mauryan king Asoka (273–236 B.C.E) of India. After the third Buddhist Council held in Pataliputra under the patronage of Asoka and Mogaliputta Tissa as president, nine groups of Buddhist missionaries from India were appointed to propagate the doctrine of the faith. Two of the Buddhist missionaries, Sona and Uttara, came to Suvarnabhumi to preach Buddhism. Suvarnabhumi had been identified with the region comprising south Myanmar, Central Thailand, and east Cambodia.

Two cities of antiquity in Thailand's central river basin have long been called Suphanburi ("City of Gold") and U Thong ("Cradle of Gold"). Buddhaghosa's *Samantapasadika* refers to the successful mission of Sona and Uttara and credits them with the authorship of *Brahmajala Sutta*. A huge stupa known as Pathom Chedi (Prathama Chaitya in Sanskrit) was built. Sona and Uttara constructed it during the reign period of Asoka to commemorate the event. The Mon settlements gradually became urbanized. There emerged the Mon Kingdom of Dvaravati with its capital in Nakhon Pathom, the largest city of the period. Dvaravati consisted of a number of city-states in the lower plain of the Chao Praya River, with its area comprising Nakhon Pathom, Lopburi, Ratchaburi, and Prachinburi in modern Thailand.

Most of the people of Dvaravati were Buddhists. India played a major role in introducing Buddhism in the region. The oldest known Mon-Buddhist inscription near Nakhon Pathom is probably not earlier than the sixth century C.E. Other Buddhist sites include Phra Pathom and Phong Tuk in Dvaravati. One of the special features of Buddhist art is the representation of Buddha descending from heaven with Hindu gods Indra and Brahma. The representation of Buddha, such as that in Phra Pathom showing *dharmacakra* (the wheel of life, symbolizing the Buddha's first sermon and teachings) with crouching deer proved the strong influence of Buddhism in this Kingdom.

In addition to Buddhist architecture, the Mons were skilled at building moats and embankments. An earthen embankment and two moats surrounded the cities of Dvaravati. The culture of Dvaravati flourished in between the middle of the fifth and eleventh centuries. Afterward the Kingdom started to decline and most of it was absorbed by the advancing Khmers. Its art and architecture would influence later Kingdoms.

Besides Dvaravati, the Mons had established other Kingdoms in central and northern Thailand. The Lop Buri Kingdom of central Thailand was also known as Lavo, and name derived from that of Lava, son of Rama, the hero of epic *Ramayana*. Famous for its art and religion, the Lopburi Kingdom was incorporated into the Khmer empire by Suryavarman I (1002–1050). Mon Princess Chamadevi had established another Mon Kingdom in the Lamphun region of northern Thailand during the years 661 to 750. Along with her went the Buddhist monks to this new Kingdom of Hariphunchai. The capital city, Lamphun, had many Buddhist relics. The two famous Buddhist temples were Wat Haripunchai (1040) and Wat Chamadevi (1218). For defense, the city of Lamphun had many *wiangs*, or outposts, such as Wiang Mano, Wiang Tho and Wiang Tha Kan. The *Chamadevivamsa* and *Jinakalamali* chronicles mentioned that the Kingdom was attacked by the Khmers in the eleventh century. Finally it became a part of the Lanna Kingdom in 1292 after King Mengrai's capture. According to the *Tamnan Hariphunchai* (History of Kingdom of Hariphunchai), Yip was the last ruler of Hariphunchai.

THE KHMERS

In the first century of the Common Era, states in Southeast Asia took part in trade relationships with India. Although trading had been conducted since the prehistoric period, trade between the two regions now became brisk. Indian art, architecture, statecraft, administration, and other cultural features arrived in many forms to create Indianized Kingdoms. The Funan (150–550 C.E.) was one such Kingdom, which was established by an Indian Brahman.

The coming of Indian cultural influence was convenient for the rulers, who used it to support their own political authority. This process of cultural interaction slowly affected not only the elite but also lower-class people in their socio-religious life. Under Fan Ch'an, the territory of Funan extended up to central Thailand. Rudravarman was the last king of Funan. The dominant religion of Funan was Hinduism but the Buddhists constituted an important community.

The Kingdom of Funan lasted from the second to sixth century. It was followed by the Kingdom of Chenla (550–802 C.E.). At its height, Chenla included southern Laos, the Vietnamese coast, and the lower valley of Chao Praya and Mun Valley in Isan region. The Chenla kings came to be deified. By tradition, its princesses were married to Brahmans who came from India. The ruling elite embraced Saivism and claimed descent from the Sun dynasty of Rama, the hero of *Ramayana*. There was "water" Chenla, which was distinct from the "land" Chenla. The former had appropriated the Funan Kingdom. In turn, the rulers of the Srivijaya and Sailendra dynasties incorporated the water Chenla.

The Khmer empire flourished in Thailand between 802 and 1431. It benefited from territorial expansion as well as cultural efflorescence. The Khmer territories covered the present northeastern region of Thailand, much of the central area, and stretched into the west up to Kanchanaburi province. Thailand received Indian cultural patterns through the Khmers and adapted these according to its needs. The Angkor dynasty was established in 802 C.E. by Jayavarman II (802–834). Its new rulers introduced the *Devaraja* cult, in which influences from India, as well as the megalithic culture of Southeast Asia, Campa, Indonesia, and China could be discerned. *Devaraja* means the "king of Gods," which is the god Siva himself. The successive rulers contributed in different ways to the cultural life of Angkor and territories under its sway.

The Brahmans continued playing an important role in the religious life of the people. In Cambodia, the *purohita*, or chief priest, had a powerful influence on the royalty. This sacerdotal office passed from uncle to nephew in the maternal line, exemplifying the indigenous matrilineal social system. The royalty was well versed in Sanskrit and acquainted with Indian epics, *kavyas* (a type of classical Sanskrit poetry), and *puranas* (A genre of important Hindu encyclopedic religious texts, depicting legends of gods, history of royal dynasties and cosmogony). Sanskrit was used for royal genealogies, panegyrics for kings and donors of various categories. In the stone inscriptions dotted throughout Thailand, Khmer, Pali, and Sanskrit were used. Many of the words from Sanskrit and Pali found their way into the Thai language during the period of Khmer dominance. In the art and architecture of Thailand today, the presence of Indian and Khmer influence can be traced back to this period. The beautiful stone temples of Phimai and Phanom Rung in northeast Thailand were examples of Khmer art in Thailand. The Khmer rulers also ordered roads built, which were wide and paved by laterite. Icons of Hindu gods and Buddha images showed artistic skill with beautifully engraved lines and exquisite finish.

By 802 the Khmers had extended their territory into the neighboring areas. Jayavarman II occupied land to the north and east of Chenla. The Khmer empire stretched to Ubon in Isan by 889 during the reign of Indravarman I (877–889). The long rule of Jayavarman V (968–1001) was marked by peace and cultural attainments previously unknown. Suryavarman I (1006–1050) extended the Khmer power into the Chao Praya River Valley in the west and Mekong Valley in the north. South Thailand was made into his tributary. He used his wealth to make donations to the religious foundations and assist in the spread of Mahayana Buddhism.

The Angkor civilization reached its apogee at the time of Suryavarman II (1113–1150), who constructed the magnificent Vishnu temple, the Angkor Wat. Pagan (in Myanmar) in the west, the Vietnamese coast in the east, and the Malay Peninsula in the south were the territorial extent of the Khmer empire during his rule. After subjugating Champa, Jayavarman VII (1181–1219) unleashed a career of conquest. Vientiane, Annam, south Thailand, north Malay, and a portion of Myanmar came under his rule. He constructed the famous Buddhist temple in the new capital city of Angkor Thom. But the royal treasury was depleted due to incessant wars and construction works.

The steady southward movement of the Thai people resulted in the emergence of new principalities held previously by the Khmers. The Chmas began putting pressure on the Khmers. The Khmer empire began to decline after Jayavarman VII's death. Warfare between the Thais and Khmers was constant, becoming a regular feature from the middle of the fourteenth century. Angkor was captured ultimately by the Thais in 1431.

CITY-STATES AND THE SRIVIJAYA EMPIRE IN SOUTHERN THAILAND

The research studies on the history of southern Thailand are not as extensive as studies on other areas of the country. However, recent studies and archaeological excavations have shed new light on the history, culture, and archaeology of the region. Situated between the Andaman Sea and the Gulf of Thailand, southern Thailand and northern Malay have occupied a strategic position in regional and Asian trading systems. The zone was the meeting point for people from China, India, Sri Lanka, and the neighboring locales.

Its history and culture were shaped by external influences and indigenous factors. The region had a rich prehistorical heritage. Discoveries of artifacts and metallurgical objects have pushed back the cultural history. Between 4000 and 1000 B.C.E., the Neolithic mode of technology appeared. Bronze and iron made their appearances from 500 B.C.E. onward. The traders from this region played an important role in the Indian Ocean. The Indian trade was intensified with a demand for goods of this region. The people were politically, economically, and culturally receptive to elements of Indian culture. According to the Chinese sources, there emerged in the beginning of the Common Era city-states like Tun-hsun, Ch'ih-t'u, P'an-p'an, Tan-tan, Tambralinga, and Langkasuka in the Thai-Malay Peninsula that were influenced by the Indian culture. The confederacy of Tun-hsun existed from the first century C.E. and it had contact with Tonking, India, and Parthia. A large number of Indian traders, Brahmans, and Buddhists made it their trading base.

The Kingdom of Ch'ia-t'u ("Red-earth land") was situated in the area of northeastern Malay. The Chinese text *Ch'ih'-t'u kuo chi* attests to the presence of Buddhists and Brahmans. P'an-p'an was on the trade route between India and China. From P'an-p'an, the Brahmin Kaundinya II went to Funan. The state of Tan-tan was situated in the region of Trengganu and its ruler sent to China gifts like the tooth relic of Buddha, painted stupas, and leaves of the bo tree.

The first century C.E. state of Langkasuka was near Patani and had access to the Gulf of Thailand. Its ruler Bhagadatta established a diplomatic relationship with China in 515 C.E. The Chinese travelers, Yi Jing (635–713, I-tsing) and Xuanzang (602–664, Hiuen-tsang) recorded their observations of Langkasuka. It was in control of trade routes to the east. The ruins of a Siva temple have been found from this place. Tamralinga, located between Chaiya and Pattani, was already in existence in the second century C.E. as evident from the Buddhist canon *Nidesa*. The Thai–Malay Peninsula, with its city-states, assumed importance in the trading network involving Rome, India, and China.

Ships of the Roman empire came to Southeast Asia from the Indian Ocean during this period. After the collapse of Roman trade, the merchants went through Kedah to southern Thailand and from there to Campa by way of northern Thailand and Cambodia. The trading activity in the region began around the second century C.E. The Hindu influence could be marked from the findings of Chaiya in southern Thailand. Trade in beads and the discovery of Buddhist votive tablets and the many Hindu icons point toward strong Indian influence in the region. The city-states lost their independence as a result of the expansion of island power of Srivijaya, which engulfed the city-states by the middle of the eighth century.

From its headquarters in Palembang in southeastern Sumatra, the regional center of Srivijaya in south Thailand was Chaiya, near modern Surat Thani. The town of Chaiya and its surrounding areas still have relics of Srivijayan art and architecture. Buddhism flourished in Srivijaya due to patronage by its rulers. Mahayana Buddhism was prevalent in the Kingdom. Apart from influences from Java, the Amaravati, Pala, and Gupta styles of India had an impact on architecture found on the eastern coastline from Surat Thani south to Songkhla. Some of the important monuments of the Srivijayan period were found in Chaiya, including Phra Borom Mathat and Wat Kaew Pagoda. Wat Mahathat could be found in the Srivijayan city of Nakhon Sri Thammarat.

Specimens of Srivijayan art with strong Indian influence are preserved at the National Museum in Bangkok, as well as the Nakhon Sri Thammarat Museum and wat Phra Mahathat Museum in Chaiya. Though adherents of Buddhism, the rulers continued to honor indigenous beliefs: one of the stone inscriptions depicted a local Malay water oath with a Buddhist icon. The Srivijayan rulers built monuments in areas as far away as Canton in China and Negapattan on the east coast of south India. Dharmakirti was the greatest Pali scholar in the first two decades of the eleventh century. He was the head of the Srivijaya clergy, for whom the Thai king had built a monastery, the Lankarama. Apart from Buddhism, Indian influence was present through Sanskrit language also. Some of the inscriptions were in Sanskrit, which was popular in Srivijaya.

INDIAN CULTURAL INFLUENCE IN THE REGION

The introduction of Indian culture into Thailand, Indonesia, Myanmar, and Indochina forms an important aspect of early and medieval history of Southeast Asia. In the modern contemporary period, some Indian cultural influence lingers on. It would not be out of context to analyze cultural interactions between Southeast Asia and India, as it has relevance in studying Thai history.

Indian art, architecture, literature, religion, and statecraft had a fundamental impact on Thai history. Some of its remnants are still extant in modern Thailand. This Indian influence in Southeast Asia is often referred to as "Indianization," and various theories look at the motives and process of this cultural impact. It is to be noted that interaction between the cultures of India and Southeast Asia resulted in the spread of Indian culture. The Indian cultural influence was by peaceful and nonpolitical methods. For a long time, the process of Indianization was regarded as an Indian initiative with Southeast Asia at the receiving end. The countries of the region were described by nationalist historians of India as colonies of India. In 1926 the "Greater India Society" was established to recover the historic role of India in Southeast Asia. Formed by nationalist historians wanting to glorify ancient Indian culture, its members referred to Indian adventurers traveling by ship and setting up Kingdom after Kingdom. The indigenous population of Southeast Asia was characterized as the passive recipient of Indian culture.

The earlier view of large-scale Indian migration "colonizing" Southeast Asia is far from the truth. The arrival of large numbers of Indians would have led to significant demographic changes, but even Indian dietary habits, such as using curry powder and milk products, did not seem to have been adopted by Southeast Asians. In addition, political allegiance toward India was not practiced by these Southeast Asian countries. Economically speaking, the states of Southeast Asia were not colonies as the opportunity for economic exploitation was missing. India did not enjoy a monopoly in the field of foreign trade.[1] Various theories regarding the motives and process of Indianization have emerged. Even the use of the term "Indianization" has been criticized because "it may suggest a conscious effort on the part of Indians to spread their culture over major parts of Southeast Asia".[2]

Some scholars have preferred the term "classical" and terms like "Indic," discarding "Indianization." One author went to the extent of saying that his objection to the term "Indianization" was "the modern prejudice against Indians in twentieth-century Burma, where because of many Indians were of a lower socio-economic status, we concluded that they surely could not have influenced Burma in the past."[3] In spite of objections in certain quarters regarding the use of the term "Indianization," the term has been retained in this book for the study of Indian cultural influence. It has been used in a broader context with due emphasis on Southeast Asian initiative or indigenization.

The general consensus is that the process of Indianization was accomplished by peaceful means and it was nonpolitical in character. The polemics is about the factors, process, and extent of Indian influence in Southeast Asia. Various theories have been propounded in spite of the fact that they are not entirely exclusive of one another. The first theory is the *ksatriya* (warrior class) theory, which proposes that the influence from Indian culture came from the large numbers of Indian warriors and conquerors who migrated to the area. The adventurous *ksatriya* immigrants established "colonies" after "colonies" (the term used by nationalist historians) in Southeast Asia. They got married into local ruling families and afterward enlisted the service of Brahmins for supporting their political authority. Due to the unsettled political condition in India, large numbers of refugees migrated to seek new places across the ocean. However, there is no proof of a large-scale migration after Asoka's conquest of Kalinga in 261 B.C.E.; rather, the war made a remorseful Asoka turn toward Buddhism. Neither the Kushana invasions of the first century C.E. nor Samudragupta's campaign resulted in the mass exodus of people.

The advocates of the *ksatriya* hypothesis have visualized the introduction of Indian culture as a result of the activities of Indian warriors playing the role of robber barons, marrying locally, and producing a society of mixed blood. It has been argued that Indian influence can be explained by colonization due to the warriors. All the above postulations are speculative and there is no real evidence for it. Indian immigration was not so massive otherwise there might have been demographic changes among the inhabitants. There is no doubt that persons of Indian origin are residing in some pockets of Thailand as in Nakhon Sri Thammarat and Bangkok. It is not known in what circumstances they came. The argument that overseas empires were colonized and administered from Indian centers can be dismissed due to the lack of evidence. In the inscriptions of Southeast Asia, one does not find any reference to the ancestry of these warriors or the reasons for their coming to distant lands. But it is plausible that sons passed over in the succession might have gone to far off places to seek glory and power, which they considered their due. This is a mere suggestion only and not supported by any fact.

The *vaisya* (merchant class) theory proposes that the Indian influence came from traders, who passed along their goods and culture to the indigenous population and even married local women in some cases. Through the trading establishments of the Indians, the culture was diffused. The traders were thus transmitters of the culture to the Indianized elite. Commerce was the prime factor behind the Indian expansion in the first century C.E. Indians came to Southeast Asia traders in search of spice and gold, married into the local families, and in some cases an Indian might have imposed himself as chief over local populations, establishing Indian-styled Kingdoms. The services of the Brahmans were enlisted, who merged the Hindu religious system with local cults and made the rulers as *avataras* (incarnations) of god. The *vaisya* hypothesis may be criticized on the following points: (1) merchants were not enlightened enough to transmit a higher culture or to have contact with royalty; (2) they were versed in vernacular language only and not in Sanskrit; (3) the scholastic character of Indian culture in Southeast Asia had been learned by the people and not brought by Indians; (4) if the traders had played a major role in spreading Indian culture, the early centers of Indian civilization would have been found in the coastal regions, whereas these were in the interior of Java and the royal abodes were also not in coastal regions; and (5) commercial contacts were not enough for the transmission of civilization. In spite of serious objections to the *vaisya* theory, it contains elements of truth. It would be wrong to assume that merchants were not competent to transmit elements of culture. In spite of the caste system in India, there was social mobility among different castes. The Brahmans performed functions other than acting as priests. If they traveled overseas despite injunctions mentioned in ancient scriptures, they could also take on vocations including trade. The *ksatriyas* were not warriors only, and there are numerous instances of kings and princes well versed in literature. So it would be wrong to say that the *vaisyas* were not at all acquainted with Sanskrit and were familiar with vernacular literature only. It is also not convincing to say that the character of Indian culture was scholastic—whether the people who had learned elements of Indian culture were locals or Indians who had come to Southeast Asia. It is also not correct to say that only interior areas were centers of Indian influence. Oc eo, Palembang, Trang, and Kedah were ports with traces of Indian influence. They were not only centers of commercial activities but places of cultural interaction. At Oc eo, archaeological excavations have proved Indo-Southeast Asian contact. Sanskrit inscriptions of earlier periods have been found from Kedah. The Amaravati sculptures were found on the sea route joining Kedah, Palembang, the east coast of Java, and Western Celebes. Among the merchant groups, the practice of Buddhism was strong. The removal of caste barriers and restrictions on maritime voyages resulted in the arrival of sailors. The *Jataka* stories dealt with maritime activities of the traders. Images of the Buddha at the Amaravati School were discovered in Southeast Asia. The sailors were devotees of Dipankara Buddha ("Calmer of Waters") and evidence of Indianization is said to be revealed in these Buddha images. The activities of Buddhist missionaries gave further impetus to Indianization because they came to the royal courts of Indonesia, converting the rulers, and establishing a new order of monks. So, on the whole, in spite of criticism against the *vaisya* theory, it contains a certain degree of historical truth as seen in the elements of Hindu and Buddhist culture known to have spread through trading centers.

The third theory, known as the *brahmana* theory, proposes that indigenous port patricians and rulers used the service of Brahmans to support their political authority through Hindu ceremonies and rituals. This view opened new perspectives by not only rejecting the earlier two theories but giving importance to local initiative.[4] Emanating from the court, the Indian cultural influence was focused on consecration formulas and royal proclamations in the sacerdotal language of the Brahmans. The priests became counselors in the affairs of the courts and provided political support to the rulers by giving them a sort of investiture and genealogical list, which elevated their position. Thus the *brahmana* theory made Indianization proceed as an initiative of the elites of Southeast Asia. Even if one agrees to the view propounded by the *brahmana* theory that it was the local aristocracy who took the initiative, nevertheless the Indian elements like Sanskrit language, the Hindu–Buddhist cults, Dharmasastras, concepts of royalty and other "gifts" from India became essential features of the early states of Southeast Asia.

Even though a small population of the region was affected by Indian culture, this aristocracy had bequeathed to the people cultural heritage in the form of literature, monuments, and icons. It is also difficult to agree with the proposition that Indian influence was confined to royalty and court. That the common people were influenced by it to a considerable extent is evident from the popularity of Sanskrit epics such as the *Ramayana*, Indian themes in dance dramas, worship of Brahma, festivals, and so on. Therefore, all three hypotheses outlined here contain some amount of historical truth.

It seems likely that the whole process of Indianization was the product of endeavors made by warriors, traders, and priests, along with some indigenous initiative. The local society produced new cultural forms out of the different cultures it received. Quite often the three types of people—*ksatriya, vaisya*, and *brahmana*—were not distinct in the Southeast Asian context. A *ksatriya* might have been a trader or a *vaisya* might have indulged in a power struggle of the court. All these classes of people also might have sought local help to serve their interests and the latter in turn would have desired assistance from the influential Indians.

Giving greater importance to the role of Indians rather than a purely indigenous initiative may be the result of a semantic disagreement. However, there certainly were interactions between Indians and local cultures. Southeast Asians were able to choose which elements of Indian culture they could apply to their own beliefs—an indication of a highly functioning civilization during this early period of history. Vishnu's consort Laksmi became the goddess promoting fertility in the rice fields of west Java. Siva was transformed to the tradition of cult of earth god in Campa. In the site of Ba Phanom of Cambodia, the goddess receiving sacrificial rituals was an amalgamation of the earlier goddess Me Sa ("white mother") with the Indian goddess Mahisasuramardini. The stories of the *Ramayana* were transformed into Thai, Lao, or Indonesian versions. In the *devaraja* cult, Hindu concepts blended with Southeast Asian mountain cult ideas. The Southeast Asian people took cultural customs from Indian elements and adapted them to fit their own indigenous traditions. Indian culture itself consists of a plurality of traditions that evolved out of interaction between Sanskrit culture and vernacular lore of dominant groups. It spread to Southeast Asia also as a result of interactions between indigenous and imported cultures, resulting in the adoption of Indian religions, ideas of kinship, administration, law, writing, literary traditions, festivals, art, and architecture. During the last 2,000 years, the region that has become modern Thailand was under the influence of major civilizations of the world—above all Indian traditions. India's contact with Thailand could be dated to the fourth century B.C.E. as is evident from the excavations in the Iron Age burial site of Ban Don Ta Phet, where bronze bowls have been found. The late prehistoric sites such as Ban Chieng, Ban Na Di, Non Muang, and Ban Tha Kea have yielded glass beads, which were tangible indicators of the contact of Thailand with the outside world.

Evidence of Buddhism coming to Thailand could be found from the discovery of an ivory comb that bears a Buddhist motif and icons of the Amaravati school of art. The Mon Kingdom of Dvaravati had Buddhist sites yielding Buddha images. The Tai conquest of the thirteenth century gave further impetus for the spread of Buddhism. In the development of Buddhism in Thailand, influences from India, Sri Lanka, Cambodia, and Myanmar were quite discernible.

One finds the impact of Hinduism on Thai society presently through festivals, music, architecture, language, and literature. The rulers have legitimized their position by taking recourse to the Hindu *dharmasastras* (religious scriptures) and brahmanical rituals. The Brahmans (priests, *phrams* in Thai) perform various rituals connected with royalty. The Thai culture has appropriated certain elements of Hinduism. Images of Hindu gods and goddesses such as Parvati, Hanuman, Ganesha, Vishnu, Indra, and Brahma adorn *wats* (temples) of Thailand. The icons of Ganesha are installed in newly constructed buildings as symbols of good omen. The Erawan shrine in Bangkok is the site of a statue of Brahma that is venerated by the Thais. The *Ramayana* (*Ramakien* in Thai) tradition is a perennial source of inspiration for the people and the performing arts forms like classical dance, masked plays, theater shows, and shadow plays have used the stories from this classic. The Thai festivals such as *Loh Chingecha* (swing ceremony), *Loi Krathong* (festival of lights), *Baruna*

Satra (rain festival), and *Songkran* (astrological New Year) possess elements of Hindu and Buddhist traditions. The Brahmans conduct family ceremonies such as births, deaths, purifications, and weddings. Nonetheless, Thai society has retained its distinct identity in spite of adapting certain Indian cultural norms.

NOTES

1. For details regarding Indianization, please see, Patit P. Mishra, "Critique of Indianization Theory", Full Article in *Proceedings of Indian History Congress*, 58th Session, Bangalore (Aligarh, 1998), pp. 799–807. See also, Presidential address of Indian History Congress, Patit P. Mishra, "A Discourse on Indo-Southeast Asian Relations: Prejudices, Problems and Perception", 65th Session, Bareilly, December 28–30, 2004, Section, IV (Delhi, 2005–2006), pp. 912–45.

2. J. G. de Casparis and I. W. Mabbett, "Religion and Popular Beliefs of Southeast Asia before c. 1500," in N. Tarling, ed, *The Cambridge History of Southeast* Asia, Vol. 1 (Singapore, 1992), p. 281

3. M. Aung Thwin, "The Classical Southeast Asia: The Present in the Past" *Journal of Southeast Asian Studies* 26 (1995), f.n. 22.

4. J. C. van Leur, *Indonesian Trade and Society* (The Hague, 1955), p. 95: "The Indian priesthood was called east-wards certainly because of its wide renown for the magical, sacral, legitimacy of dynastic interest and the domestication of subjects, and probably for the organization of the ruler's territory into a state."

3

The Emergence of Thai States: Sukhothai and Lan Na

There are many hypotheses about the origin of the Thai race. One theory postulated is that they migrated from the Siachun province in central China and set up a Kingdom in southern China called Nanchao (Nanzhao/Dali Kingdom). The Nanchao rulers occupied parts of Myanmar and North Vietnam. It was incorporated into the Mongol empire in 1253 by Kublai Khan (1215–1294). This theory argued that the migration that proceeded southward into northern Thailand was slow early on but was sped up by the Mongol conquest. Based on evidence from archaeology and anthropology, another theory claims that the Thais were living in Thailand for a long time. They were forced by the Mons and Khmers northward into what is today the Yunnan area of China. Once again the Thais migrated to their original homeland in Thailand. Another hypothesis argues that the Thais migrated from the Malay archipelago northward. Another claimed that they came from southern Chinese provinces, including those we know today as Guangdong, the former Guangxi Zhuangzu, and Yunnan. The Thai migration from these three provinces has been accepted by most scholars. The Thais belong to the Tai ethnic group living in neighboring areas of Laos, Vietnam, Myanmar, China, and northeastern areas of India. Before the establishment of Kingdoms, the Thais resided in *muangs* or clusters of villages grouped together in principalities. These consisted of the ruling aristocracy, cultivators, and slaves.

Since the *muangs* were established on river valleys, rice cultivation was their main source of revenue. The Thai principalities were established in areas such as Chiang Saen, Chiang Rai, and Chiang Mai in northern Thailand. Gradually, more fertile lands in the central plains came under the occupation of these principalities, who were able to maintain a large army out of economic surplus. By the thirteenth century, the Thais became the dominant force in the area, making a dent on the Khmer and Mon powers. Thailand came to be ruled by the Thais, ending any previous non-Thai Kingdoms. The Thais took advantage of the decline of Khmer power after the death of Jayavarman VII in 1219.

SUKHOTHAI KINGDOM

The local Thai princes Pho Khun Bang Klang and Pho Khun Pha Muang, who were governors of Ban Yang and Rad, revolted against the Khmer rule. They established the independent Kingdom of Sukhothai ("Dawn of Happiness") in 1238. In the Thai imagination, Sukhothai was seen as the first Thai Kingdom to have material prosperity and cultural blossoming. Bang Klang became the King of Sukhothai with title of Sri Indraditya (r. 1238–1270). The wave of migration after the Mongol victory over Nanchao in 1253 reinforced the nascent Thai state. The army was bolstered due to an influx of Thai soldiers from Nanchao. The formative stage of Thailand's history began with powerful monarchs operating from Sukhothai on the banks of the Mae Nam Yom River. The Kingdom of Sukhothai's dominance was due to the fact that it had tremendous potential for agricultural production. It controlled water resources for the entire Chao Praya basin, as it was situated at the top of the main flood basin. A surplus of production in this fertile land made it possible to have a large army. The minor Thai princes lent support to Sukhothai, which increased the strength of the Kingdom considerably. Indraditya was succeeded by his second son Pho Khun Ban Muang (r. 1270–1277). The territorial extent of Sukhothai was the area between the rivers of Ping and Nan.

There was further expansion under Rama Khamheng (1239–1298), who ruled from 1277 until 1298. A younger bother of Ban Muang, Rama Khamheng, also known as Rama the Great, was one of the greatest monarchs of Thailand and at the time of his death he left a vast Kingdom. His domain in the north extended up to Luang Prabang and to Nakhorn Sri Thammarat in the south. Substantial parts of the lower Chao Praya, the upper Mekong, and the lower Salween Valleys came under his subjugation. He adopted both diplomacy and warfare to expand Sukhothai's domain. The stability of Sukhothai was assured by friendship with China. A Chinese mandarin named How Chow Chi came to Sukhothai in 1282 and a treaty of friendship was signed between

China and Sukhothai. Rama Khamheng visited Peking (Beijing) in 1282 and brought Chinese potters back with him, establishing a ceramic industry that was economically important for a long time. The kilns of the Kingdom produced glazed ceramic wares known as *sangkhalok*. These were exported to countries such as the Philippines and Indonesia, where specimens of this type of ceramic have been found. Rama Khamheng was determined to check any future Khmer aggression and developed friendly relations with Lanna ruler Mangrai (r. 1259–1317) and Prince Ngam Muang of Phayao. Sukhothai was secure in the west through friendship with Makato, the ruler of Pegu. Rama Khamheng's Kingdom was larger than present-day Thailand. However there was no direct control of outlying provinces, which acknowledged his suzerainty.

Rama Khamheng's reign was marked by general peace and prosperity for the people. He was a benevolent monarch. A bell hung in front of his palace bore testimony to his sense of justice. The king would listen to grievances after the ringing of the bell. Rice and fish were in abundance so that his subjects did not have any food shortages. There was no road tax. People did not have to pay tax on merchandise and inheritance. Trade in horses, silver, and gold was brisk. Rama Khamheng was interested in moral education for his subjects and persuaded them to lead a life following Buddhist precepts. The Thai society that evolved in the Sukhothai period was elitist in nature with the presence of a non-Thai slave population. The Thai aristocracy resembled that of the Mongols.

Many important facets of Thai culture developed under Rama Khamheng's reign. Sukhothai was one of the early Kingdoms that emerged in Thailand integrating traditional *muang* administration with the Indian *mandala* concept of a centralized state. It also borrowed from the Khmer various art forms and administrative structures. The impact of the Mongols could be discerned in military units beginning from 10 onward to 20, 30, and so on. Legal traditions came from the Mons. In spite of influences from India, Sri Lanka, and neighboring regions, Sukhothai evolved its own cultural pattern, still maintaining its identity. The legacy of Sukhothai was in the realm of language, script, and religion that became an essential part of Thai culture.

The Mons, Khmers, Indians, and Sri Lankans had close cultural contact with Sukhothai. The Sri Lankan variety of Buddhism (Theravada Buddhism) became predominant in Sukhothai. Rama Khamheng invited monks from Sri Lanka to come to Sukhothai to free existing Khmer-dominated Buddhism. The monks of Sukhothai went to Sri Lanka to learn about Buddhist cannons. Nakon Sri Tammarat became an important center of Sri Lankan Theravada philosophy. It had close religious ties with Sri Lanka, with which contact was established through Nakon Sri Tammarat. In continuity with the indigenous tradition of worshiping spirits, Rama Khamheng continued to make offerings to Phaya Khaphung, the *phi-thewada* or spirit deity located on a hill south of Sukhothai, even after adopting Theravada Buddhism. His inscription of 1292 mentioned the link between the prosperity of Sukhothai and respect for Phaya Khaphung. Thus two religious traditions were merged. The art and architecture received inspiration from Sri Lanka, India, and neighboring regions but retained a separate identity. The artistic excellence of artisans could be visualized in Sukhothai, Si Satchanalai, and Kamphaeng Phet. The Buddha images of the period denoted elegance, calmness, and serenity. In the monasteries in the major cities of Sukhothai, the monks led a disciplined lifestyle. The bell-shaped stupa, stucco decoration, and lotus-bud spires were testimony to Thai genius.

Rama Khamheng was the originator of the Thai script. He changed the Khmer alphabets and adapted it to the sounds of Thai words. The Thai alphabets invented by him in 1283 are basically still in use with some modifications. The written languages of the Burmese, Khmer, Sanskrit, and Pali had greatly influenced his innovation. A common written language gave the Thais an identity of their own. Rama Khamheng's famous inscription dated 1292 was written in the new script and bears testimony to the prosperous Kingdom of Sukhothai. The reign of Rama Khamheng, the warrior and benevolent monarch, is rightly called the "golden period" in Thai history as mentioned in Chapter 1.

After the death of Rama Khamheng, his son Lo Thai (r. 1298–1346) ascended the throne. Decline of the Kingdom had begun and successors of Rama Khamheng could not check the process of disintegration. During the reign of Lo Thai, most of the vassal Kingdoms seceded from Sukhothai. Uttaradit, Suphanburi, Luang Prabang, and Vientiane declared independence from the yoke of central rule. In 1321, the ancient town of Tak was wrested by the Lan Na Kingdom. Thus Sukhothai was much reduced in size. A struggle for power followed the death of Lao Thai, and the next ruler, Pho Khun Nguanamthom, ruled only for some months in the year 1346. Lao Thai's third son Pho Khun Luthai ultimately became the ruler with title of Mahathammaracha I (r. 1346–1368). A great scholar and patron of Theravada Buddhism, the king was more involved in religious affairs than his title suggested. The *Lankavong* form of Buddhism reached its high-water mark under Mahadhammaraja Lithai, who even entered the monastic life of a Buddhist monk for four months. He did not pay much attention to the affairs of the state. A treatise on Buddhist cosmos entitled *Tribhumikatha* has been attributed to him.

The emergence of the powerful Lan Xang Kingdom in Laos and Ayudhya in southern Thailand resulted in the loss of a sizable territory of Sukhothai. Fa Nagum (r. 1353–1373) had established the first unified state of Lan Xang in 1353. The Kingdom of Ayudhya founded by Rama Tibodi (r. 1350–1369) in 1350 dominated Thai power and culture for four centuries. Neither

Mahathammaracha I nor his successor, Mahathammaracha II (r. 1368–1398) could check the acquisition of Sukhothai territory by Lan Xang and Ayudhya. In 1371 Boromaraja I (r. 1370–1388) of Ayudhya, bent upon a policy of doing away with his Tai rivals, invaded Sukhothai and captured several towns. Four years afterward, the important town of Phitsanulok fell into the Ayudhya king's army. The frontier city of Chakangrao was also taken. Sukhothai became a vassal state of Ayudhya in 1378 after 140 years of independent existence. In 1400, there was a flicker of hope for Sukhothai, when Mahathammaracha III (r. 1398–1419) declared independence from Ayudhya's subjugation. It was suppressed and a new king, Mahathammaracha IV (r. 1419–1438), was installed by Ayudhya. Phitsanulok was the new capital of a much smaller Sukhothai. It became a province of Ayudhya after the king's death. The princes of the royal family generally became the administrators of the Sukhothai region. The ruins of the Sukhothai capital of Tambon Muang Kao are now a historical park in Thailand. Apart from weak rulers, who were more interested in religious affairs and building activities than the defense of the Kingdom, the decline of Sukhothai was due to the emergence of the powerful Thai state of Ayudhya.

LAN NA KINGDOM

The Lan Na ("land of a million rice fields") Kingdom, another contemporary Thai state, emerged in northern Thailand in the middle of the thirteenth century. Its founder, Mangrai (r. 1259–1317), hailed from the Yuan Tai family that ruled over the Chiang Saen region. The ancient city of Chiang Saen was called by various names such as "Nakhapun Singhanuwat Nakorn" and "Yonok Nakorn Chaiburi Sri Chiang Saen." It was established by the Tai chieftain King Singha Nuwat, who had migrated from Yunnan around the middle of the sixth century. For about 500 to 600 years, it had been difficult to construct a reliable history of the region due to a paucity of materials. But it can be safely assumed that small principalities were in existence in the upper Mekong River region, stretching from Lu in Yunnan to Lunag Prabang in Laos. The advent of Mengrai, a person of intellect, farsightedness, and valor, changed the scenario. His heritage was impeccable, as his mother was the daughter of the ruler of Lu in Yunnan. After the death of his father in 1259, Mangrai ascended the throne at Chiang Saen (Yonok Nakhon). His first task was to unify various warring tribes from different principalities into the Lanna Tai Kingdom. The leaders of various communities came to Chiang Saen to pay homage, and any recalcitrant fief was subjugated. After extending the territorial boundary of the new Kingdom, Mengrai established the capital city of Chiang Rai in 1262. But Chiang Saen remained as an outpost for defensive purpose in the northern area. Its location was strategic as the Mekong River formed a natural border in the east. Troop movements to Chiang Saen were easier due to its location among waterways of rivers such as the Mekong, Mae Chan, and Mae Ruak. It had eight watchtowers and eleven gates. The Ping River Basin came under control of the king, who named it Khwaen Ping. The Chiang Khong area was captured in 1268, and four years afterward the capital was moved to Fang, from where further expansion of the Kingdom would be carried out.

Another factor that facilitated the security of Mengrai's Kingdom was the close alliance with the powerful Thai rulers of Phayo and Sukhothai. Apart from Sukhothai, the Phayao Kingdom was another autonomous Thai state, although not as powerful as Lan Na or Sukhothai. Until its annexation to Lan Na in 1338, the independent Phayo Kingdom east of Chiang Mai, with its capital near Phayo Lake, was famous for Wat Sikhom Kham. Mengrai, Rama Khamheng, and Muang became close allies and never fought against one another. Mengrai turned his attention toward the south, where the Mon Kingdom of Haripunchai (Lamphun) was located. The Mons tried to extend their territory in the Ping River Basin. The capture of the prosperous trading city of Haripunchai would bolster trade and enrich the treasury of Lan Na. Mengrai knew that a war with the Mons would be disastrous, and he devised a plan to capture Haripunchai. Ali Fa, a merchant and confidant of the king, was sent to the Mon Kingdom to foment discontent and rebellion against the Mon ruler Phaya Yi Ba. At the opportune moment, Mengrai seized the city of Haripunchai and, after staying in the city for three years, appointed Ali Fa as his representative to rule over the Mons. Mengrai looked for a new capital city. Muang Cha Wae, located northeast of Haripunchai, was chosen. But frequent flooding compelled the king to search for another capital. The fertile basin of the Oing River was chosen and the city of Wiang Kum Kam was set up. Mengrai stayed in the new capital for five years, but heavy flooding forced him to look for another site again. The relics of this ancient capital are present in the Sarapee district of the Chiang Mai province.

In 1296, Mengrai discovered a meadow near a mountain that had many waterfalls. The legends surrounding the place spoke of the Hindu god Indra's order for a city that would be free from any misfortune. Although mythology and favorable omens were responsible for the choice of the site, its strategic position between the Kok and Ping rivers, abundance of fertile land for agriculture, and location along the north-south route weighed heavily in the mind of Mengrai for building the new capital. He was still not satisfied with all these, and invited close friends Ngam Muang and Rama Khamheng to help with the planning of the new capital, ultimately giving his final approval. In 1287, the three kings took a vow to never invade each other's Kingdom. Phayo, Sukhothai, and Lan Na had expanded their domain and were assured of each other's neutrality. The new city named Nopburi Sri Nakorn Ping Chiang Mai was constructed in 1296. Shortened to Chiang Mai, the city became the center of a unique northern Thai culture and a tourist attraction in modern times. In the center of the capital city, a monument was built for the three kings. It currently adorns the facade of the Chiang Mai City Hall. Within four months the construction of the rectangular shaped city, which was 1,000 *wah* (one *wah* equals two meters) in length and 900 in width, was completed. The city walls had gates on each side, eight meters in width. A royal monastery was constructed in the garden adjacent to the Western gate of the city, where relics of Buddha brought from the Sukhothai Kingdom were preserved. A threat, however, was looming at large from the northern direction.

The Mongols were constantly harassing Mengrai's Kingdom and in 1301 the combined army of Sukhothai and Lan Na repulsed the Mongol attack. Mengrai was not only a warrior, who expanded the territorial boundary of the Kingdom, but also a compiler of law codes known as *Mangraisart*. The king also established markets in the cities of Chiang Mai and Wiang Kum Kam. He patronized and brought skilled artisans from the Pagan area. He organized the administration by parceling the Kingdom into rice-growing areas. A prince was to get 1,000 rice fields apart from getting territories in outlying areas for defense purposes. A commoner was to get cultivated fields for growing 5 *muen* (about 60 kilograms). After his death in 1311, 17 kings and queens after Mengrai ruled over Lan Na.

Phaya Chai Songkhram, son of Mengrai, ruled over the Kingdom from Chiang Rai. Songkhram's successor Saen Phu constructed a city in Chiang Saen, which was made into the royal abode. The notable event during the reign of Phaya Kham Fu (r. 1334–1345), successor of Saen Phu, was the annexation of the Phayo Kingdom in 1338. Pha Yu (r. 1345–1367), the next ruler, was instrumental in spreading Buddhism in the Kingdom. He shifted the capital to Chiang Mai and built the Wat Li Chiang. Keu Na, the sixth ruler (1367–1385), introduced the *Lankavong* Buddhism of Sri Lanka and invited the Sukhothai monk Phra Sumana Thera. The Wat Buppharam, constructed in 1373, became the disseminator of the *Lankavong* sect. He also assisted King Mahathammaracha II in 1372 in Sukhothai's war with Ayudhya. Keu Na's successor, Phaya Saen Muang Ma (r. 1385–1401), made an abortive attack against Sukhothai. There was also a war with Ayudhya King Boromaraja I (r. 1370–1388) in 1387. The invading forces of Ayudhya were defeated at Sen Sanuk near Chiang Mai. The victory was mainly due to the bravery of the Lan Na princess Nang Muang, who fought with the invading army on the back of an elephant dressed as a man. Muang Ma also began the construction of the Phra Chedi Luang. He was succeeded by his son Phaya Sam Fang Kaen (r. 1401–1441), who forced the retreat of the Haw toward Sipsong Panna. Kaen's son Phaya Tilokaraj (r. 1441–1487) was a notable ruler of the Lan Na dynasty.

The Nan Kingdom was inhabited by Tai Lao and Tai Lu, and had come into existence in 1368. It was incorporated into Lan Na in 1449. Tilokaraj also fought an indecisive war with Ayudhya in 1470s. However, the Lan Na-Ayudhya warfare consolidated the Kingdom of Tilokaraj and bolstered his image. The Shan state in the west and Chiang Rung in the north were the territorial extent of Tilokaraj's Kingdom. His reign was important for construction work and the building of monuments such as Wat Jed Yot, Wat Pa Tan, and Wat Pa Daeng Maha Vihar. In 1477, the Eighth Buddhist Council met in Wat Pa Daeng Maha Vihar near Chiang Mai to review the Buddhist scripture, the *Tripitaka*. This proved the power and prestige that Lan Na enjoyed. Lan Na declined due to political instability beginning in the first decade of the sixteenth century, and ultimately it became a vassal state of Myanmar in 1558 during the reign of Phaya Mekuthi of Muang Nai. The period of occupation by Myanmar continued until 1774. Chiang Mai became a tributary state of Thonburi and of Ratanakosin afterward. It became a province of Thailand in 1932.

The Lan Na Kingdom had remarkable artistic achievement. Its literature flourished during the reign of Phaya Mueang Kaeo (1514–1525). The important Pali text *Khamphi Mangkhalatha Thibani* was composed by Phra Siri Mangkhalajan. The kilns at Wiang Galong of Chiang Rai were famous for the ceramic industry. Archaeological excavations have yielded exquisite Galong ceramics, which were traded locally and outside the country. The architectural genius of Lan Na artisans was reflected in innumerable Wats dotting the Kingdom. A unique Lan Na pattern emerged out of blending various styles from eastern India and the Mon and Khmer Kingdoms. There were also influences from Pegu and Ava from Myanmar. A Buddhist temple, Wat Ku Kham (Temple of the Golden Chedi) was built in the capital city of Wiang Kum Kam by Mengrai in 1288. The *wat*, one of the oldest extant structures of Lan Na with its *ratna cetiya* (jeweled chedi), was constructed on the bank of the river Ping. The relics of Buddha were kept in a chedi (stupa). Mengrai also constructed the first monastery in Chiang Mai, the Wat Chiang Man in 1297. Built in 1385 in Chiang Rai, the Wat Phra Singh was an example of classic religious Lanna architecture. The Wat Phra That Haripunchai, which represented the Mon-style *ratana cetiya*, was built in 1418. The Wat Phra Kaeo, located in the city of Chiang Rai of the late Lan Na period, was famous for its statue of the Emerald Buddha, which was later enshrined in Bangkok. The Kingdom of Lan Na was also famous for bronze Buddha icons in different postures. After becoming a vassal state of Myanmar, the artisans lost their royal patronage, and for the next 200 years styles from Myanmar dominated the region. With its various manifestations and cross cultural influences, the culture of Lan Na had become a part of Thai culture as a whole.

LAN XANG KINGDOM

The history and culture of the neighboring countries of Thailand and Laos are interwoven to a great extent. The majority of the population in both regions is of Tai stock, who shares a common tradition. In fact the Tai Loa people of northeastern Thailand are greater in number than of those in Laos. Before the emergence of Tai states in Thailand and Laos, these areas were under domination of the Mons and Khmers. Prince Fa Ngoum (r. 1353–1373), a Tai Lao, founded the first unified state, Lan Xang ("land of a million elephants"), in 1353. He occupied the Korat plateau in northeastern Thailand. In the middle of the fourteenth century, the Tai kings of Lan Na, Lan Xang, Ayudhya, and Sip Song Panna (in China) had agreed not to disturb each other's territories. The powerful Lan Xang Kingdom ruled Laos, northeastern Thailand, areas of the Cambodian plateau, and parts of Yunnan.

In the first two decades of the sixteenth century, Lan Xang rulers began to interfere in internal matters of the Lan Na Kingdom. The ruler of Lan Xang, King Phothisarat (r. 1520–1548), occupied Chiang Mai in 1545 while an intense power struggle was going on in Chiang Mai. He installed his son Settathirat (r. 1548–1571) upon the throne of Lan Na. While going back to Lan Xang after his father's death, Settathirat took the Emerald Buddha along with other Buddha images, religious scriptures, and texts. He enshrined the Emerald Buddha in Wat Phra, Vientiane, after keeping it in Laung Prabang for some time. Only in 1778 did the image come back to Thailand. Internal dissension and powerful neighbors brought Lan Xang's decline in 1713, and it splintered into the three Kingdoms of Luang Prabang, Vientiane, and Bassac.

4

The Kingdom of Ayudhya

From the middle of the fourteenth century, Thai political power shifted farther south with the emergence of the Kingdom of Ayudhya, which lasted for the next four centuries. Ruling over much of the former Angkorean empire, it became the most powerful political entity of the peninsula. Dominating Thailand as well as mainland Southeast Asia, the capital Ayudhya was an island-city located at the meeting point of the Chao Praya, Lopburi, and Pasak rivers. It was well protected from invasion due to its strategic location on an island. One of the most famous metropolises of the middle ages, Ayudhya was a well-developed city with its monasteries, buildings, international settlements, and waterways. A major tourist attraction today, the city was declared by UNESCO as a World Heritage Site in 1991.

RAMA TIBODI I

The Ayudhya Kingdom was founded by General U Thong after capturing some principalities held by Sukhothai. He assumed the title of Rama Tibodi (r. 1350–1369) at the time of his coronation in 1350. He named the new capital city Ayudhya after the capital of the Kingdom of Rama, the hero of the

Ramayana. From a modest settlement of teakwood houses, the city became the center of imperial grandeur. Known as Rama Tibodi I in Thai history, adventurous Rama Tibodi had matrimonial alliances with royalty in the cities of Lop Buri and Suphan Buri. The king followed a policy of expansion, taking advantage of the weakening power of Sukhothai and Angkor.

The strategic location of the capital Ayudhya facilitated the task of attacking the Khmers. The control of people living in the borderlands of the two Kingdoms had become one of contention. Tibodi also was bent upon claming overlordship of the region. He began to exert pressure against the Kingdom of Angkor, which was followed by his successors until the complete subjugation of the Khmers. Beginning with Jayavarman VII's death in 1219, the decline of the Khmer empire continued. Warfare between the Thais and Khmers continued from the middle of the fourteenth century onward. The expedition against the Khmers in 1352 under the king's son Ramesuan ended in a disastrous defeat at the hands of Khmer king Jayavaman Parameswar (r. 1327–1353). Tibodi went on exerting pressure against the Kingdom of Angkor. The second attack was led by the king's brother and Angkor was subdued by it in 1369. The important consequence of the victory was an influx of Khmer bureaucrats, artisans, and brahmins to Ayudhya. Tibodi extended his domain to the lower Chao Praya River, the Gulf of Martaban, and the Malay Peninsula. He had to suppress frequent rebellions in Chiang Mai and Sukhothai.

Composed of self-governing principalities, the Kingdom had to be held together by the monarch's sagacity and vigilance. Rama Tibodi had to buttress authority and legitimize his claims by following the practice of Indian kings, who declared themselves to be the *devaraja* or divine king. The laws promulgated by Rama Tibodi continued in principle for six centuries. A combination of indigenous practices and Indian legal concepts, this legal system exhibited characteristics of the society of that time. The royal decrees were added to the legal code written in Pali, and it was operational until the last decade of the nineteenth century. In administering the Kingdom, the king was assisted by ministers such as the *khun klahng* (minister of finance), *khun muang* (minister of local government), and *khun nah* (minister of agriculture). A deadly outbreak of cholera spread in 1357, resulting in innumerable deaths. Tibodi embraced Theravada Buddhism in 1360, which became the state religion of Ayudhya. The monks came from Sri Lanka to spread Buddhism.

FROM RAMESUAN TO BOROMARAJA II

After the death of Rama Tibodi I, his son Ramesuan (r. 1369–1370), the governor of Lopburi, ascended the throne. He abdicated the throne in favor of Boromaraja I (r. 1370–1388), who was popular among the people of Ayudhya because of his successful expedition against Angkor. He gave priority to establishing dominance of Ayudhya over the upper Chao Pray Valley. Sukhothai raised the banner of independence, and a series of invasions, beginning from 1371 ultimately led to the submission of Sukhothai king Mahathammaracha II. He ruled as a vassal of Boromaraja. Ayudhya's expedition against Lan Na in 1387 failed due to the valor of its princess, Nang Muang. The troops of Boromaraja were defeated at Sen Sanuk. Thonglun, a boy of 15, became king after Boromaraja's death but would rule for a week only. The ex-king Ramesuan seized the throne and ruled Ayudhya again from 1388 to 1395. Ramesuan defeated the Lana Thai ruler in 1390 and seized Chiang Mai. The victory attributed to the Ayudhya king was described in the Thai chronicle the *Pongsawardan*, but it does not find favor with some historians.

Ramesuan took up the task of subjugating the Khmers. The control of Ayudhya ended after the Khmer ruler Kambujadhiraj (r. 1377–1383) recovered Angkor. Among the rulers of Ayudhya, two different thoughts had alternated regarding policies to be followed toward the Khmers. The Lopburi faction wanted to establish hegemony over the Khmers. But the Suphanburi faction was interested in subduing the Thai Kingdoms in the north and visualized Sukhothai, rather than Angkor, as a rival. Boromaraja I, who was from Suphoburi, did not follow an active policy toward the Khmers and concentrated his energy in subduing Sukhothai. Rama Tibodi I and his son Ramesuan were from Lopburi and perceived the threat from Angkor as more menacing than that from Sukhothai.

The immediate cause of the invasion by Ramesuan I in 1393 was the capture of Chonburi and Chantaburi by the Khmer ruler Dharmasokaraj (r. 1383–1389), who had also taken away a majority of the population. Angkor fell to the Thai army and 90,000 people were taken as prisoners. Rama Raja's rule for the 15 years from 1395 to 1409 was comparatively peaceful. A palace revolt resulted in the emergence of Prince Nakorn Intra, son of Boromaraja I, from Suphanburi. He defeated Rama Raja and became king of Ayudhya (r. 1409–1424) with the royal title of Somdej Phra Nakorn Intrathi Raja. Intrathi Raja had visited China in 1377, which resulted in an influx of Chinese to Ayudhya. He suppressed a rebellion by the Sukhothai king Mahathammaracha III and installed a new king, Mahathammaracha IV, in 1419. After the death of Intrathi Raja, a war of succession ensued among the princes. The winner was Prince Sam Phaya, who became the ruler of Ayudhya as Boromaraja II (r. 1424–1448). He led a large army against the Khmers in 1431 and occupied the capital city Angkor Thom after killing the ruler Srey (according to some Tammasok).

The sacking of the Angkor Thom (Sri Sothonpura) by the Thais led once again to a burgeoning of Khmer culture in Ayudhya. The Khmer features in the social and cultural domains percolated throughout Thai society. But the

Ayudhya occupation was only for a brief period, as Prince Intaburi, who had been installed as the new king by his father, Boromaraja II, died within a few months. The Khmers relocated the capital to Phnom Penh in 1434, as Angkor Thom was close to the Thai border. The sacking of their capital incurred heavy losses in terms of men and material for the Khmers. But from the Thai viewpoint, they had gained supremacy by these invasions and Ayudhya was safe from any attack from the Khmers.

A general pattern also was emerging in the internecine wars between Cambodia, Thailand, and Myanmar. Apart from ransacking the towns and imposing tributes, the victorious power would take much of the local population to make up for persons killed in the wars. One result produced is the ethnic mix now found in mainland Southeast Asia.

Sukhothai formed a part of the Ayudhya Kingdom by becoming a province of it in 1438, with Prince Ramesuan appointed as governor. Four years afterward, Boromaraja II led an unsuccessful campaign against Phaya Tilokaraj of the Lan Na Kingdom. His army was defeated by the Chiang Mai forces. Boromaraja II developed an illness during the campaign and died in 1488. His eldest son, Prince Ramesuen (Trailoknath), the governor of the Phitsanulok province since 1438, became the next king of Ayudhya.

TRAILOKNATH

The reign of Trailoknath (r. 1448–1488) formed an important period in the history of Ayudhya. After the beginning of Thai migration from Nan Chao, the Thai princes established small principalities independent of one another and constantly at war. The control of central authority was nominal. The absence of a unified state resulted in losses of revenue and the neglect of both forest and agricultural lands. Trailoknath turned his attention toward the administrative problems faced by the expanding nation because the existing structure was not adequate. The king brought all the Thai principalities together under centralized control and divided the Kingdom into a number of provinces, each headed by a *Chao Phraya*, or governor. He organized the central administration on a departmental basis with a high-ranking official in charge of each department.

The five *krams* (departments) were established in the capital city so that the king could have direct control over them. A chief minister headed the Ministry of Interior. The city and province of Ayudhya was under the ministry of the local government. The Ministry of Finance looked after taxes and state income. In light of growing maritime commerce, a separate branch for foreign affairs and trade was created under this ministry. Cultivation, food supplies, and land tenure were under the Ministry of Finance. The *Kalahom*, or head of military affairs, with the same status as that of a minister, looked after a separate category of military administration that was different from civil affairs. The army chiefs were brought under one royal command.

Trailoknath overhauled the Thai bureaucracy by assigning lands to different categories of people. The nobility having varying amounts of *sakdina* (honor marks) were categorized into seven grades. At the top was the *Chao Phaya* followed by *Phra, Luang, Khun, Muen, Pun*, and *Tanai*. The *Chao Phaya* was reserved for princes who were entitled to about 4,000 acres. In contrast, the share of the lowest category, the *Tanai*, was 10 acres. Thus economic holdings determined the status of a person. Except for the *Chao Phaya*, the rest of the ranks were nonhereditary. The nobles were supposed to maintain their livelihood from revenue collected from the land.

In 1450, the king codified the *Kot Montien Ban* (palace law) pertaining to royal families and tributary states. It created a hierarchy for royalty, each rank having separate laws. There were altogether five classes of queens and princes as per their rights and duties. The rituals, ceremonies, and functioning of the royal court were enacted. Details of punishment were meted out to royal families in cases of violations of the laws. Execution was the fate for a lady indulging in adultery. A member of the royal family was to be beaten to death by a sandalwood club. Death was prescribed for whispering at the time of royal audience and for shaking the boat of the king. Trailoknath saw to it that succession was peaceful and therefore created the post of the heir-apparent, *brah maha uparaja* (Vice King). Generally the heir apparent, who was the eldest son or the younger brother of the king, received the privileges of having a separate palace and 40,000 acres of land. The innovations of Trailoknath continued for centuries in Thailand. Some of the reforms of the king violated the principle of equality before law, but they gave stability to the Kingdom within the parameters of an absolute monarchy.

Trailoknath continued the policy of his predecessors in subduing the Lan Na Kingdom. The ruler Phaya Tilokaraj had besieged Phitsanulok but was driven out by Ayudhya troops. From 1463, Trailoknath began to reside in the city of Phitsanulok in the north of the Ayudhya realm, leaving his son Prince Boromaraja in charge of the capital city Ayudhya. Traiolknath and Tilokaraj fought indecisive wars throughout the 1470s, and both kings agreed for a peace settlement. Chiang Mai remained outside the reach of Ayudhya. Meanwhile, the rulers of the port city of Melaka had become Islamized and came into conflict with Ayudhya rulers bent upon extending influence over all of the Malay Peninsula.

During the reign of Muzaffar Shah (r. 1445–1459), Tun Perak, the *bendahara* (chief minister), had to fight a naval as well as a land battle with Trailoknath in 1456. The Thai forces were repulsed. Ayudhya and Melaka made peace afterward. The Melaka Sultan Mansur Shah (r. 1459–1477) was given a queen from Ayudhya.

Trailoknath also did much to encourage the arts and literature. He was a devout Buddhist and his palace was used for activities of the Buddhist Sangha. The king also built Buddhist monasteries and trade centers in the city of Ayudhya and other places of the Kingdom. A new sect of Buddhism, named *Vanaratnavong* or the Pa-Kaeo, became popular during the reign of Trailoknath. He joined the Buddhist seminary as a monk at Wat Chulamanee in Phitsanulok, where he died in 1488.

FROM BOROMARAJA III TO CHAI RAJA

Boromaraja III (r. 1488–1491), who managed the affairs of the Kingdom during Trailoknath's absence from Ayudhya, became the ruler after his father's death. There were no significant events during the three-year reign of the king. He was succeeded by his younger brother Prince Jutta, the governor of the Phitsanulok province. Jutta assumed the title of Somdej Phra Rama Tibodi II (r. 1491–1529). He introduced conscription for male citizens from the age of 16. Those unable to serve had to provide ivory, saltpeter, and hides. Between 1507 and 1515, a number of clashes occurred between Rama Tibodi II and the Lan Na rulers Phaya Yot Chiang Rai (1485–1514) and Phaya Mueang Kaeo (1514–1525). But these did not change the status quo.

The Portuguese victory over Melaka in 1511 had important consequences for the history of Southeast Asia as well as Thailand. The entry of the Europeans into Thailand forced the Thai ruling class to find means for maintaining its independence in the face of colonial expansion. Aflonso de Albuquerque, the conqueror of Melaka, sent Duarte Fernandez to Ayudhya to advance Portuguese commercial interests. Fernandez became the first European to make contact with the Thais. A treaty signed in 1517 with the king permitted the Portuguese to carry out trade and establish a Roman Catholic church. In return, the Portuguese provided firearms and military training. Some Portuguese soldiers even joined the army of Ayudhya.

Boromaraja IV (r. 1529–1533) made peace with the Lan Na rulers during his short reign. He appointed his brother Chai Raja to be the governor of Phitsanulok. The king died due to smallpox and his son Rasadathi Raja, a child of five years, was placed on the throne. Chai (r. 1534–1546) killed Rasadathi and became the king of Ayudhya. Such palace revolts and usurpations of the throne by murdering child kings occurred frequently in the history of Ayudhya. Chai developed water communications by finding the shortest route for transportation on the Chao Praya River. The bend of the river in Bangkok has become the main course of Chao Praya since then. Disputes over succession in the Lan Na Kingdom witnessed the involvement of the Ayudhya, Lan Xang, and Toungoo dynasties. The Lan Xang ruler of Laos Phothisarat claimed the throne of Chiang Mai and occupied it in 1545.

His son Settathirat was installed as the king. Chai intervened but was repulsed by the Chiang Mai army and afterward by Lan Xang troops while retreating. Chai Raja died in 1546, to be succeeded by his 11-year-old son, Keo Fa (r. 1546–1548). But the real power was with his mother, Queen Sri Suda Chan, who acted as the regent. There were palace intrigues, adultery committed by the queen, and assassinations. A younger brother of Chai, Prince Tian Raja, became the king of Ayudhya with the title Maha Chakraphat (r. 1548–1568). He along with his queen, Suryothai, fought against the Myanmarese menace from the west.

THE AYUDHYA–TOUNGOO WARS

The ruler of the Toungoo dynasty in Myanmar, Tabinshweti (r. 1531–1550), followed an expansionist policy, which went beyond Myanmar and toward the east. Lan Na, Lan Xang, and Ayudhya were on his agenda of conquest. After the unification of Myanmar, Tabinshweti became confident of bringing the eastern Kingdoms under his domain. The immediate cause of the war with Ayudhya was over white elephants, highly venerated figures in Hindu and Buddhist mythology. Tabinshweti's desire was to become a *chakravartin* (conqueror of the world) of the white elephant myth of Buddhist legends. The Ayudhya king possessed white elephants and he was bent upon having a number of these animals. Another reason to wage war by the rulers of Myanmar and Thailand was to augment the population with prisoners, who would be used as slaves. The earlier conflict between Chai and Tabinshweti were border skirmishes only between the respective troops. In 1548, the real war began with an invasion by Tabinshweti with a large army after the rainy monsoon season was over. The dispute over succession and violent happenings in the palace made the king confident of an easy victory. Both armies met near the city of Ayudhya. Queen Suryothai fought along with her husband dressed as a male soldier on an elephant. In an act of unsurpassed valor, she put herself between Chakraphat and Tabinshweti, when the former was losing the combat. She was slain by Tabinshweti, who afterward retreated. His troops returned to Myanmar through the Mae Lamow Pass, but not before being ambushed by Thai soldiers. Her saga of bravery and courage has been immortalized in the Hollywood movie *The Legend of Suriyothai* (2003). The Thai version released in 2001 became one of Thailand's biggest box-office hits. The ashes of Suriyothai are preserved in the *chedi* of the Suan Luang Sobsawan temple.

The second attack occurred during the reign of Bayinnaung (r. 1551–1581), the brother-in-law of Tabinshweti. After occupying the states of Myanmar and Bayinnaung, "the conqueror of ten directions," moved toward the east. The Lan Na Kingdom was ruled by Phra Mekuthi of Muang Nai (r. 1552–1558), who surrendered to the invading army in 1556 and agreed to pay an annual tribute. But Mekuthi had to face invasion from Lan Xang, the ruler of Settathirat. In 1558, Bayinnaung defeated the Lan Xang ruler. Settathirat and Chakraphat made a formal alliance after Bayinnaung's departure to his homeland. In 1563, Bayinnaung invaded Ayudhya. The pretext was the Thai king's refusal to surrender two elephants to him. But the real motive was to control the northern and central Thai states. He launched a two-pronged attack. Bayinnaung himself led a large army and reached Ayudhya after passing through the Sittang Valley, Chiang Mai, Kampengphet, and Sukhothai.

Another army from Myanmar came through the Mae Lamow Pass in the Tak province. The war resulted in the defeat of Ayudhya so that Bayinnaung was forced to return with four white elephants and some hostages from the royal family. Chakraphat's son Mahindra ruled as a vassal ruler with a Myanmarese garrison controlling him. When Bayinnaung reached Pegu, he found Pegu burning along with the palace. The rebellion caused by the Shan and Thai prisoners of wars was crushed ruthlessly and the capital was built again. A split in the royal family of Ayudhya in 1565 facilitated an attack from Myanmar again. Chakraphat and Mahindra wanted a close relationship with Lan Xang. But Tammaraja, holding the second most powerful position in Ayudhya as the governor of Phitsanulok, was well disposed toward Bayinnaung. Mahindra and Lan Xang, the ruler Settathirat, joined forces and attacked Phitsanulok. Chakraphat, held as a hostage in Pegu, was eventually allowed to return to Ayudhya on a pilgrimage. But he discarded the saffron robe of the monk and joined the attack against Phitsanulok. Another attack was launched in 1568 by Bayinnaung, who marched through the Mae Lamow Pass. After capturing Phitsanulok, he besieged the city of Ayudhya in 1568.

Chakraphat died and his son Mahindra succeeded him. Ayudhya soldiers offered fierce resistance, but ultimately the city fell due to the treachery of Phaya Maha Thamraja and Prince Chakri. Ayudhya was plundered and the victorious king returned with a large number of prisoners. Maha Thamraja (r. 1569–1590) was installed as a vassal ruler and his son Naresuan, a boy of nine years, was taken as a hostage to ensure the loyalty of Thamaraja. Mahindra had died while being taken as prisoner to Pegu. Ayudhya remained under Toungoo occupation for 15 years, until 1584.

The *Dhammathat* based on Manu's code of law was introduced in Ayudhya. The Thai also adopted the Era of Myanmar beginning from 638 C.E. The system remained in force until the adoption of the Gregorian calendar in 1887.

Naresuan was allowed to return to Ayudhya in 1576. He was put in charge of Phitsanulok. A capable leader, Naresuan organized an army and was waiting for the opportune moment to make Ayudhya independent. He successfully repulsed the Khmer during the years 1575 to 1578. Nandabayin became the ruler after the death of his father Bayinnaung in 1581. A rebellion had broken out in the Shan states and Naresuan suppressed it after his help was requested by Nandabayin. The success and popularity of Naresuan created jealousy in the mind of Nandabayin. He wanted to get rid of Naresuan before he proved to be too dangerous. Naresuan was again requested by Nandabayin to quell the rebellion of Prince of Ava and a plan was hatched to murder him. Naresuan became aware of it on the border area and in a declaration before his soldiers proclaimed his intention to throw off the yoke of servitude.

After killing the leader of Myanmar's army, Naresuan reached Ayudhya in 1584. Ayudhya was once again free and was put in charge of the defense of the Kingdom by his father, Maha Thamraja. Naresuan undertook the task of strengthening Ayudhya by building a strong army. He persuaded people from the northern area and the Shan states to join him. Nandabayin mounted another attack in 1584, but Naresuan defeated the invading troops. The second invasion three years later was also abortive. Naresuan also repulsed an attack by the Khmers, pursuing the army to the capital of Lovek.

Naresuan became the king of Ayudhya with the title Somdej Phra Naresuan Maharaj (r. 1590–1605) after the death of Thamaraja. Trade agreements with European powers were made during his reign. After the Portuguese, the Dutch and Spanish signed similar agreements with Ayudhya. A similar treaty in 1592 gave the Dutch a privileged position in the rice trade.

Spain had brought the Philippines under its colonial rule in 1598. Don Tello de Aguirre, the Spanish envoy came from Manila to Ayudhya to sign the Treaty of Friendship and Commerce. Nandabayin launched the fifth attack against Ayudhya in 1593. Naresuan marched to Nong Sarai to meet the troops of Crown Prince Min Kyawsaw. Both fought on elephant back, and Naresuan killed the prince.

Commemorating the victory, the King of Ayudhya erected a pagoda at Don Chedi in Suphanburi that is still extant. There is a fair on January 25 each year in honor of Naresuan. It is also Thailand's National Armed Forces Day. Some of the weapons and belongings of Naresuan find a place in Royal Regalia even now. The king then took the initiative and attacked Myanmar.

For her maritime commerce, Thailand needed ports in the Indian Ocean, and in 1593 two armies under Generals Chao Chakri and Phaya Praklong were dispatched to southern Myanmar. Chakri seized Tenesserim and Praklong occupied Tavoy. Naresuan wanted to secure the southeast frontier and marched against Cambodia. The Khmer king Raemea Chung Prei fled from the capital in 1594 and Naresuan returned with prisoners of war to be relocated in the depopulated northern provinces. Naresuan received an appeal from the Chiang Mai ruler, Tharrawaddy Min, a son of Bayinnaung, for help after an attack by Lan Xang. In 1595, Lan Na came under suzerainty of Ayudhya again, but Myanmar regained it after 20 years. Naresuan made an abortive attack against Pegu in 1595, repulsed by the arriving forces of Nandabayin arriving from Toungoo.

In 1599, Naresuan launched another attack against Pegu, while internecine quarrels took place among Prome, Ava, and Toungoo, all ruled by brothers of Nandabayin. Pegu was in ruins when Naresuan arrived. He marched further toward Toungoo but was defeated. Naresuan returned to Ayudhya. According to some sources, the king marched in 1605 for the last time against Myanmar and crossed the Saleween River. But he died after falling sick with a carbuncle on his face. The lower portion of Myanmar from Martaban onward was in control of Ayudhya. King Naresuan the Great not only freed Ayudhya but also made the Kingdom very powerful. The history of Ayudhya from the seventeenth century onward will be explored in the next chapter.

THE ADVENT OF ISLAM AND THE SULTANATE OF PATANI

The important religions of the world thrive side by side in Southeast Asia. Religion has been an important factor in shaping the destinies of the people of the region. Brunei, Indonesia, and Malaysia are predominantly Muslim countries. The Philippines and Thailand include sizable Muslim populations. At the time of the decline of the Indianized Kingdoms of Southeast Asia, Islam began to penetrate the region. The Arab traders played an active role in bringing the region under the spell of Islam. They purchased pepper from Sumatra and spices of Maluku (Moluccas) and Bandas.

After the advent of the Turks in India, the Islamization of Southeast Asia was rapid. The conquest of north India by the Turks was an event of far-reaching consequences for Southeast Asian countries. The spice and pepper trade to the Mediterranean by the Gujrati traders resulted in the establishment of Muslim settlements in Southeast Asia. From Gujarat and the Coromandel Coast, the traders traveled through the region, spreading their beliefs about Islam as they went. As it was the Indian Muslims who spread the religion, Islam in Southeast Asia was not the orthodox Islam of Arabia. The Indian traders were themselves newly converted, so the religion that they brought was not completely alien. Southeast Asia preserved some of the Hindu–Buddhist characteristics long acquired by its contact with India.

The progress of Islam in Southeast Asia became rapid after the rise of Melaka. The earliest evidence of Islamic presence in the Malaya Peninsula is a stone inscription found at Trengganu that says that the local people have converted themselves to Islam. Paramesvara, a rebel refugee from Palembang, founded Melaka and began to rule from 1403 to 1424 with the new name of Iskandar Shah. Earlier, in 1390, he had killed the ruler of Singapore (Tumasik), Tamagi, whose father was a Thai prince and whose mother was a daughter of the Patani noble. Singapore was under the suzerainty of Ayudhya from 1364.

Patani, along with Ayudhya, dispatched a navy to capture him, but Paramesvara escaped. Melaka soon became prominent politically as well as commercially. The spice trade route was from Maluku to India through Melaka. This port attracted traders from neighboring areas as well as India, and many of the traders were Muslims. The Gujratis, Parsis, Arabs, Bengalis, Kalingans, and others constituted the trading communities. The Tamils were also involved in politics and rose to high positions. These Marakkayars from the Coromandel were playing a major part in politics as well as trade. Melaka was also becoming the main diffusion center of Islam in Southeast Asia. On the eve of the Portuguese conquest of Melaka in 1511, Islam had been firmly entrenched in Southeast Asia.

Islam came to Thailand from various regions including China, India, the Middle East, the Malay–Indonesian archipelago, Myanmar, and Cambodia. As noted, Muslims as a whole constitute about 10 percent of the total population today. But Malay-speaking Muslims, who inhabit the southern provinces bordering Malaysia, make up about 3 percent of the population. In the four southern provinces of Thailand—namely Patani, Narathiwat, Satul, and Yala— about 76 percent of the people adhere to the Islamic faith. In its initial phase, roughly between the seventh and twelfth centuries, the Muslim traders played an important role in propagating Islam. Maritime commerce was an important activity of the Thai states.

The southern ports played major roles in oceanic trade. The traders from the Middle East, South Asia, and neighboring Kingdoms began to arrive and south Thailand witnessed the advent of Islam through trade. The religion was not confined to south Thailand only, as the city of Ayudhya was a center of commerce that had international settlements, including the Muslim traders. The indigenous traders as well as people of Thailand were attracted to Islamic preaching, its egalitarianism, and its belief in one god. Islam, with its prohibition of idol worship and images, presented a new form of faith. The prosperity of Muslim traders coming to Thailand might have been an added factor. But it was the creation of states ruled by Muslim sultanates that was responsible for making southern Thailand Islamized. Islam began to hold its sway here as compared to other areas of Thailand. The Hindu–Buddhist tradition was not as firmly established here as it was in north and central Thailand.

In the beginning of the Common Era, city states like Tun-hsun, Ch'ih-t'u, P'an-p'an, Tan-tan, Tambralinga, and Langkasuka emerged in the Thai–Malay Peninsula. The first century C.E. state of Langkasuka was the predecessor of the Patani sultanate established in 1374. The Langasuka and Tambraling areas witnessed its continued importance in regional and international trading network. The Melaka sultanate and Ayudhya Kingdom desired to bring it under their sphere of influence. Tamralinga, located between Chaiya and Pattani, was already in existence in the second century C.E. It was the precursor of the Nakhon Si Thammarat Kingdom. With the decline of Srivijaya, it became dominant in the region.

Nakhon Si Thammarat was paying tribute to the Sukhothai Kingdom and afterward to Ayudhya. In turn Songkhla was a vassal of Nakhon Si Thammarat, and according to Royal Thai chronicles its ruling aristocracy were Muslim landlords. Farther south was Patani, which assumed much more importance in the history of southern Thailand. The greater distance from Ayudhya facilitated the Islamization of Patani. Islam came to Patani even before the Melaka sultanate was established. Patani, like the Malay states of Kelantan, Trengganu, Kedah, and Pahang, had a tenuous relationship with Ayudhya in the sixteenth and seventeenth centuries.

Kedah had contact with Ayudhya, as is evident from sources of Kedah, which had a Muslin name for Rama Tibodi I, Sultan Mad Zafar Syah III. One of his sons was buried in Alor Setar, Kedah. When the central authority was strong enough, the Malay states had a vassal status. But most of the time they enjoyed almost an independent status.

After the Islamization of Pasai on the island of Sumatra toward the last decade of thirteenth century—as is evident from Sultan Malikul Saleh's tombstone dated 1297—Patani had Pasai Muslims living there in a village called Kampung Pasai. Patani was not unknown to the Islamic world before it was Islamized. Local legends mentioned in the chronicle *Hikayat Patani* state that Patani was Islamized toward the latter part of the fourteenth century at the time of its ruler Raja Indra. The name, "Patani" came into vogue at the time of his father, Raja Sri Wangsa. The state was prosperous due to trade and it was visited by merchants from different regions. A learned Pasai Muslim named Sheik Syafialudin once cured Raja Indra on the condition that he would be converted to Islam.

The sheikh began to indoctrinate members of royalty in Islamic laws and precepts. Raja Indra took the name Mahmud Shah with the title of sultan. Incorporating the neighboring provinces of Narathiwat, Yala, and Satun gradually, the state came to be known as Patani Raya. In the fifteenth century, Melaka, Ayudhya, and Patani endeavored to dominate each other as well as the Thai–Malay peninsula. Sometimes it resulted in war and at other times friendship. The Melaka sultanate under Iskandar Shah and his successors spearheaded the spread of Islam and cultivated a relationship with the royalty of the peninsula.

The Sultan of Patani, Mahmud Shah, sent ambassadors to Melaka, who returned with gifts for him. The two Muslim sultanates became allies. Patani became known to the outside world, and traders from Ayudhya, China, Japan, India, Arabia, and Persia came to the sultanate of Patani. Rivalry between Melaka and Ayudhya became intense, with trade and religion playing important parts. The Thai king Trailoknath had attacked Melaka in 1456 but did not succeed. Patani threw its lot with Melaka, keeping in view the long-standing enmity with Ayudhya. Both wanted to have mastery over the isthmus of Kra so that it would be easier to control the Straits of Melaka. Ayudhya also had an eye on the lucrative trading port of Melaka in the fifteenth century and the Malay states south of Nakorn Sri Thammarat.

From the isthmus of Kra, Patani began to launch attacks against Ayudhya, and the latter left no stone unturned to bring Patani under its control. Under the rulers of the Ayudhya dynasty, southern Thailand and particularly the Patani region enjoyed alternate phases of independence and subjugation.

The population of Patani increased, as did the progress of trade. Ships carrying goods came through the mouth of the Patani River. In 1516, a Portuguese ship loaded with different commodities came from Melaka for the first time to the Sultanate of Patani, who was very much impressed with the arms and ammunition that the Portuguese brought. Afterward the Portuguese ships came regularly for trade. There were about 300 Portuguese living in the city of Patani. Sultan Mahmud Shah, a capable ruler, died in 1538, to be succeeded by his son Muzafar Shah. Muzafar visited Ayudhya during the reign of Maha Chakraphat but was not treated well. However, the sultan was presented with slaves from Pegu and Cambodia. As they were Buddhists, a monastery was built for them in a village called Kedi (monk's house), and the Kampung Kedi still exists today.

Taking advantage of Ayudhya's war with King Bayinnaung, the sultan launched an attack against Ayudhya in 1563 with warships. His younger brother Raja Mansur and some chiefs accompanied the sultan. But the attack proved inconclusive and the sultan died while retreating. Raja Mansur became the next sultan with the title Sultan Mansur Shah. Then, after a palace revolt, Raja Bahadur, son of Mansur Shah, became the sultan. He had three daughters named Raja Hijau, Raja Biru, and Raja Ungu (Green Princess, Blue Princess, and Purple Princess).

After Bahadur died, Raja Hijau became the first female sultan to govern Patani. At this time, Patani had become virtually independent from Ayudhya. Hijau governed with skill and to the best of her ability. She was quite well known in the chancelleries of Europe, Ayudhya, and Japan. She sent her representatives to these places. The king of Japan sent envoys asking for permission to have trade and commercial relations with the sultanate of Patani. Hijau granted the request in 1592. She also sent emissaries to Japan in the years 1599 and 1606 requesting friendship and a trade relationship.

In spite of a rivalry with Ayudhya, the trade relationship was not hampered between the two. There were also exchanges of friendship missions. Ayudhya kings always referred to the queens of Patani by the honorable title *Pra Nang Chau Ying* (Her majesty, the female Raja). But beneath the surface, there was the lurking desire of Ayudhya as well as Patani to subdue each other.

5

History of Thailand, 1605–1782

The remaining 162 years of rule by Ayudhya kings were eventful in Thai history. The Kingdom was consolidated by absorbing Malay states and thwarting invasion by neighbors. International contact increased, and the name Siam became familiar among royalty, travelers, adventurers, and scholars of the world. After 1767, the Kingdom of Ayudhya ceased to exist, but its name and culture remained.

FROM EKATOSROST TO PRASART THONG

After the death of Naresuan, his younger brother Prince Ekatosrost became the ruler with the title of Somdej Phra Ekatosrost (r. 1605–1620). He reaped the benefit of a consolidated Kingdom created by his elder brother, but due to constant wars the royal treasury was almost empty. Therefore he took avid interest in commerce and administration. He introduced the payment of taxes. The revenue of the Kingdom increased as shop owners and traders had to pay taxes. Ayudhya was in control of export items like ceramics, timber, gemstones, and other commodities. The king brought Thailand into the sphere of international trade by exchanging ambassadors with other nations. He was interested in the Netherlands, where the telescope was invented. In 1608, the king sent a delegation to the Hague with a letter and gifts. The Prince of Orange was impressed by the Thai ambassador's espousal of Thai–China friendship, as the Dutch were also interested in China.

The first Portuguese Jesuit missionary, Balthazar de Seguerra, arrived in the year 1609. Shortly afterward, in 1612, the British and Dutch established trading factories in Thai territory. In June 1612, the first British ship, *The Globe*, sailed from Java to Patani, from where the merchants could reach Ayudhya for trade. A Japanese settlement in Ayudhya called *Ban Yipun* was inhabited by traders, unemployed Samurais, and Christian converts from Japan. Commodities like silver and handicrafts were being imported from Japan in exchange for Thai deer hides. Some of the Japanese were military men and there was a department in the administration for these "volunteers" called *Krom Asa Yipun*. Yamada Nagamasa (1590–1630), a Japanese adventurer, became the chief of *Ban Yipun* around 1610. He rose rapidly in the hierarchy of Thai nobility, becoming *Okya Senaphimuk*. During the reign of Ekatosrost, the Anglo–Dutch rivalry was intense and both fought between 1618 and 1620 in Patani and Ayudhya.

Sri Sauvapark, a son of Ekatosrost, became the next ruler, in 1620. He was killed and Indraraja, his stepbrother, became the king as Songtham (r. 1620–1628). In 1624, the Portuguese had captured a Dutch ship but had to return it after Songtham's intervention. The king began the tradition of paying homage to footprints of Buddha in Saraburi province. Songtham also wrote books on Buddhism. The king proclaimed Prince Jeta as the successor to the throne, and he ruled as Phra Jetathiraj from 1628 to 1630.

Sri Voravongse, an uncle of King Songtham, was powerful, and he became the *Chao Phya Kalhom* (head of military). He murdered the king, and afterward the younger brother King Atitaya ruled for about a month. The *Kalhom* proclaimed himself to be the king of Thailand as Phra Chao Prasart Thong (r. 1630–1655). Thong turned his attention toward the southern sultanate of Patani. Ayudhya was bent upon subjugating Patani because of its commercial value. A sovereign ruler in the south that could block access to Ayudhya was not to be tolerated. King Naresuan had made an abortive attempt in 1603, when a Thai armada landed in Kuala Patani. The attack was repulsed by Patani's ruler, Raja Hijau (Green Princess). In 1632, during the reign of Raja Biru (Blue Princess), Ayudhya attacked Patani for the second time. The promised help of the Dutch company based in Jakarta did not arrive and the Thai forces suffered defeat at the hands of the combined army of Patani and Jahor. The next year, at the time of the reign of Raja Ungu (Purple Princess), Patani was attacked again under the same commander, Okya Decho. The Thai armada battled with Patani-Jahor troops for some months and had to retreat due to shortage of food and affliction of diseases. The six warships of the Dutch arrived very late. Thong sent an emissary to the new ruler of Patani in 1635 to submit. But Kuning, daughter of Ungu, the new ruler, declined.

Yamada Nagamasa, who had been given the charge of the Nakhon Si Thammarat province, was asked by the king to attack Patani, but he also failed. Afterward, there was no major conflict between Ayudhya and Patani for quite a long time. Both sides were exhausted by the continuous warfare. The local history mentioned that Patani remained independent. But according to some sources, the Patani ruler in 1636 accepted nominal suzerainty of Ayudhya in light of Dutch advice.

THE REIGN OF NARAI THE GREAT

After Yamada's death in 1630, Thong destroyed the *Ban Yupin* and Japan ended its trade relationship with Ayudhya. The Dutch replaced the Japanese as Ayudhya's closest trading partner. A disagreement over the supply of rice caused the relations between Ayudhya and the United East India Company (*Vereenigde Oostndische Compagnie*, VOC) to deteriorate, but good relations were eventually restored again. The king received a letter from Batavia along with valuable gifts. The Dutch had helped Thong in his war against neighboring countries by sending warships. Cambodia, which was under the vassalage of Ayudhya, had declared its independence during the reign of Songtham, but Thong brought it under Thai control. With the Dutch help, the Thai army subdued a rebellion in Songkla.

After ruling for 25 years, Thong died and was succeeded by Prince Chai, who ruled for some months only. The brother of Thong, Sri Suthamraja, also ruled for a short time. King Narai (r. 1656–1688) occupied the throne after a palace revolt. Narai the Great was a notable ruler. He became preoccupied with a rebellion in the northern states and European powers. In 1660, the Chinese had invaded the Kingdom of Ava successfully and Chiang Mai, the vassal state of Ava, sought the help of Narai. The ruler of Chiang Mai soon changed his mind, and Narai returned to Ayudhya after capturing the town of Lampang. The following year, Narai checked an invasion from Myanmar successfully. In 1662, Narai led a successful invasion of Chiang Mai, bringing it under Ayudhya's control. He also married a Chiang Mai princess, and their son, Sorasak, became the king of Ayudhya afterward. But Ava captured Chiang Mai again in 1664 and kept it under its control for 63 years.

The Dutch were becoming the dominant power in Ayudhya, demanding more privileges in trade. In spite of being allowed to establish a processing plant, the Dutch desired a monopoly in deer and cow hides. Narai did not yield to this. The Dutch seized an Ayudhya merchant vessel in the Gulf of Thailand and blockaded the mouth of the Chao Praya River. In August of 1664, Narai had to succumb to pressure and signed a treaty with the Dutch, which gave the latter monopoly of trade in hides and China–Ayudhya trade as well as extraterritorial rights of jurisdiction. Like a wise strategist Narai began cultivating relations with the British and French in order to countervail the Dutch dominance. The British factory at Bantam urged London to assist Narai. But the Ayudhya factory was under the jurisdiction of Madras (Chennai) in India, and London did not want to interfere in Thai affairs.

Roman Catholic missionaries had arrived from France around 1664. Narai was not interested in their religion but took the help of Father Thomas, an engineer, to build forts in Thonburi, Nonthaburi, and Ayudhya. The French were allowed to open a trading station in Songkhla. De Lamar, a French engineer, put 18 guns around the city as a deterrent against hostile forces coming from the Gulf of Thailand. The French built a church and for some time Ayudhya was their headquarters in Southeast Asia. The king also shifted his residence to Lopburi and constructed a new palace. All these moves were for the purpose of weakening the Dutch influence in his Kingdom. In 1673, Pope Clement IX presented a letter to Narai urging him to convert to Roman Catholicism; however, the attempt under the auspices of French Jesuits to convert Narai failed.

A British ship, the *Phoenix*, arrived in Ayudhya in 1675 with Constantine Phaulkon (1647–1688), a Greek adventurer, as one of its trading staff. A linguist and thoroughly pro-French, Phaulkon began his remarkable career in Songkhla. He was known as the "Falcon of Siam" as his personal seal carried the image of a falcon. Phaulkon became the Superintendent of Foreign Trade and afterward a close confidant of the king. His advice to the king concerning trade affairs with Europeans was accepted. Marrying a Portuguese–Japanese Roman Catholic woman, Phaulkon discussed with the king the merits of Catholicism. The extravagant lifestyle, hobnobbing with royalty, favoring private traders, and other shortcomings would eventually come back to haunt him later.

The exchange of diplomatic relations between Ayudhya and France began. In 1680, a ship was sent by the French East India Company to trade with Ayudhya. A second Thai embassy embarked for the court of Louis XIV (r. 1638–1715) in 1684, as the first one sent four years before had been lost at sea. Chervalier De Chaumont (1640–1710) came to Ayudhya as an ambassador of France in 1686. He accompanied the Thai ambassador Phra Wisutsuntorn in the Kingdom's third diplomatic mission to France. Narai was not interested in changing his religion to Christianity, but he desired a trade agreement. Songkhla was ceded to the French and they monopolized the tin trade on Phuket Island. There was also a tax exemption of the French East India Company. France was the predominant trading partner with extraterritorial rights in Ayudhya. Meanwhile, the India Company had claimed compensation from Ayudhya for damage to British ships along the Indian Coromandel coast caused by ships sailing under the Thai flag.

In August 1687, Narai declared war against the EIC upon advice of Phaulkon. King Louis XIV decorated Phaulkon in 1687 and he became a Knight Order of St. Michael and St. Peter because of his services to France. The unlimited power wielded by Phaulkon had made him a hated figure among certain sections of the nobility of Ayudhya. The pro-French attitude of the king along with stationing of the French soldiers in Bangkok and Mergui (situated on the southern Myanmarese coast but under Thai control) were also resented. A powerful general and foster brother of Narai, Phetraja became the leader of an anti-foreign group. Sentiments against the *Farangse* (French, abbreviated to *Farang* afterward, which is used until now for a foreigner in Thai) rose to a high point. When the king became seriously ill with dropsy in 1688, Phetraja used the king's weakness to keep him as a virtual prisoner in the palace of Lopburi. Phaulkon was executed for treason. Phetraja killed the royal heirs and proclaimed himself king with the title Somdej Phra Phetraja (r. 1688–1703), after the death of Narai in July.

Narai was one of the greatest Thai kings. He cultivated international relations and diplomatic contact with rulers from Asia and Europe, putting Ayudhya on the map of oceanic trade. In 1664, he had a sent a mission to the Golconda sultanate of south India. After five years, another went to court of the Safavid ruler, Shah Solayman (r. 1666–1694). The legacy of a close relationship with France remained. The French accounts of Chevalier de Chaumont, the Abbe de Choisy, Fr. Tachard, Claude de Forbin, and de la Loubere regarding Ayudhya became important source materials for historians. In the French cities of Brest and Marseilles, streets were named Rue de Siam in honor of diplomatic missions of the king. The cannons given as a gift to Louis XIV by Narai were functional at the time of the French Revolution on July 14, 1789. However, he allowed Phaulkon unlimited powers and in the process alienated the majority of the nobility, leading to his downfall as well as Phaulkon's execution. An anti-foreign feeling began, which developed into a policy of isolation. It continued until the middle of nineteenth century.

FROM PHETRAJA TO BOROMAKOT

It became the policy of Phetraja and his successors not to allow any foreigner like Constantine Phaulkon to wield unlimited power. Also in the future no foreign power was allowed such privileges. The French fortification in Bangkok was seized and its troops left Ayudhya in November 1688. Phetraja also had declined the French offer of a new treaty one month earlier. The European missionaries were taken as hostages but released after the return of the Thai embassy from Europe. The king again allowed religious freedom. A new agreement with the Dutch was signed. Phetraja faced internal disturbances during his reign from different provinces of the Kingdom.

In 1690, an imposter by the name of Tam Tien, claimed to be a brother of Narai and rose in rebellion from the Nakhon Nayok territory. Although he was captured and executed afterward, many people fled to Myanmar in fear of persecution. The following year, the provincial governors of Korat in the north and Nakhon Si Thammarat in the south made abortive attempts to become independent from Ayudhya rule. Both rebellions were suppressed with an iron hand and much cruelty. In the battle for Korat, kites were flown over the city with flaming torches that landed on rooftops and burned houses. Nakhon Si Thammarat's governor escaped with the assistance of the chief of the navy of Ayudhya. The latter's head was placed on the city gate as an exemplary punishment. In 1699, a rebellion of 4,000 broke out again in Korat, spearheaded by a fanatic and magician, but it was crushed.

Cambodia had acknowledged Ayudhya's sovereignty and its king, Chettha IV, presented Phetraja with a white elephant. The neighboring Kingdom of Lan Xang of Laos experienced a succession dispute after the death of its king, Souligna Vongsa (r. 1637–1694). The Kingdom was fragmented into Luang Prabang, Vientiane, and Bassac. The Vientiane ruler received help from Nguyen and Ayudhya, which became rivals for dominance of Lao territory.

A son of Phetraja, Luang Sorasak, the *Phrachao Sua* ("king tiger") became the king of Ayudhya in 1703. He was a psychopath, debauched and cruel. Nothing significant occurred during his reign of six years. The king was fond of hunting, fishing, and *Muay Thai* (Thai kickboxing). After his death, his son Taisra (r. 1709–1733) succeeded him. Taisra appointed his younger brother, Phra Bantunnnoi, as *uparat*, or heir apparent, to the throne of Ayudhya. In 1714, the king of Cambodia, Prea Srey Thomea (Sri Timmaraja), took asylum in Ayudhya after being deposed by his uncle Keo Fa with assistance from Vientiane and Hue. The Thai army attempted to restore him but was defeated by Fa twice. However, the 1717 invasion was successful and Ayudhya reestablished sovereignty over Cambodia. The *uparat* became the king of Ayudhya with title of Maha Thammaraja II. Usually referred to as Boromakot (r. 1733–1758), his reign was fairly peaceful and prosperous. The only discordant note was an attack by 300 Chinese settlers in 1733, who were executed. The king was a great patron of Buddhism. It was now the turn of Ayudhya to send monks to Sri Lanka, which in 1753 requested Boromakot send priests to establish the Buddhist Sangha. Buddhism was in a state of decline in Sri Lanka. Under the leadership of Upali Mahathera and Ariyamuni Theras, 15 monks went with a golden image of the Buddha and a royal letter in Pali and gifts. The group set up in Sri Lanka the *Siyamopali Vamsa* (a Thai sect), which is still present to this day. The king also constructed monasteries in his Kingdom. The monasteries received lavish grants and became the center of religious ceremonies. These were places to impart teaching to monks and students. Uthumpon, the youngest son of Boromkat, succeeded to the throne in the year 1758. He was of religious temperament and enjoyed living in a monastery. Called by his subjects *Khun Luang Ha Wat* (The King of Buddhist Inspiration), he abdicated to lead the life of a monk in Wat Pradu Rongtham. His older brother Prince Ekatat became the ruler of Ayudhya, assuming the title of Boromaraja V (r. 1758–1767).

END OF AYUDHYA

A Kingdom or dynasty cannot last forever. Myanmar was now in an expansionist phase and Ayudhya bore the brunt of its growing power. A new and powerful dynasty was emerging in the west, which would close the Ayudhya period in the history of Thailand. In 1752 Alaungpaya (r. 1752–1760) was recognized as the king of Ava and founded the Konbaung dynasty. He captured Pegu five years afterward and in 1760 launched the first attack against Ayudhya. After regaining the cities of Tavoy, Mergui, and Tenesserim, Alaungpaya besieged Ayudhya for about a month. Uthumpon was recalled by Boromaraja V to rule on his behalf as the latter felt that he was not competent enough to protect Ayudhya. Meanwhile Alaungpaya had been wounded severely and died while retreating.

The next ruler was his eldest son, Naungdawgyi (r. 1760–1763), who was succeeded by his brother Hsinbyushin (r. 1763–1776). He followed the policy of his father, with attempts to conquer Ayudhya. He planned to attack it from the north after overrunning Lan Xang and Vientiane. In 1764, he began his campaign by subduing both Kingdoms in the north and marching south with the intention of capturing Ayudhya. A supporting army marched toward the east from Myanmar. By October 1765, much of the southern, Western, and northern territories of Ayudhya had come under Hsinbyushin. The siege of Ayudhya began in February 1766, and after a year it capitulated in April 1767. Hsinbyushin declined the offer of Boromaraja V to become a vassal king and unleashed a reign of plunder, destruction, and devastation after storming the city gate of Ayudhya on April 8, 1767.

Hsinbyushin's marauding army of 1.5 million soldiers and 6,000 elephants destroyed everything in Ayudhya and burned the city to the ground. Ayudhya's soldiers and civilians perished along with Buddha icons, royal chronicles, temples, and literary works. The destruction reduced the heritage of Ayudhya to ashes. Thus ended one of the most beautiful cities of the world and its history of 417 years. The body of Boromaraja V lay in the west gate of Ayudhya. Uthumpon was a prisoner of war in the city of Pegu, where he penned the book *Khun Luang Hawat* (*The Priest Monarch*).

THE LEGACY OF AYUDHYA

The Ayudhya Kingdom had ceased to exist, but its legacy remained imprinted in Thai history and culture. The city became a cosmopolitan center with the advent of traders, scholars, travelers, and adventurers. Ayudhya was an international city with many settlements of foreigners as well as an emporium of international trade. The diplomatic missions sent to countries like China, Japan, Golconda, Persia, the Netherlands, Britain, France, and the Vatican put Ayudhya on the international map. The growth of trade with Asia and Europe made it wealthy. The Chinese, Persian Muslims, Indians, Japanese, and European traders as well as merchants from Pegu, Cochin–China, and the Malay Peninsula gave the city a true international color. The foreigners also obtained high positions in the court of Ayudhya and became advisors of the king like Phaulkon. Shaikh Ahamad Qomi, a Persian merchant, rose to a high rank of *Chularajmontri* at the time of King Ekatosrost. He supervised Thailand's trade with the Middle East and with the Deccan sultanates of India.

Ayudhya was the city where merchants exchanged goods from China and Japan for commodities brought from Malay, Indonesia, India, and Persia. The Chinese and Muslim merchants dominated the scene to a great extent. Even the foreign department had Chinese and Muslim sections. There were Hindus, Christians, Buddhists, Muslims, and cult worshippers in Ayudhya. The Muslim population in Ayudhya up to the last decade of the seventeenth century was overwhelmingly Shi'ite Persians. They came from Persia (Iran) proper and also from the Shi'ite Deccan sultanates of India. The lingua franca of the Muslims of the Ayudhya was Persian, unlike the Malay language of the southern Kingdoms of Thailand. The king sponsored the *tazia* procession of the Muslims, as is known from the account of the French traveler and diplomat Guy Tachard.

The Sino–Thai trade thrived in Ayudhya. While dealing with other traders from Southeast Asia, the Chinese sometimes used the Thais as intermediaries. The Chinese enjoyed a privileged position in Thai society because they did not participate in *corvee*, or forced labor. They were free to engage themselves in trading activities. Some of the persons from foreign countries also obtained high positions in the court of Ayudhya.

The Kingdom of Ayudhya excelled in literature with novel content as well as forms. The title denoted the content; *kamsuan* would be a poem dealing with the pathos of departed lovers and *nirat* described the journey of separated lovers. Originating from the folklores of north Thailand, the *Lilit Yuan Phai* was about war between Ayudhya King Trailoknath and Tilokraja of Lan Na. The poem, the *Lilit Phra Lo*, was a love story between the ruler of Suang city Phaya Lo and Princesses Phuan and Phaeng of Song city. The romance between the three lovers of rival cities ended in a tragedy. The *Mahachat Kham Luang*, story of Prince Wetsandon, was a commissioned work ordered by King Trailoknath.

Literature developed a great deal during the reign of King Narai. Phra Horathibodi wrote the first textbook on the Thai language, entitled *Chinda Mani*. The didactic literature of the period included works such as *Khlong Phali Son Nong*, *Khlong Thotsarot Son Phra Ram*, and *Khlong Ratchasawat*, which discussed principles for entering into royal services and the art of governance. The festivals of each month, royal as well as public, were described in the chronicle *Phraratcha Phongsawadan Krung Si Ayutthaya*. In the *nirat* tradition, the work *Khlong Nirat Hariphunchai* described the poet's longing for his beloved while going to Lampun located in the Kingdom of Haripunchai. The *Samutthakhot Kham Chan* (The story of Prince Samutthakhot) and *Sua Kho Kham Chan* (The Tiger and the Cow) were also written during King Narai's time. The former had beautiful couplets such as *"Cease heart, heart without joy, heart with its everlasting memories of her beauty/memories that remain with me."* The life of Narai as an exile was depicted in *Khlong Kamsuan* (*A Mournful Journey*), written by Si Pat. In the reign of Boromakot, Thai literature flourished with the coming of excellent work like *Kap He Ruea* (boat song), written by Prince Thammathibet in the *nirat* tradition. The description of natural beauty while on a boat journey influenced later-day poets. In the procession of royal barges, the verses of this work are recited. Phra Maha Nak's poetic work entitled *Punnowat Kham Chan* was about a visit to Phra Phutthabat (Buddha's Footprint Shrine) located in the Saraburi province.

Art and architecture flourished brilliantly in the Ayudhya period. It was influenced by traditions from Cambodia, Sri Lanka, and India. The impact of Sukhothai lingered on for sometime. But the Ayudhya artisans developed a unique style producing masterpieces. In spite of the destruction caused by the events of 1767, many had survived, reflecting the resilience of Ayudhya art. Religious architecture became massive and the structures were imposing. Steep-roofed Ayudhya temples had their own pattern with elaborate ornamentation. The spires of the chedis became elongated. Wat Phutthaisawan, Wat Mahathat, and Wat Phra Ram were some of the earlier constructions of the Ayudhya period. The Wat Mahathat was a royal monastery and excavations in 1956 yielded relics of Buddha, Buddha images, votive tablets, and plaques made of gold. The Wat Phra Si Sanphet was constructed during the period of Trailoknath. Rama Thibodi II installed a standing image of Buddha, Phra Buddha Chao Sri Sanphet, 16 meters in height. The icon was covered in gold. The Wat Chaiwatthanaram, an imposing structure, was built by King Prasat Thong in 1630.

The gilt-lacquered Buddha images of the gallery in *mara vijaya mudra* ("victory over evil posture") were exquisite. The Buddha icons of the Ayudhya

Kingdom had a unique hair frame and small line engraved above the upper lip and eyes. The Buddha figures were made of stone in the early Ayudhya period, which gave way to gilted bonze icons. One of the best specimens was found in Wat Phra Sri San Phet, which was shifted to Hor Phra Nag and afterward was enshrined in the temple of the Emerald Buddha. The Buddha images were in various postures, such as reclining and standing. In the late Ayudhya period, the Buddha icons were adorned in royal attire and the base of sitting images was profusely ornamented. The scenes of *Ramakien* and *Jataka* stories were also found in the bas-relief of temples. The Ayudhya sculptures encompassed icons of Hindu gods and the Buddha. The inscription of Rama Tibodi I is mentioned in the installation of images of Siva and Vishnu from the Hindu pantheon. Many of the beautiful artworks in bronze, woodcarving, and stucco were lost to posterity because of destruction by the army from Myanmar in 1760s.

The performing arts also reached greater achievements. The dance, *khon*, based on the *Ramakien* was popular. The artists used masks for the first time during the Ayudhya period. The royalty encouraged *nang yai* (shadow puppet), *hun* (marionette), and *piphat* (musical orchestra).

THE THONBURI INTERIM

After the Burmese devastation of Ayudhya in April 1767, it was the half-Chinese general Phya Taksin (r. 1767–1782), governor of Tak province, who restored the pride of Thailand. Taksin had become famous in 1763 when he along with 500 followers resisted an army of the king of Ava, Hsinbyushin. Before launching a full-scale invasion against Ayudhya in 1765, another contingent of forces of Hsinbyushin had been turned back from Petchburi by Taksin. While Ayudhya was being destroyed in April 1767, Taksin had left the doomed capital and reached the safe sanctuary of the eastern shore of the Gulf of Thailand. With an expanded army of 5,000, he became the leader of resistance against Hsinbyushin's army. Taksin instructed soldiers of the novel method of using a sword in each hand while fighting the adversary. The province of Rayong came under his occupation, and afterward in June 1767 Taksin overran Chanthaburi. He was now the master of a sizable territory. His armada sailed along the Chao Praya River and proceeded toward Thonburi.

Taksin established himself as the king of Siam (Thailand) in the town of Thonburi after defeating both the army of the renegade Nai Thing-in and later Suki, the Myanmarese Commander of Hsinbyushin. Taksin had become the "Liberator of Siam" and people lovingly called him *Phaya Chao Taksin*, or King Taksin. Thonburi became the new capital, and the Chinese from Taksin's paternal home of Chaozhu supplied the labor force and building materials for building the capital. Strategically located near the mouth of the Chao Praya River, Thonburi was a suitable port. Trade was essential to revive the Thai economy. There was much maritime commerce, and the Chinese-Thai traders took a large part in it.

Taksin took recourse to guerrilla warfare against the troops of Hsinbyushin and occupied many towns. Bangkok and finally Ayudhya came under his sway. He had complete control over central Thailand areas like Bangkok, Ratchaburi, Nakhon Pathom, Jaksi, Prachin, Chantaburi, and Nakhon Sawan. There were independent rulers as well, such as Chao Nakorn controlling Nakhon Si Thammarat and other southern provinces. The governor of Phitsanulok named himself as King Ruang. Korat and the adjoining eastern area were under control of a son of Boromakot named Prince Pimai. The extreme northern part was under the control of the "Priest King," Chao Phaya Fang, who also seized Phitsanulok in 1768. At the outset, Taksin defeated Pimai along with his Myanmarese commander and brought the Korat area under his control. The following year, Nakhon Si Thammarat came under Thonburi. But his Cambodian adventure failed. The exiled king, Ang Non, had come to Thonburi in 1769 and Taksin had asked Ang Tong, ruler of Cambodia, to pay tribute. An army was sent to restore Ang Non, but it did not succeed. Taksin led a large army against Fang and it was successful. Afterward he marched to Cambodia and installed Ang. Ang Tong ousted the Thai army in 1772 with help from Vietnam, but he could rule for a year only. The next year, the Thais again controlled the affairs of Cambodia and Ang Non was made ruler of Cambodia. Taksin repulsed the attack of Myanmar against Chiengmai and Chiensen in 1774 and 1775. Hsinbyushin and his troops no longer posed any threat to Taksin.

The Kingdom of Luang Prabang under Inta Som became an ally of Thailand in 1774, throwing off the Myanmarese domination. Vientiane, whose ruler Ong Boun had defied Taksin by maintaining an alliance with Myanmar, was occupied in 1778. The famous Emerald Buddha, in Vientiane's possession since 1564, was brought to Bangkok at that time.

The frequent campaigns took a toll upon the health of Taksin and he began to show signs of insanity. He grew ever more paranoid. He had fantasies of becoming an enlightened figure like Buddha. Taksin also claimed he had mystical powers and desired sainthood. By the year 1782, he had become depraved and brutal. The hostility of Buddhist monks against Taksin's demand of respect and homage led to his downfall and imprisonment. General Chao Praya Chakri and his younger brother Chao Praya Surasi, the commanders of the Thai army, declared Taksin insane and deposed him. The historical consensus is that he was executed, but one Thai tradition mentioned that he was dispatched secretly to Nakhon Si Thammarat, where he passed the remaining years of his life as a Buddhist monk. Nevertheless,

Taksin became a symbol of Thai resistance against the marauding forces of Myanmar. He was the savior of the Thais after Ayudhya was burned to ashes. One of the most remarkable kings of Thailand, he had rallied the Thais against alien occupation. He was not only a warrior, but also a lover of arts and literature. The equestrian statue of Taksin adorns the big circular grounds of Thonburi.

6

The Chakri Dynasty: Rama I to Rama IV

The Chakri dynasty was established on April 6, 1782, when Chao Phaya Chakri was crowned the king of Thailand as Rama I (r. 1782–1809). In the history of Thailand, what is known as the Rattnakosin or Bangkok period began with Rama I's rule. The rulers belonging to the House of Chakri have been kings of Thailand ever since. The present ruler, Bhumibol Adulyadej (Rama IX), the ninth ruler of the Chakri dynasty, became the king in 1946. They have built up the administrative institutions of the illustrious rulers of the past and also made new contributions. The country has remained united ever since. The illustrious Chakri rulers have managed to steer clear of the difficulties faced by the country during the troubled times of earlier colonial rule. They have modernized Thailand with a great vision.

RAMA I

Thong Duang was born on March 20, 1737, to Phra Aksorn Sundara Smiantra, a noble of the Ayudhya Kingdom. After finishing his education in the Buddhist temples, he served in the royal household for some time and finally joined Thaksin's army. He conquered Vientiane in 1778 and it became a vassal of Thonburi. The famous Emerald Buddha, which was in Vientiane's possession since 1564, was brought back to the capital of Thonburi. Taksin having been declared insane, it seemed that the newly established peace and order of the Kingdom would pave the way for a civil war and anarchical situation. Thong Duang rose to the occasion. He returned from the military campaign of Cambodia. He assumed the royal title after restoring order and came to be known as Rama I.

Rama I decided to move the capital from Thonburi to the opposite bank of the Chao Praya River. It was a vast stretch of land with scope for future expansion. Earlier there were only a few trading settlements, a French garrison, and some villages. The king planned the layout for a new city of Bangkok. It has remained the capital of Thailand ever since. On the eastern side of the Chao Praya, he made a strong defense layout for the capital with fortification. Taksin's capital Thonburi was on both the banks of the river so as to make a gateway in case of an invasion by water. Rama I did not have any plan for escaping and concentrated on checking any future attack from the capital itself. A large Chinese community residing on the eastern side was transferred half a mile downstream to Sampheng. (It is now the location of a famous Chinese shopping area.) Rama I built a palace, which is still in existence. He was residing in a temporary abode made of wood. Within three years, the Grand Palace was constructed. In tune with the earlier Thai monarchs, connections with Indic-style Sanskritized epithets were retained as is evident from a host of adjectives used for the new city such as "Impregnable City of god Indra," "Grand Capital of the World," and "A City given by Indra and built by Vishnukrma." The Emerald Buddha was installed in Wat Phra Kaew. On both sides of the Chakkrabhat Piman Hall, a splendid residential complex was built up. The new capital was inaugurated in 1785 with the very long official title *Khrung Thep Maha Nakhon Amorn Rattanakosindra Mahin-drayutthaya Mahadilokpop Noparattana Radchhani Burirom Udom Rachnivet Mahastan Amorn Pimarn Avatarn Satit Sakatuttiya Vishnukarm Prasit* (City of Angels, Great City and Residence of the Emerald Buddha, Impregnable City of god Indra, Grand Capital of the World, Endowed with Nine Precious Gems, Abounding in Enormous Royal Palaces which Resemble the Heavenly Abode where Reigns the Reincarnated god, a City given by Indra and Built by Vishnukrma).

The reign of Rama I witnessed a consolidation and expansion of the Kingdom by extensive warfare. The king of Myanmar, Bodawpaya (r. 1781–1819), was determined to bring the neighboring state of Thailand under his submission. He arranged nine armies and sent them in three directions, which were successfully repulsed in 1785 and 1787 respectively. In 1793, Rama I invaded Myanmar provinces that extended into the Malay Peninsula but failed to capture it. Chiang Mai and Chiang Saen were once again under Thailand.

The Kingdom of Vientiane of Laos acknowledged the vassalage of Thailand. Chao In (r. 1792–1805) of Luang Prabang remained as a vassal of Rama I. Thus Thai control extended over to Laos. In 1795, Rama I installed the exiled ruler Anh Eng (r. 1779–1796) in Bangkok as king of Cambodia. Eng was sent back to the Cambodian capital Udong under protection of a Thai army. Rama I annexed provinces of Battambang and Siem Reap as a price for help rendered to Eng. When the powerful Gia Long (r. 1802–1820) unified Vietnam, Cambodia had to acknowledge suzerainty of both Thailand and Vietnam. The sultans of the Malay Peninsula such as Kedah, Kelantan, and Trenggannu acknowledged the suzerainty of the Thai monarch. They used to send *bunga mas* (gold leaves) as a mark of insubordination to the Thai court. When the British began to control the sultanates in 1909, the practice of offering *bunga mas* stopped. Chao Praya Surasingha Nath, the *Uparaja*, or Second King, and younger brother of Rama I, led an expedition to Patani in 1785. He was in southern Thailand resisting the troops of Bodawpaya. The sultanate of Patani had declared its independence in the 1760s, when Myanmar was attacking Ayudhya. Sultan Muhammad II was defeated. He had two gigantic Phya Thani canons, which were captured and taken to the capital. They are now displayed in front of the building that houses the Ministry of Defense. The prisoners of war, numbering around 4,000, were employed in digging the *klongs* (canals) of Bangkok. A rebellion in Patani in 1791 as well as 1808 was crushed, and Patani was formally annexed into Thailand in 1902.

Rama I revamped administration in the provinces as well as in the capital, thus making his rule very much centralized. The incessant Myanmar invasions of the eighteenth century had made bureaucracy and the monkhood corrupt and lax. During the years 1784 to 1801, Rama I restored the moral standard of the Buddhist monks by a series of royal decrees. The Buddhist scripture the *Tripitaka* (Three Baskets) and Thai civil law had been destroyed during the sacking of Ayudhya. Rama I called a Buddhist council in 1788, attended by 250 monks and Buddhist scholars who participated in reconstructing the *Tripitaka*. The Thai king was the defender of Theravada Buddhism, the pillar of Thai governance and society. Rama I performed his obligation to the fullest extent. A post designated as Supreme Patriarch of Thai Buddhism was also created. Rama I appointed a commission in 1795 that consisted of 11 jurists and scholars to look into the laws promulgated by Rama Tibodi I, the founder of the Ayudhya dynasty. The code of laws comprising indigenous practices and Indian legal concepts was changed to a certain extent. The new Code of 1804, known as *Tra Sam Duang* (Laws of the Three Seals), categorized the 48 provinces of the Kingdom. The governors were generally appointed from the royalty for a term of three years only. The ministries of *Mahat Thai* (North), *Kalahom* (South), and *Khlang* (Finance) oversaw provincial administration. The code also enumerated provisions for civil and military administration. The king took special care in appointing persons to head the ministries. Some of the appointees in the ministries were not Thais, as they were actually the Brahmans from India and Bunnag family from Persia.

There was a flowering of Thai literature under Rama I. He had initiated the royal writings known as *Phra Rajanibondh*. He was the author of the Thai version of the Indian epic, the *Ramayana*, which depicted the hero, Rama. The *Ramakien* of Rama I differed significantly from the original, with many interpolations throughout. Prose literature developed during this time as well. The Sri Lankan *Mahavamsa* was translated. The *Unarut*, based on the Indian epic the *Mahabharata*, depicted the life history of Krishna's grandson, Aniruddha. In the performing arts, apart from the *Ramakien*, dance dramas such as *Dalang* and *I Noa* were adapted from Javanese *Panji*. Verse recitals accompanied by musical instruments were also fairly common. Rama I died on September 7, 1809, in Bangkok, leaving 42 children from 29 wives. Many of his children renovated 23 temples in Bangkok and Thonburi. He was succeeded by his son Prince Isarasundorn as King Rama II (r.1809–1824). Rama I had left his mark in Thai history as a patron of literature, lawgiver, benevolent ruler, and empire builder.

RAMA II

The Kingdom held by Chakri rulers was fairly strong, with Thai suzerainty extending over most of Laos, part of northeast Myanmar, west Cambodia, and the northern portion of the Malay Peninsula. Rama II ruled smoothly during a time of peace and stability. The king appointed his confidants from among the royal relations and especially from the side of his mother, Queen Amarindra, strengthening his power base. Myanmar invaded the Peninsula region in 1810 and occupied Takau-Pa and Thalang in Phuket. But it was repulsed soon by a contingent of 20,000 soldiers. The town of Talang was devastated and depopulated by the army of Myanmar. It took quite some time to bring back normalcy. There was much increase in Sin-Thai trade with the important export of rice to China. Rama II asked the traders to import Chinese ceramics. The king also made Buddha images. He introduced the Niello ware and artisans were sent to Nakorn Sri Thammarat to set up a manufacturing center.

Thai literature reached its pinnacle of glory due to the writings of the king and the court poet Sunthorn Phu (1786–1855). The *Ramakien*'s two episodes were scripted by Rama II for dramatic performance. Authorship of the epic poem *I Nao* also was credited to him. Much of Thai social history pertaining to the early nineteenth century could be gleaned from this work. He was the author of the story titled *The Prince in a Conch Shell*, which is still read by students in Thai schools today. The *Sang Thong* and *Kraithong* were written for dramatic performance as well. Sunthorn's life was a colorful one. He had a love affair with a lady of the court and he married her afterward. He became a court poet. Sunthorn was jailed in 1821 due to his involvement in a brawl. After Rama II's reign, he lost his royal patronage and became a monk. His poetic romances were in the *sepha* (a type of ballad) style. His magnum opus, the *Phra Aphai Mani*, narrated the romantic adventure of Prince Aphai in ancient Thailand. Sunthorn also penned nine *nirats*. He wrote in a simple language for the common people. The *Khun Chang Khun Phaen* was another epic poem of the period. The story behind the poem's 30,000 lines originated in the folk tradition. It was indigenous in origin without influence from India or Java. The story revolves around two male characters, Phlai Kaeo and Khun Chang, who love Nang Phim. The three pass their lifetime amid happiness, sorrow, love, and war. They are not from royalty and belong to ordinary families. The story ends in tragedy with the heroine's death.

The reign of Rama II witnessed the resurrection of relations with the European power once again. The Thai monarchs had the difficult task of dealing with colonial powers expanding in Southeast Asia. Due to the sagacity and willingness to compromise of the kings, Thailand would remain free from Western imperial domination. The European countries had undergone dramatic changes after the Industrial Revolution. Development of technology had put them ahead of Asian countries. From traders, they became colonial masters. The Indian subcontinent had become a British colony. Southeast Asia was coming under their sway gradually. Penang Island and Melaka were acquired in 1786 and 1795 respectively. When the Napoleonic Wars were over, there was a renewed political and commercial offensive. After the reign of King Narai, Thailand had avoided having any treaty with European countries. It was Rama II who once again started signing treaties. From Macao, a Portuguese representative named Carlos Manoel Silveira arrived in Thailand in the year 1818. He became the Portuguese consul in Thailand after signing a trade agreement. The only expansionist act of Rama II was ousting the Sultan of Kedah, who fled to Penang in 1821. The mission of John Crawford in 1821 to Thailand failed and no treaty could be signed, as there was disagreement over Anglo–Thai trade procedures and the status of the Kedah sultanate.

RAMA III

Rama II died in 1824 and his son Prince Tub began to rule Thailand as Rama III (r. 1824–1851). Myanmar was no longer a threat to Thailand as it was directing its attention toward the west, and the first war between Britain and Myanmar broke out (1824–1826) because of a dispute along the border between Myanmar and India. The British wanted the support of Thailand against their common enemy Myanmar as well as for an extension of the British expansion to the northern Malay states of Perak and Selangor. At the same time, they desired to have Thai influence in Malay states. The British East India Company (EIC) sent Captain Henry Burney to sign an agreement with the Thai king. The June 1826 Treaty of Commerce and Friendship did not alter the Thai position as far as the Malay states were concerned. It also did not withdraw troops from Kedah. Any trading activity or building of factories would be done with the permission from the king only. The export of rice as well as the import of opium was forbidden. The Thai court did not accept any British consul and the king retained his monopoly over most of the export items. At least for some time Thailand did not succumb to outside pressure. But a relationship with the British had been established by a treaty. In 1818, American missionaries came and were allowed to provide medical treatment to the Thais. They established the first printing press in 1833. It was Dan Beach Bradley who set up the press for printing in Thai alphabets. In 1833 Edmund Roberts was sent by the American President Andrew Jackson to sign a Treaty of Amity and Commerce Friendship with Thailand. However, another attempt by the United States to exact concession from the Thai court did not succeed. Rama III did not receive the America envoy Joseph Balestier personally and asked the finance minister to confer with him. Balestier's mission thus failed. Another British mission came in 1851, hoping to establish a favorable trading agreement with Thailand. Rama III was ill and did not receive the emissary of Queen Victoria, Sir James Brooke. The White Raja of Borneo (Sarawak) instead met the finance minister, who did not want any change in the status quo. Brooke had no other alternative but to leave fuming. Had Rama III lived longer, things might have been different. These are big "ifs" of history. Probably Britain and Thailand would have come closer.

The military might of the Bangkok Kingdom was unleashed against Laos in 1826–1827. The splinter Kingdom of Vientiane was maintaining a balance between Vietnam and Thailand, showing allegiance to both. The ruler Anuvong (Chao Anou, r. 1805–1828) had wanted his son to be the ruler of Champassak, but the Thais resisted. Anuvong was determined to throw off the Thai yoke. He crossed the Mekong and attacked Korat, hoping that the Lao-speaking people would support him. Luang Prabang did not side with him but supported the Thais. He marched against Bangkok in 1827, but the Thai retaliation resulted in the depopulation of a major part of the Kingdom and the destruction of Vientiane. The following year Anuvong was captured and he died as a prisoner in Bangkok. The Vientiane Kingdom was abolished and it became a part of a Thai province. In 1831, Rama III sent an expedition against Cambodia down the southern shores of the Tonle Sap and the Thai troops occupied Phnom Penh. But the Emperor Minh-Mang (r. 1820–1841) of Vietnam sent a large army that expelled the Thais from the newly occupied territory. Thailand's hold over west and east Cambodia, however, remained unchanged. Its ruler, King Ang Chan II (r. 1806–1834), no longer sent the *bunga mass*, a symbol of vassalage status. The eastern portion was under Vietnamese domination. In late 1840, a large-scale revolution occurred in Cambodia against the Vietnamese, when Thieu Tri (r. 1840–1847), Emperor of Vietnam, began to impose a direct rule. In 1841, the Thai troops again invaded and installed Ang Duong (r. 1841–1859) as the king. By a compromise formula, the ruler showed allegiance to both Vietnam and Thailand. The distant vassals like Terenganu, Perak, and Kedah continued to pay tribute to the Thai court. In 1838, the mutiny by way of an attempt of the Sultan of Kedah to be independent was crushed.

The trade and commerce of the Kingdom continued to flourish and its income rose. Rama III strengthened the economic base of the Kingdom. The Chinese trade had developed to its fullest extent with the export of rice, tin, pepper, and cardamom, among many other things. Bangkok imported silk, paper, tea, porcelain, and saltpeter. Rama III had kept the profits from the Chinese trade in bags near his bed called "red bag money." The production of tobacco, sugarcane, and pepper increased manifold. Industries connected with sugar, tin, iron, and shipbuilding developed tremendously. The royalty and the emerging Chinese commercial elite had befriended each other. The Chinese could buy land and property. Emphasis on money and the economy had started a new age. It gave Thailand the semblance of a modern state in the context of a changing world. It was further developed by his successors. Although the threat from Western colonialism was renewed later, skillful negotiations by the king preserved Thai dominance in the outlying provinces. The king diplomatically avoided war and disallowed preferential trading privileges to Europeans. Rama III preserved his Kingdom in Southeast Asia at the time the region was being dominated by a Western presence, the British. He neither succumbed to Western pressure nor alienated Western countries completely. Rama III was a devout Buddhist. During his reign, about 50 temples were constructed and others received major renovations. He died in 1851 and was also known as Nangklao posthumously. As the king had not named a successor, the Council of Ministers decided to put Rama III's half-brother Prince Mongkut on the throne.

MONGKUT (RAMA IV)

Mongkut (r. 1851–1868), the grandson of Rama I, was son of Rama II and Queen Sri Suriyendra. Mongkut donned the garb of a Buddhist monk at the age of 19 and led the life of an ascetic until the day of his coronation as Rama IV. As a monk, he had founded the *Thammayut Nikaya* reform movement. He devoted his time to studying Western science and humanities. He was a renowned scholar on Buddhism. Mongkut had mastery over Pali,

Sanskrit, and major languages of mainland Southeast Asia. Well versed in European affairs, he learned Latin and English. He was an occasional contributor to the local *Siam Times*. Mongkut had traveled throughout the Kingdom as a monk and knew about the people. While on a pilgrimage in 1833, he discovered the famous inscription of the Sukhothai king Rama Khamheng. After becoming the king, he appointed his younger brother Prince Pinklao (Chudamani) as the vice king, who advised the king frequently. The king had an open mind with an incessant quest for knowledge, which ranged from the classical scriptures of Pali language to Western science and culture. Retaining the fundamentals of Thai culture, he began to modernize the country in a way best suited to Thailand. There was blending of tradition and modernity.

Without compromising his status as a benevolent despot, Mongkut undertook major reforms. He initiated major changes in building activities, health, education, administration, and court etiquettes. The king appointed Western experts as well as advisors to facilitate the task of modernization. In the royal army two Frenchmen were in charge of the drill and band. The mercenary police force was headed by a British commander. The customs service was looked after by an American. Mongkut also was in correspondence with the heads of state from France, the United States, Britain, and with Pope IX (1792–1878). He had invited foreign dignitaries to his coronation ceremony and frequently met with them in the royal palace. No persecution of Christians in the capital and other provinces was allowed. Freedom of religion was granted. Mongkut had developed a personal rapport with some of the missionaries as well as his tutors in Western languages and sciences. Chudamani, the vice king, equally matched the zeal of his brother with his interest in Western technology, the English language, and European manners. He named his eldest son George Washington. Chudamani built ships with steam engines and repaired watches. The reign of Mongkut witnessed massive construction works in the form of bridges, brick buildings, canals, and roads. The roads in Bangkok such as the Fuangnakorn road, the Charoen Krung road along Chao Praya River, and the Bumrung Muang road were constructed. The capital also was connected with the Moulmein–Singapore telegraph line. On the rivers, steamers appeared. A royal mint was established and for the first time currency in the form of metal coins was produced to meet the demand of the economy. The reign also saw a relaxation in the rigid court manners. The nobles were encouraged to put on shirts. Foreigners were exempted from crawling while going to meet the king. A prevailing ancient custom making it mandatory for persons to close windows and doors at the time of a royal entourage's passage was abolished. As a ruler with special concern for his subjects, the king granted them the right of petition directly. He appeared in public on a weekly basis to listen to the grievances of the subjects. Mongkut believed in Western medicine. Bradley, who had established the printing press at the time of Rama III, was also a doctor credited with introducing the small-pox vaccination in Thailand. Mongkut received it from the doctor's hands. He also encouraged medical work of the missionaries.

With his love of English language and Western knowledge, Mongkut wanted the members of the royalty to be trained in English. Initially, the wives of the missionaries like Ms. Bradley and Ms. Jones taught the ladies of the court religious texts in an effort to convert them to Christianity. Afterward the king recruited the services of Ms. Anna Leonowens (1834–1914), a British widow from Singapore. She arrived in Bangkok in 1862 to teach English to Mongkut's children. She taught them English language skills, science, literature, and history. All the sons and daughters of the king, numbering 60, were taught by her. One of her promising students was the Crown Prince Chulalgkorn. The role of Leonowens in influencing the modernization program in the nation has generated much debate. The king had set the agenda of modernizing Thailand much before he came into contact with her. Her exaggerated claim has been disproved by modern research and her autobiographical account, *The English Governess at the Siamese Court Being Recollections of Six Years in the Royal Palace* (1870), contained lies and half truths. At best, it could be said that Leonowens made the royal children educated in the English language and the king had respect for her as she was the tutor of his beloved children. Her "favorite" student Chulalongkorn did not invite her to the Kingdom after she had left in 1867. But the saga of Anna Leonowens had caught the imagination of novelists and moviemakers. In certain quarters, her story is much more important than the life and philosophy of Mongkut himself. The king was an erudite scholar and an enlightened person. By no stretch of the imagination would he have been influenced by the tutor of his progenies. In 1944 Margaret Landon wrote *Anna and the King* and screen versions of it came afterward. There was a movie entitled *Anna and the King of Siam* (1946). The Broadway play *The King and I* (1951) is still banned in Thailand for distorting Thai history and portraying Mongkut to the point of ridicule. More recently, the motion picture *Anna and the King* (1999) generated further controversy in Thailand. The Thai Censor Board ruled that Thais should not see the movie, which was said to misrepresent the monarchy and exaggerate the extent of impact of Leonowens on Mongkut.

One of Mongkut's greatest accomplishments was to keep Thailand free from colonial rule by use of diplomacy, treaty arrangements, and grants of concessions. Rama III had just begun this policy, but it was left to Mongkut to make a major breakthrough. He had already done his homework and knew very well that the times had changed and that Thailand must keep pace with them. The king had created an atmosphere of amity and trust by removing suspicion from the minds of foreigners. John Bowring (1792–1872), an author of repute and the fourth governor of Hong Kong, was the emissary of Her

Majesty's Government to sign a new treaty with Thailand. London was determined to square up the unfinished task of James Brooke. He arrived from Singapore in the warship the HMS *Rattler* and desired attendance with the king and not with the finance minister. Bowring was greeted by the king, whose demeanor charmed him. The 1855 April Treaty of Friendship and Commerce between Britain and Thailand was the precursor to treaties signed with other European countries and the United States. These treaties were more or less similar with the agreements that China signed with foreign powers. The advantage was with the foreign countries as they received the status of most-favored nation, extraterritorial jurisdiction, and tariff control. Therefore, these unequal treaties were abrogated afterward in the reign of Rama VII (r. 1925–1935). The Thai treaty with Britain allowed British nationals to own land property in Bangkok. The import of opium was made duty-free, rice trade was opened, and for the rest of the imports from Great Britain the customs duty was 3 percent only. The British Consul only would handle cases concerning offenses committed by the British subjects in Thailand. The Thai laws and courts did not have any jurisdiction over them.

Mongkut had no other way out but to sign a treaty with Britain. By 1852, the southern provinces of Myanmar had become a part of the British empire, making Britain an immediate neighbor of Thailand and establishing itself as the most powerful colonial power on the Asian continent. It was a judicious decision of the king, lest the British might expand their territorial aggrandizement further. The other colonial power, France, rival of Britain, had to be contained, too. A similar treaty was signed with France in 1856, when an envoy of Napoleon III (1808–1873), the vice-consul of Shanghai de Montigny, arrived in Bangkok. The Thais were apprehensive of French designs on Cambodia. In fact, the French interests were a combination of economic, political, and religious motives. In 1867, Thailand recognized Cambodia as a French protectorate and annulled earlier treaties between the two countries. The century-old Thai domination of major parts of Cambodia had ended except for its ports in the provinces of Siem Reap and Battambang. A few months before the French treaty, a Treaty of Amity, Commerce, and Immigration had been signed with the United States in May 1856 and Stephen Mathon became the first American consul in Thailand. Similar treaties were signed with Denmark (1858), Portugal (1859), the Netherlands (1860), Prussia (1862), Sweden–Norway (1868), Belgium (1868), and Italy (1868). One of the major consequences of the treaty system was the end of Chinese dominance in the foreign trade of Thailand. The British gained a major foothold and profited from trade, investment, and shipping. The foreign trade of Thailand increased phenomenally from the middle of the 1850s, most of it going through Singapore. British companies opened branches in Bangkok. Investments were made in the tin and timber business. The so-called free trade benefited the British. Remittance abroad became easy, as the British had abundant reserves in gold. The British economic predominance over Thailand continued until the 1940s and the Thais continued its policy of allying with the most powerful regional power.

An avid astronomer, Mongkut had invited the courtiers and foreign communities to Thailand to observe the total solar eclipse, which he had calculated two years earlier. After observing it in 1868 in malaria-infested Sam Roi Yod, Mongkut and Prince Chulalongkorn were stricken with the disease. The king died a few days afterward and Chulalongkorn, who survived, became the next king of Thailand. Mongkut is venerated in Thailand for his modernization program and introduction of Western science and technology. An astute statesman and one of the most remarkable kings of Thailand, he ruled the country with dignity and preserved its independence.

7

King Chulalongkorn (Rama V)

As we saw in the previous chapter, it was Mongkut and his son Chulalongkorn who preserved the independence of Thailand at the time of Western colonial expansion in Southeast Asia. Both father and son ushered in an era of modernization and propelled the country toward a new age. Mongkut had laid the foundation and Chulalongkorn followed his father's footsteps. He demolished the power brokers of the earlier regime and built a support base to assist him in his schemes. Gradually, Thailand began to free itself from the late medieval age and entered into the modern period.

EARLY LIFE AND NEW ORDER

Chulalongkorn was born in the year 1853 as the eldest son of Mongkut and Queen Debsirindra (1834–1861). He received a traditional education as well as instruction from European tutors, including Anna Leonowens. In fact he was a favorite student of Leonowens and thanked her profusely after she had left the Kingdom. Chulalongkorn became the king of Thailand at the age of 15 after his father's death in 1868. Due to his tender age, the Kingdom was placed under the Regency of Chao Praya Siri Suriyawong (1808–1883) until 1873. During this period, Chulalongkorn traveled widely. While in

Singapore, Java, and India, he acquainted himself with the administration of the colonial powers. This was the second visit of a Thai king abroad, the first being the visit of Sukhothai king Rama Khamheng to Beijing in 1282. Chulalongkorn knew about the history and cultures of other countries. This exposure helped him a great deal in modernizing his Kingdom. The king was now at the helm of affairs after the end of Regency, but the direct influence of the old guards was still there. He had differences of opinion with Suriyawong over the pace of reforms. The latter belonged to the powerful Bunnag family, who were under the services of Thai kings for more than 200 years. His father had been the *Phra Khlang*, or finance minister, under Rama III. Suriyawong was in charge of military (*Kalhom*) command under Mongkut. Many persons belonging to the higher echelons of the administration had a stake in maintaining the status quo. In 1875 the *hua boran* (conservative) forces, in fear of losing privileges by the reforms of the king, staged an abortive palace revolution and tried to put Prince Wichaichan on the throne. The king began to induct his younger brothers and persons amenable to reforms. Prince Damrong Rajanubhab (1862–1943), a stepbrother of the king who was with the Royal Bodyguard Regiment, undertook major administrative reforms of the provinces. He became the deputy commander-in-chief of the army, minister of education, and afterward headed the ministry of interior. Devawongse Varopakar (1858–1923), another stepbrother of the king as well as a brother-in-law due to his sisters' marriages with the king, was the personal secretary of the king in 1878. After the resignation of Chao Praya Phanuwong, a member of the Bunnag clan, Varopakar took charge of foreign affairs. He was mainly instrumental in maintaining Thai independence by diplomacy and balancing Anglo–French interest. It took the king about 10 years to undertake changes without any opposition as advisors were persons of the king's choice. In the 1870s, the reform process was slow, but in the 1880s it was all pervading in administration.

REFORMS

Chulalongkorn reformed Thai society. His changes in administration, education, and the judicial system had a lasting impact on the country. In 1873, the system of prostrating before the presence of the king was done away with. By a royal proclamation it was declared that any person born during the king's reign was a free man, which was the first step toward the abolition of slavery. Children born of slave parents would be free by the age of 21. It took 31 years for the complete abolition of slavery. Gradual abolition of slavery did not raise protests from any quarters, not even from conservative elements. In 1874, privy councils were created. The lower one was in an advisory capacity, bringing important matters to the court. The higher council, composed of princes and nobles, was an advisory body regarding matters of revenue and loyalty of the subjects. It was presided over by the king. With consultative functions only, these bodies did not represent the will of the people, and it would take a long time for democracy to arrive in Thailand.

The king was deeply committed to educational reforms. A school was established to impart secular education. It became the Royal Pages School in 1902. In addition to offering training in civil services, its curriculum included international relations, engineering, medicine, and commerce. It was named the Civil Service College in 1911 and after seven years the famous Chulalongkorn University came into being. In 1887, a separate department of education was created. The king instituted a scholarship program for students. The princes and scholars were sent abroad for higher education. In 1880, the king established the first public museum inside the Grand Palace; after seven years it was converted to the National Museum. A medical school was also established. James W. McKean, an American doctor and Protestant missionary, did yeoman service in the Thai medical field. He supplied quinine tablets, vaccinated for smallpox, and helped persons afflicted with leprosy. In Sirirat, the first public hospital was established in 1887. It offered services in both indigenous and Western medicines. Prince Damarong set up a medical school in 1890 that afterward became a college. Thai students benefited a lot after the printing of a textbook entitled *Paetsart Sonkhra* in 1895. The printing press of the state provided school textbooks and a *Royal Gazette* was also published. Damarong and British civil servant Robert Morant (1863–1920) did much for educational improvement during the reign of Chulalongkorn. Morant also was in charge of tutoring the royal family. Press freedom was guaranteed by royal decree and nonlibelous writing against the royalty was tolerated to a certain degree. Chulalongkorn announced religious toleration in 1878. Sunday was declared a holiday. With the abolition of the traditional lunar calendar, Thailand followed the Western pattern of calendar.

From the 1880s, the administrative apparatus of Thailand was changed drastically and most of it was at the behest of the principal advisor and most trusted person of the king. Prince Damrong had been Minister of Education and afterward Minister of Interior. The provincial administration was overhauled, with the division of the Kingdom into *monthon* (circles), which were subdivided into *changwat* (provinces) and *amphur* (districts). The *samuthathespiba* was the head of circles. Provincial autonomy was curtailed a great deal with nominated governors, who received their salary from the ministry. Thus central control over outlying regions was ensured. The districts were under control of *nai amphur*, or district officers, who were appointed by the center. The village was the smallest unit and the *kamnan* or chief belonged to the local community. Generally a leader represented a hamlet of about 20 families and he would have a major say in the appointment of *kamnan*. The ministries were also revamped.

The trusted persons of the king were appointed in important ministries such as the interior, foreign, justice, and military affairs. In 1892, the ministers met as a cabinet for the first time. In 1891, the king ordered organization of the mining industry and entrusted the task to Herbert W. Smyth (1867–1943). He became the secretary and afterward director of the newly constituted Department of Mines. Smyth traveled widely throughout Thailand and reported about mining potentiality. He also arbitrated conflicts among different mining companies.

In 1888, a separate department for the army was created and the Thai army was strong enough to suppress any local rebellion. A modern army on the pattern of European countries was created and Chao Phra Surasakmontri (1851–1931) was placed in its command. Chulalongkorn introduced conscription in 1902. The king gave special attention to creating a strong army, and the defense expenditure rose from 1 million baht in 1898 to 13 million in 12 years. The outburst of rebellions from minority areas was easily crushed. The nation's martial power, consisting of the Thai army of 20,000, navy of 5,000, and 50,000 reserves, was strong enough to crush any internal dissension. About 2,500 rebels of Ubon in northeast Thailand had revolted under the leadership of Thao Thammikarat. He styled himself as the Messiah and began a millenarian movement. The rebels sacked Khemmarat in 1901. But soon the Thai army suppressed them. The Shans of Phrae in the north rose in rebellion, aided by local rulers. The latter were in distress over the loss of privileges by the sweeping reforms. Phrae was captured and Lampang was attacked. It was also crushed by a Thai army led by Danish adviser H. M. Jensen and Surasakmontri. The sultan of Patani, Abdul Kadir Kamaruddin (r. 1899–1902), revolted in 1902. The seven provinces of Patani had been regrouped as one unit called *boriween chet huamuang* (area of the seven provinces). Loss of autonomy and sending of revenue to the central treasury resulted in a rebellion against Chulalongkorn by the sultan. The revolt was suppressed and the sultan was arrested. In 1902, Patani was incorporated into the Thai Kingdom. Reform in judiciary was undertaken on a large scale. A Ministry of Justice was created in 1892, headed by Oxford-returned Prince Rajeburidirekrit, who set up law courts in districts, provinces, and at the country's center. Multitudinous cases had been piled up, and to clear the backlog special courts were also set up. The profit of middlemen and officials was curtailed to a great extent. Five years afterward, a law school was established for training lawyers and judges. In 1908 the Thai laws were codified. The following year, the penal code of Thailand was passed. Apart from the prince, a Belgian advisor, Gustave Rolin-Jaequemyns (Chao Phraya Aphai Raja, 1835–1902), helped in bringing about judicial reforms. In 1891, the Belgian solicitor had met Prince Damrong in Cairo and accepted the post of a general advisor with an annual salary of £3,000. In 1897, he helped in the establishment of a law school to provide training facilities to Thai lawyers and judges. Rolin-Jaequemyns was of the opinion that traditional laws of the countries should be maintained while the legal system was updated. Some of his reforms in accountancy and public projects led Thailand toward the foundation of a modern state. A statue was erected at the Law Faculty building of Thammasat University in his memory.

Chulalongkorn brought about major changes on the financial front. For all financial transactions, auditing, budgeting, and bookkeeping were introduced by Prince Damarang. The bureaucracy was centralized for financial as well as other departments. While recruitment of the staff was made, the modern educational background was always kept in mind. Alfred Mitchell-Innes (1864–1950), a British diplomat, was appointed the financial advisor of the king in 1896. The flat silver coin was replaced by introduction of paper money in 1902. Baht was the official currency. Tax collection was given to parties by public auction and not to private individuals. The corrupt middlemen were ousted as the taxes were paid directly to the state. Revenues from taxes were deposited in the treasury and all expenditures were accounted for. The revenue increased from 1.6 million baht in 1874 to 57 million in 32 years. Agriculture was the main source of livelihood for the majority of the population. For the benefit of cultivators, title deeds were given for the land. The land tax became more equitable. Due to canal projects, new areas were brought under cultivation. The uncultivated lands of the landlords were given to peasants and the latter occupied it during the period of cultivation. The production of rice increased from about a million *piculs* (1 *picul* is about 60 kgs) in 1950 to 11 million by the year 1900. During the reign of Chulalongkorn, technological advancements were made with new roads, bridges, canals, and water gates. In the capital city, new roads, avenues, and boulevards were constructed. The traffic on canals gave way to roads. Bangkok looked like any modern city, with European-style houses, pavement, and tree-lined roads. The famous Rajadamnoen Avenue was built linking central Bangkok with Dusit Palace. European technicians also installed electricity in the palace of the king. In 1875, the royal telegraph was established. The transport system was revolutionized with the introduction of railway track from Bangkok to Paknam at the mouth of the Chao Phraya River, over which travelers could travel a distance of about 12 miles within an hour. Both goods and passenger trains plied between the two terminals covering 10 stations. Within a few years, the return from the capital invested in the rail system was high because of its regular traffic. It took five years to complete it in 1893. No single European country was given monopoly in railway construction in spite of Queen Victoria's desire. The railway track was completed with help from foreign technicians belonging to different nations. The railway was a joint enterprise of Belgium and Denmark with locomotives constructed by the Kraus of Germany. In 1905 the British government provided the king loans for meeting expenses connected with the railways.

Thailand was increasingly known to the outside world due to the influx of foreign advisors and opening of Thai consulates in major cities of the world. Out of a total of 549 advisors, the majority belonged to Great Britain. They were mainly in the field of finance, education, police, and mining. Rolin-Jaequemyns from Belgium had helped in the Thai judicial reforms and foreign affairs. The Americans helped the government in medical advancements and negotiating Thailand's treaty system with colonial powers. Francis B. Sayre, an American lawyer, was a foreign office advisor. The Danes, French, Belgians, Germans, and Italians worked in various projects of the state. The role of the Europeans was in an advisory capacity and ministries were headed by the Thais. Loyalty to throne was a must for any person residing in Thailand. Chulalongkorn was in correspondence with the heads of state from different countries in Asia and Europe. He traveled around Europe in 1897 and 1907. Czar Nicholas II of Russia (1868–1918) and the German Kaiser Wilhelm II (1859–1941) supported Thailand's endeavor to be a part of the international system. Chulalongkorn became the first Thai monarch to visit Europe. The major cities of the world like Berlin, Tokyo, Paris, St. Petersburg, London, and Washington, D.C., had Thai consulates. The foreign office under knowledgeable and efficient foreign Minister Varopakar was reorganized. By skillful diplomacy, he made a harmonious balance between Anglo–French interests in Thailand and preserved the nation's independence.

TRANSFORMATION OF THAI SOCIETY AND THE ECONOMY

The sweeping reforms of Chulalongkorn changed Thai society and the economy a great deal. The influx of Western culture made a lasting impact on the country. The society was not going to be the same. Although most of the benefits reached the elite, it also percolated to other classes of the society over the course of time. Common people did not have money and they were busy in earning their livelihood. The city of Bangkok thrived with a population increase from 100,000 during the reign of Rama III to 500,000 in the year 1909. With the improvement in communications, people from all over the world came and many resided in the city. The Chinese population in the capital city increased considerably. The Chinese from all over Thailand constituted about 10 percent of the total population. The Thai aristocracy began to don Western apparel, and foreign shops like Bad Man Store, Windsor Store, Ramsey Store, Kim Seng Lee, and S.A.B. Store opened in Bangkok. The women wore Western-style makeup and cut their hair short. The *mahatthai* (parted topknot) of men was no longer seen as it was being replaced by a short hairstyle. The Ramsey Seck Field on Bamrungmüang Road was a famous shop for Western-style dressmaking. The capital became one of the biggest markets in Southeast Asia, with imported consumption goods flowing. Watches, jewelry, perfumes, German beer, canned milk, typewriters, and liquor were sold by different shops. The lifestyle of urban people changed with *boriphok niyom* (consumerism) becoming the catch word for rich people of the cities. Clubs and holiday resorts also sprang up. The wealthier people constructed Western-style houses with materials imported from abroad. Concrete, iron, and chandeliers came from Britain. Singapore, Italy, and Belgium supplied cement, marble, and glass, respectively. Skilled artisans came from abroad. The popular sayings about cuisine were *kinkhao kin pla* ("eat rice and fish") and *numprik phaktom* (referring to a sauce of shrimp paste, chili, and boiled vegetable). After the establishment of rice mills, white rice became popular. In the cities, the age-old custom of betel chewing gradually fell out of favor. The use of spoon, knife, and fork was much in vogue. Chulalongkorn asked his minor wives to prepare soup, stew, steak, salad, sandwiches, and desserts. Soda and ice were becoming popular in certain quarters. The first ice factory was the Nai Loet ice factory. The rich mainly adopted Western values and purchased luxurious goods. Consumerism came to society because of the remarkable changes during the reign of Chulalongkorn.

The Thai economy witnessed the impact of reforms in all its ramifications. International trade expanded, becoming the biggest source of state income. Rice was the major item of export. Teak, tin, textile, pepper, gemstones, rhinoceros leather, ginger, nutmeg, wax, and lead were other items of export. Rice business was under the Chinese, and the European companies controlled teak production. The imported commodities were mostly of consumer goods for the elite. These were opium, copper sheets, tea, eyeglasses, mirrors, metalware, liquor, chinaware, face powder, camphor, pigments, perfumes, ceramic ware, and paper. For monetary transactions the British opened banks between 1888 and 1894. In 1897, the French opened *Banque de l' Indochine*. Goods were imported and exported mainly in ships, with the British and German ships providing most of the shipping facilities. The prices of land for residential and shopping purposes increased. Investment in land became a profitable business. The unused land between Silom Road and Ban Thawai in Bangkok was developed for the Chinese and Europeans, who constructed houses as well as shops. There was demand for rental housing for the floating population of Bangkok, many of whom came to the capital only for a short time. Apart from economic reforms, the era saw developments in Buddhist religion and literature. Vachirayan, half-brother of the king, was appointed as head of a new Buddhist academy in 1893. By the Sangha Act of 1902, the monks were organized into a single order under the king. The Supreme Patriarch was Vachirayan. The Thammayut order of King Mongkut spread to different provinces of Thailand. In 1899 the king ordered the construction of a Buddhist temple in Bangkok. The Wat Benchamabophit (Marble Temple) was one of the most magnificent examples of modern Buddhist architecture, with its Italian marble and orange tiered roofs. The Thai epic poem *Khun Chang Khun Phaen* had another revision by Prince Damrong in 1910. It became the standard text with, including interpolations and deletions from the original.

SOCIETY AND THE ECONOMY ANGLO–FRENCH ADVANCES

Thailand survived without becoming a colony of either Britain or France due to the sagacious policy of Chulalongkorn. When imperialism was at its height in Southeast Asia, the neighbors of Thailand had succumbed to colonial onslaught. Mongkut had signed unequal treaties of friendship and commerce, allowing extra-territoriality rights. Chulalongkorn followed his father's footsteps with some changes and retained the country's independence. With his farsightedness, knowledge of the English language, and deep study of European history, he knew well that the best course for Thailand would be to maintain friendly relations with colonial powers even at the cost of Thai territory. Chulangkorn also was aware of the limitation of his military prowess against the might of colonial powers and made several land concessions to the French and British, keeping Thailand as a buffer state between the two. Britain was the master of the whole of Myanmar in 1885, and it reigned supreme in the southern Malay Peninsula. France had established its stronghold in Indochina save for Laos. There was a rivalry between Britain and France in Southeast Asia and Africa. The last two decades of Chulalongkorn's reign witnessed the impact of the European alliance system over Thailand. In the 1890s, Anglo–French relations had deteriorated over what was known as the Fashoda incident in Africa, and only in the beginning of the twentieth century did they begin to improve. The *entente cordiale* of Britain and France in 1904 would have its impact in Thailand as well. It settled the two Western nations' disputes over Africa, Canada, and Southeast Asia. Between British Myanmar and French Indochina lay the independent Kingdom of Thailand. Both colonial powers thought it judicious to keep Thailand as a buffer state rather than bringing it under colonial hold. Neither France nor Britain would remain as a silent spectator were the other to gobble up Thailand. France as well as Britain wanted to seize as much Thai territory as possible. Chulalongkorn exploited the Anglo–French rivalry and he was prepared even to "bend with the wind"—that is, he was prepared to sacrifice territories for the sake of the independence of Thailand. The territories that Thailand ceded to colonial powers did not belong to the core area, where ethnic Thais were living. These were the outlying periphery zones where Thailand had forced suzerainty. The king thought it better to give up the claims. By sacrificing a little, he thought the country would achieve more. Its sovereignty would be preserved.

France was determined to extend its hold over Laos after controlling Tonkin, Annam, Cochin–China, and Cambodia by 1885. A clash between French ambition and Thai suzerainty over Laos was inevitable. Four years afterward France proposed to Britain that Thailand be declared a buffer zone between the spheres of influence of both the countries along with division of Thailand along the Mekong River. Britain declined the proposal. France planned for conquest of Laos, which was the last stage of French imperialism in Laos. Thailand had reduced the king of Luang Prabang, Oun Kham (r. 1872–1887 and 1889–1895), to the status of a governor following the French advance. In 1885, it also sent a military expedition to Luang Prabnag under the pretext of protecting it from Ho tribes. The French were alarmed over the events as they did not want Laos coming under Thai authority. An agreement with Bangkok in May 1886 resulted in the creation of the post of a vice consul in Luang Prabang. Auguste Pavie (1847–1925), a famous explorer who was responsible for bringing Laos under French colonial rule, joined the post in 1887. The Thai army chief had made another raid to Luang Prabang, but the Ho tribes sacked the city after it had left. Pavie decided to take initiative with the backing of *Parti Colonial* in France and he received additional staff and financial support for his mission. In 1892, Pavie was appointed the chargé d'affairs with the rank of a consular general in Bangkok. He was determined to acquire territory east of the Mekong River and used force to secure the compliance of Bangkok. Thus the Paknam incident began.

The Paknam (Phra Chulachomklao) fort at the estuary of the Chao Praya River had been completed in 1893 and the French navy was fired upon from the fort in July. The 25-minute battle resulted in the loss of 151 Thai soldiers. The casualty figure for the French was 32. Afterward, the French moved 15 miles upstream to Bangkok, threatening to bombard it. The guns of the two ships, the *Comete* and the *Inconstant*, were targeted at the royal palace. The king received an ultimatum of two days to recognize the French rights to territories east of the Mekong River, withdrawal of Thai garrisons and a compensation of two million francs. The Thais did not receive any support from Britain and agreed for a treaty in October by establishing the French protectorate over Laos. The French empire extended from the coast of Vietnam to the Mekong across the whole of Laos. It was further noted in the agreement that Thailand would not use the Mekong River for warships, and on the west bank of the river on a width of 16 miles, military activity was disallowed. France acquired the right over disputed land, where 600,000 people were living over an area of 55,000 square miles. The Paknam clash also demonstrated the weakness of the Thai army. Although it was strong enough to quell local rebellions, it was no match for a Western army. In many quarters of Thailand, the incident is taken as a cause of grief due to territorial loss after the humiliating treaty. An Anglo–French agreement of 1896 guaranteed the integrity of central Thailand, leaving northeast Thailand and the Mekong basin for furthering French interests as well as the Malay Peninsula for the British. In spite of British noninterference in the Paknam incident, Bangkok did not want to lose the support of Britain and agreed for a British proposal not to give concession to any other power except London south of the 11th parallel, where the Kra Isthmus and southern Malay states of Thailand were situated. This agreement of April 1897 also stipulated that Britain guaranteed rights of Thailand in this zone. The Kra Isthmus was of strategic importance to the British. A canal over it would reduce the importance of Singapore. The French were planning to build a canal over it. Therefore, the Anglo–Thai agreement of 1897 secured the British position south of the 11th parallel. The states of southern Thailand as well as the isthmus were free from dominance by any country other than Britain. Chulalongkorn also had visited Europe in the same year to garner support of Russia and Germany for Thai independence. Thailand had to cede territories further in the first decade of the twentieth century to preserve its independence.

In February 1904 France acquired territories on the west bank of the Mekong including Xainyaburi and part of Champassak and retained commercial establishments in towns like Nongkhai and Khemmarat. The earlier mentioned April 1904 agreement between Britain and France finally brought the archrivals together in the face of increasing cooperation between Germany, Austria-Hungary, and Italy. Britain came out of "splendid isolation," so that its position in the world would be secure. It had already come to an understanding with the United States and Japan. An alliance with a European country was a necessity as Germany, Austria-Hungary, and Italy had already signed the Triple Alliance in 1887. The final declaration of the *cordiale* was about Madagascar, the New Hebrides, and Thailand. Britain and France agreed on the point of Thailand's status as a neutral buffer zone between the British territories of Myanmar as well as Malaya and French Indochina. The British and French zones of influence in Thailand were outlined as it suited both. London and Paris also agreed not to annex any Thai territory. However, France and Britain signed further treaties with Thailand in 1907 and 1909 respectively. Thailand gave up the northwestern Cambodian provinces of Siem Reap, Battambang, and Sisophon, and France in turn renounced the extraterritorial privileges. It also withdrew from the eastern Thai province of Chanthaburi. By the Anglo–Thai Convention of 1909, Thailand gave up its suzerain rights over the four southern states of the Malay Peninsula: Kedah, Perlis, Kelantan, and Trengganu. Britain recognized the Thai control over the Muslim-dominated Patani province and gave up extraterritorial privileges in Thailand. The convention thus fixed the present existing boundary between Malaysia and Thailand, which has become one of the factors for a rise of Islamic terrorism in Thailand.

The Malay States gave a loan amounting to £4 million for a railway line between Thailand and Malaya. The treaty was a turning point in the history of southern Thailand and the Malay states. Patani, Narathiwat, Songkhla, Satun, and Yala (Jala) remained under Thailand. Bangkok gave up its suzerainty over four Malay states and paved the way for the transformation of Malay into a unified state. Thailand survived the onslaught of new imperialism by a precarious balancing act. The heartland of Thailand was preserved by any means at the expense of peripheral territories in Laos, Cambodia, and the Malay states. Chulalongkorn and his team played the diplomatic game very well. Thailand ceded territories but remained free from colonial rule.

LEGACY OF CHULALONGKORN

A remarkable change had taken place in Thai society. The society and economy had changed beyond recognition due to the advent of Western culture, increase in international trade, changes in the taxation system, and the reforming zeal of Chulalongkorn. He intensified the reforms that had started during his father's reign and took Thailand toward the threshold of a modern age. A feeling of Thai nationalism took incipient form. The Thais looked toward his reign with pride. A national identity had been formed. The Thai language was taught in all the provinces, where new schools had been established. The reign of Chulalongkorn has often been criticized as undemocratic, with the king resisting the move toward a representative form of government. Actually, the movement started during the reign of the king. This was suppressed or sometimes even ignored by the throne. Anybody involved in writing against the government was punished. A journal, *Sayam Praphet*, was edited by Kulap Kritsanon. It reached a circulation of 1,500. Thianwan Wannapho, an advocate, was jailed in 1882 for criticizing the ruling aristocracy for corruption and exploitation. In 1885, a memorandum signed by a group of foreign-returned students and three princes urged the king to move toward democracy under a constitutional monarchy. It also called for equal rights and freedom of the press. Chulalongkorn replied that the country was not ready for constitutional monarchy and that benevolent despotism suited Thailand the best. Chulalongkorn had written to the Crown Prince Vajirunhis in July 1893, saying that the monarchy was not for wealth and pleasure. A king should try to reduce the sufferings of his subjects. The reward would be fame and glory after death. The letter aptly summed up Chulalongkorn's notion of monarchy. Although he was not prepared to pave the way for democracy, his policy of modernization bore fruit and subsequently became a contributing factor in taking Thailand toward the revolution of 1932. When Chulalongkorn died on October 23, 1910, in Bangkok, he had left a modern state to his successor, Vajiravudh (1881–1925), who ascended the throne as Rama VI. In commemoration of Chulalongkorn, October 23 is observed as a national holiday. In 1997, a pavilion was constructed in honor of Chulalong-korn at Ragunda in Sweden. The 150th anniversary of the king's birthday, in collaboration with the UNESCO, was celebrated with all pomp and show in Thailand in April 2004.

8

Democratic Transition

A new Thai identity was emerging in the first few decades of the twentieth century as we saw in the preceding chapter. The centralized, bureaucratic, and strong state sans slaves had intellectuals as well as a ruling aristocracy who were westernized. The different groups such as intellectuals of urban areas, ambitious generals, Thai–Chinese businessmen, and communists wanted a share of the nation-state. There was clamor for a democratic transition. The changes in China, World War I, the 1917 Bolshevik Revolution of Russia, and the world depression of 1929 had a profound impact on the course of Thai history. The above events generated internal dynamics in the country transforming its society and economy. Thailand became a constitutional monarchy with a parliamentary form of government in 1932. This was a period of great developments in education and literature. Thailand also enhanced its international standing by joining the Paris Peace Conference and League of Nations. The extraterritorial rights granted to the United States and European nations were done away with.

VAJIRAVUDH

Vajiravudh (Rama VI) became the king of Thailand after his father Chulalongkorn died in 1910. He was born in 1881 to Queen Sri Bajarindra (1864–1919). The crown prince since 1894, Vajiravudh was educated at the Royal Military College, Sandhurst and Christchurch College, Oxford. He had great love for traditional Thai drama as well as Thai and English literature. His coronation in Bangkok on December 2, 1911, was attended by royalty from Japan and European countries. Vajiravudh preached his notion of social relations and patriotism through his plays and writings. The state-sponsored nationalism of the king was eclectic, with elements of Western values and Thai traditions. The king emphasized three parameters of nationalism: *Chat*, *Sasana*, and *Phramahakasat* (Nation, Religion, and Monarch). These were worth defending and dying for all Thais. These ideals were propagated through public addresses and the writings of the king. Whatever demerits might have accrued from Vajiravudh's idea of nationalism, he is revered in many circles as the "father of Thai nationalism." During Vajiravudh's reign, monarchies were abolished in countries like China, Russia, and Turkey. The overseas Chinese were feeling a sense of nationalism with allegiance to China. The Chinese society was pushing for Chinese education. The Thai capitation tax law of 1910, which was applicable to all residents, was resented by the Chinese of Thailand. A general strike was announced for three days in Bangkok, bringing Chinese business to a standstill. There was, however, Thai resentment against them. The king published a pamphlet, *The Jews of the East*, criticizing the Chinese. Writing under the penname Asvapahu, he mentioned that the Chinese had enjoyed the privileges of citizenship but were not showing loyalty to the adopted country. The Chinese, who were the largest minority group, felt alienated by the king's emphasis on Thai nationalism.

The king ignored the advice of state councilors and succumbed to the flattery of a group of courtiers. He had alienated many of the powerful princes of his earlier reign. Vajiravudh was also profligated and his lifestyle was not in conformity with the tradition of Thai aristocracy. His extravagant expenditure on his coronation, official functions, and travels had depleted the state coffer. There was criticism against the king because of his luxurious living, which included constructing the Sanam Chal palace and importing expensive horses from Australia. Much of his time was being spent on literary and dramatic activities. In spite of his stay in Britain, the United States, and Japan, where he inculcated Western values and learned about a representative form of government, the king remained a diehard conservative as far as monarchy was concerned. He believed in absolute monarchy and propped up a figurehead to buttress his position as an absolute monarch. In May, the king established the *Sua Pa* (Wild Tiger Corps), a paramilitary organization designed to protect him as well as the throne. It became the mouthpiece of His Majesty. King Naresuan of Ayudhya had an army called the *Sua Pa Maew Morn,* and in line with that Vajiravudh created an organization providing advance scouts for the regular Thai army. It would assist the regular army only. Military training was to be imparted to civil servants by the White Tiger Corps. There would be unity of the Thais as peoples from various backgrounds would be inducted into the organization. It would also maintain law and order in the Kingdom. Throughout the country, the Tiger Corps in their black uniforms became conspicuous figures. Children also were indoctrinated and a junior division of Wild Tigers was established. It was known as the *Lok Sua,* or Tiger Cubs, and was similar to the U.S. Boy Scouts. But it was militaristic in its program. It was expected that when children would grow up they would be an asset to the nation with their notion of duty and service. It became quite popular and the number of *Lok Sua* reached 38,735 in 1925. Opposition to the king's reign was growing due to his policies that alienated important sections of the society, and in March 1912 an abortive coup was led against him by junior army officers. Increasing the power of *Sua Pa* was perceived as a threat to the army. The leaders of the coup along with 92 persons were arrested. After a trial, only 23 were put behind bars, until 1924. The rest were granted royal pardon.

REFORMS OF THE KING

The king had only five wives and he abolished the royal harem. He introduced monogamy and asked women to adopt a Western style of dress. Free mixing between men and women was encouraged. Women's fashion styles and apparel changed during the reign of the king. Women's hair was neck-length, and sometimes long hair for women with a Western-style bun became a fashion. Blouses had high necks and long sleeves. Women were encouraged to don tube skirts called *phathung.* The king ordered the use of the term "Buddhist Era" (B.E) for the official records in 1912. The era was counted from the date of death of Buddha. He also introduced the new tri-color red, white, and blue national flag in September 1917. The three colors symbolized sacrificial blood for the defense of the nation, religion, and monarchy, respectively. This was in conformity with the king's three pillars of Nation, Religion, and Monarch. The king took steps to popularize the Western system of medicine. He and the royal family looked into the health problems of the subjects. In 1911, construction of Chulalongkon Hospital began, and it started functioning only three years later. Another health center named the Vajira Hospital became operational in 1912. A research institute named after the queen mother, Sri Bajarindra, began to produce vaccines against cholera and antidotes for poison in 1913. The earlier practice of studying Thai as well as Western systems was abolished. The Medical License Act of 1923 brought Thai medical practices to an end, finding them "nonscientific." Smallpox vaccinations were given free in the clinics established by the king's order. Vajiravudh ordered the creation of surnames for every Thai family in 1913 and a deadline of six months was given to the head of the family for registering the surname. He began the process of simplifying the names of his predecessors by using the name Ramathibodi for all the kings. His name became Rama VI. The king also banned lotteries and gambling in the same year. In December 1923, the metric system of weights and measures was introduced. The game of soccer was encouraged. Thai Buddhism developed during the reign of Vajiravudh. Prince Wachirayan Warorot (1860–1921), the head of the *Thammayut* sect, became the supreme patriarch of Buddhism (1910–1921). The Thai Sangha had been centralized in the previous reign, linking the capital with the 80,000 monks of the whole country. There was also reform in Sangha education. Wachirayan made the study of the Pali language somewhat simpler by writing the textbooks in six volumes, *Bali Waiyakon*. Buddhism had become one of the three pillars of Thai nationalism. Nation, Religion, and Buddhism became interdependent in the scheme of the king. In education and public morality, the *Thammayut* order had done commendable service. Presently it wields a lot of influence. The social status of a person became interlinked with the education he or she had, and King Vajiravudh had done yeoman service for Thai education. He introduced compulsory education in 1921 and Thailand became the second country after Japan in Asia where boys and girls were required to join schools. In March 1917, the first University of Thailand was established. The Chulalongkorn University became the premier educational institution of the nation. It had been formed out of a merger of the Civil Service School and other institutions. The Thai students, numbering 303, went abroad for higher studies. The king also sent royal officers for training in foreign countries. In November 1918, the king outlined a program for female education. Women could now pursue subjects like medicine, education, law, and science. Female enrollment in schools increased rapidly, from only 7 percent in 1921 percent to 38 percent four years later. Apart from state-run schools, private schools also were available. A text entitled *Sombat khong phu di* (*The Qualities of Gentlefolk*) by Chaophraya Phrasadet emphasized the moral character of students. He established the Department of Municipal Affairs and improved upon the *skuhaphiban* (local government). Some of the other measures taken were the setting up of the Sam Sen power plant, a population survey, the registration of vehicles, and improvement of the water supply.

LITERATURE AND THE PRESS

Vajiravudh was a distinguished writer and his notable works were *Phra non Kham Luang* and a collection of nationalist articles entitled *Muang Thai Chong Tun Thoet* (*Wake up, all Thais*). He also wrote plays including *Matthanaphata* and *Sakuntala* and frequently acted in the theater. The king translated works of Shakespeare, including *The Merchant of Venice, As You like It, Othello,* and *Romeo and Juliet* into the Thai language. He also translated *School for Scandal* of Richard B. Sheridan (1751–1816) and Jean-Baptiste Poquelin's (Molière, 1622–1673) *Le Médecin malgré lui* (*The Doctor in Spite of Himself*) into Thai. The king started the Enhancement of Knowledge Club, which staged plays and published magazines. In 1915, the first Thai novel, *Khwammaiphayabat* (No Vendetta), by Luang Wilatpariwat, was published. Gradually, fiction, short stories, and books on Buddhism also came out. Prince Damrong Rajanubhab, who was the interior minister until 1915, was a well-known literary figure writing on Thai history, culture, and arts. He began the practice of distributing books at funeral ceremonies as a mark of respect for the departed soul. The two outstanding books written by him on history were *Our Wars with the Burmese: Thai–Burmese Conflict 1539–1767* and *Journey through Burma in 1936: A View of the Culture, History and Institutions.*

Vajiravudh's reign was important for the development of newspapers and magazines. Tienwan and K. S. R. Kulap were prose writers and essayists writing with political themes. Articles came out on subjects like the clash between Thai and Western civilization, modernization, social order, and economic problems. The newspapers began to play an important role among the public, ruling circles, and educated elite. During the First World War, newspaper articles urged the king to join with the Allies against the Central powers to end the unequal treaties signed during the reign of Mongkut and Chulalongkorn. There were altogether 149 newspapers and magazines in 1920, including some exclusively meant for women. In 1925, seven women's magazines in Thai and three each in English and Chinese were published.

THAILAND AND THE FIRST WORLD WAR

Countries such as Thailand, Turkey, Japan, China, and the Asian colonies of the imperial powers were involved in the First World War fought between the Allied (Britain, France, the United States) and Central (Germany, Austria–Hungary, the Ottoman empire, Bulgaria) powers. Its impact was immense in unleashing forces of nationalism and self-determination. The local elite were influenced by the ideas of democracy and self-determination of American president Woodrow Wilson (1856–1924). The only military action by the

Central powers in Southeast Asia was the naval raid by the German cruiser *Emden* off the Penang coast of Malaysia. The German agents were active in Batavia and Bangkok with arms and money to incite anticolonial insurrections. But its impact was very limited.

The Oxford- and Sandhurst-educated Vajiravudh knew the advantage of joining the Allied cause. He was hopeful of revoking extraterritorial rights imposed by France, Britain, and the United States. It would also assist Thailand in getting equal status with other nations of the international community. The Anglophile king donated large amounts to the British war effort. Moreover, he was an honorary army general of the British army. The Thai neutrality was only for official purposes and the king was looking for an opportune moment to join the war. The American entry on the side of the Allies in April 1917 turned the tide against the Central powers. King Vajiravudh sided with the Allied powers and made his independent country a belligerent nation on July 22, 1917. Immediately, the unequal treaty signed with Germany was canceled and German citizens were arrested. The 12 ships of the North German Line were seized.

Major-General Phya Pijaijarnrit (afterward Lieutenant-General Phya Devahastin) led an expeditionary force of 1,284 persons to fight the battle on the Western front along with Allied battalions. A medical unit was dispatched and its nurses served in the trenches of the Western front. Thailand also had sent a contingent of the Army Air Corps, which underwent training at the French Army Flying Schools at Avord and Istres. The pilots were further trained in bombing (Bomber School, Le Crotoy), reconnaissance missions (Reconnaissance School, Chapelle-la-Reine), gunnery (Gunnery School, Biscarosse), and conversion courses at Piox. The Thai Air Force had just been established and the three most important officers—all of whom had finished their training in France in 1913—were Major Luang Sakdi Sanlayawut, Captain Luang Arwut Sikikorn, and First Lieutenant Tip Ketuthat (afterward Air Marshal Phraya Thayanpikart). The three officers completed their training in August 1913. The movie *First Flight* (2007) depicted the exploits of the pilots and Thai–French cooperation in aviation. The Thai soldiers did not experience any combat as the war had ended in November 1918 before its training was over. But, this had been disputed and the Monument to the Expeditionary Force was erected in Bangkok, where the names of 19 soldiers killed during the First World War battle were engraved. The Thai troops, along with the victorious troops of the Allied countries, paraded on July 19, 1919, in Paris. They came back home on the ship, and each one was decorated by the king.

The end of the war on November 11, 1918, and the defeat of the Central powers formed a watershed in Asian history. The prestige of some of the Western powers suffered drastically. The mutual bickering and fratricidal struggle among European powers convinced the Asian countries that the Western nations were not at all superior. A new Asian self-consciousness developed. Arabs, Jews, Indians, Vietnamese, and others felt deceived by the double-dealings of the colonial powers. With renewed zeal, they strove hard to oust the imperialists. The Fourteen Points of U.S. president Woodrow Wilson, particularly the principle of self-determination, had raised high hopes. However, these ideas were applied in Eastern Europe only. Thailand received most of the direct benefit due to war.

The country participated in the deliberations of the Paris Peace Conference. The Articles 135, 136, and 137 were devoted to it in the provisions of the Treaty of Versailles. Thailand became a founding member of the League of Nations in January 1920. The First World War was an excellent opportunity for Thailand to be treated on par with other countries. Its international prestige increased. Thailand had lobbied in the Versailles palace for ending the extraterritoriality rights granted to Western countries during the earlier regimes. Prince Devawongse Varopakar, the Foreign Minister since the reign of Chulalongkorn, endeavored hard for an end to extraterritoriality and unequal treaties that infringed upon Thai sovereignty. The United States gave up its extraterrestrial rights and tariff restrictions in 1920 without any condition. The treaty was to be over after 10 years and finally the treaty was abrogated in 1930. President Wilson's son-in-law, Francis B. Sayre (1885–1972), who was an adviser to the Thai foreign office (1920–1927), helped a lot with the revisions of the unequal treaties. Tokyo acquiesced in March 1924. Sayre went to Europe in 1925 in hopes of persuading France and Britain to abrogate the unequal treaties. France relinquished its rights in February 1925. Britain was the largest trading partner of Thailand, with 30 percent of exports and 67 percent of imports. Tariffs on goods such as cotton yarn, fabric, and iron and steel products were limited to 5 percent for 10 years. The British advisors at law courts were withdrawn. In 1925 Sayre concluded the treaties ending extraterritoriality rights with five more European countries. The following year, four countries signed the treaties. By 1939, all the special treaties had been abrogated. For his work, Sayre was endowed with the title *Phya Kalyan Maitri* (Pyha means Royal/a honorific title, Kalyan Maitri means a kind friend).

The Thai economy was affected in various ways by the war. In fact economic conditions after the war were quite bad. As the value of silver had increased, the exchange rate between the pound sterling and the Thai baht was 1 to 9.54. Previously it was 13 baht. A bad harvest after the war contributed to the economic malaise. In 1922, Thailand borrowed 2 million pounds at 7 percent interest and after two years another 3 million at 6 percent from Britain. In 1923, the exchange rate was at 11 baht per pound sterling. There was also a huge trade deficit. The expenditure of the Kingdom went unabated with the military consuming 23 percent of state's budget. A cruiser (a type of large warship) was purchased in 1920. Vajiravudh remained adamant and did not reduce any expenditure. Moreover, there was a strike by the workers of the tramways in 1922–1923. The king also curtailed press freedom to a considerable extent. Stories, rumors, and gossip went around the capital about the king's fondness for men and dislike for the opposite sex. Nonetheless, he married late at the age of 38 and a daughter was born to Queen Pra Nang Chao Suvadhana (1905–1985) just two days before the king's death in November 1925. The king was only 44 years old.

PRAJADHIPOK

Prajadhipok became the next king of Thailand under the title Rama VII (r. 1925–1935). A younger brother of Vajiravudh, he was born in 1893 to Queen Sri Bajarindra. Educated at Eton as well as the Royal Military Academy at Woolwich and afterward in France at the Ecole Superieure de Guerre, Prajadhipok came back to Thailand in 1924. As per the law of succession, since Vajiravudh had no male heir, the sons of Chulalongkorn would be the next king. The elder brothers of Prajadhipok had died, and thus he became the king in November 1925. He was quite unprepared for it and the elderly princes of the royal family advised him in administration. They began to hold top positions. He was thorough with all official papers and listened to the suggestions of experts. The king was a liberal and intelligent man. The strident nationalism of Vajiravudh had mellowed down to an extent with an emphasis on "Thailand for the Thais" only. He would have governed very well, but the time and circumstances were against him. The king was inclined toward political reforms. He was aware of the fact that these were necessary and an absolute monarch could not last long. In 1927, he wanted to enlarge the Privy Council and the Supreme Council of the State. In the Council of the State, five important members of the royal family were appointed due to pressure from the princes. Prince Damrong Rajanubhab was a member of the Privy Council and wielded a lot of influence. He dissuaded the king from taking radical measures. The king lacked self-confidence and also was not willing to go against the advice of senior members. The princes began to monopolize the prized posts in the administration, much to the chagrin of the rising educated intelligentsia. Thailand was in disarray after the end of the First World War and the continued financial chaos became one of Prajdhipok's pressing problems. He had to take measures that led to discontentment among many sections of the society. Moreover, the world financial crisis of 1929 was approaching.

The king had brought about notable changes in the country before he was ousted from power in 1932. He cut down the expenditure of the royalty to 40 percent. During his reign, the Civil and Commercial Code was promulgated in 1925. He believed in monogamy and had one wife only, Queen Rambai Barni (1904–1984). He encouraged cooperative farming, enacting a law in 1928 benefiting the farmers. The king enacted legislation such as the Land Expropriation Act and amended the Marriage Law. The king took special measures toward the improvement of libraries, publication of Buddhist textbooks, and preservation of ancient monuments. Thai literature developed to a great extent during the reign of Prajadhipok. Many novels came out centering around the theme of lovers with a happy ending. Various social problems including inequality, polygamy, and prostitution, among others, also formed the theme of the writings of the period. *Manutsayatham* (humanism) was one of the dominant themes in Kulap Saipradit's (1905–1974) novels. Writing under the pen name Siburapha, his *Khang Lang Phap* (*Behind the Painting*) has become a classic in Thai literature. It revolved around the tragic love affair between a student and an unhappy Thai aristocratic woman. In 1928, he wrote *Luuk Phuu Chai* (*A Real Man*). He published another important work entitled *Songkhram Chiwit* (*Life Struggle*), dealing with poverty and inequality. *Phajon Barb* (*Facing Sin*), a novel whose theme was religion, was written in 1934. Akatdamkoeng Raphiphat penned the popular novel *Lakhon haeng chiwit* (*The Circus of Life*) in 1929, describing the struggle for social change by a foreign-returned young man. Wichit Wathakan's *Prawatisat sakhon* (*Universal History*), written in the genre of nonfiction analyzed Thai nationalism. The publishing industry experienced a proliferation, with 14 publishers and 127 printing presses in the country. A journal on agricultural affairs was started by Prince Sithiporn Kridakara.

TOWARD THE 1932 REVOLUTION

Like any other revolution, the Thai revolution of 1932 had immediate and outlying causes. The slashing of the salaries of civil servants as well as cutting down on the number of posts made the king the targets of the attack. They ignited the fire, becoming the immediate causes of the revolution. There was simmering discontent against the monarchy for the last two decades. The newly emerging intellectuals, bureaucrats, and army officers were clamoring for more shares in administration and the decision-making process. In a world full of new ideas, absolute monarchy was incongruous. It had neither appeal nor any legitimacy. The world economic crisis and its result on the Thai economy became added factors.

The first two decades of the twentieth century were full of new ideas stimulated by events in China, Russia, and Asian colonies and by the ideology of democracy. Monarchy had become a thing of the past in countries like Turkey and Russia. Thailand had participated in the First World War and it had become the theatre of operation for the nationalist struggles of neighboring countries. The exploits of Ho Chi Minh (1890–1969) in northeastern Thailand in the 1920s and his blending of communism and nationalism had not escaped the attention of many intellectuals. The Chinese communists had also become active in Thailand, particularly after the boycott of Japanese goods in the late 1920s. The new elite studying abroad were imbued with Western ideas of a democratic government. They found outmoded institutions after returning home, which were not in conformity with the modern world. A sense of disenchantment with the absolute monarchy had developed, along with rising anger against the princes, who had acquired the top posts of the state. There were also regular meetings of Thai students in Paris. The venue was the house of Prayoon Phamornmontri (1897–1982), who took part in the 1932 revolution. The students were advocating for ending the absolute monarchy and the promulgation of a new constitution. Pridi Phanomyong (1900–1983), the future leader of the revolution, was studying at the Sorbonne in France. In February 1927, he along with five others founded the *Khana Rasdr* (People's Party) with an agenda of economic planning, liberty, equal rights, and an end to royal privileges. After his return in 1927, he headed a group of 50 officials who wanted to bring about a constitutional monarchy.

Thailand reeled under the impact of the world economic crisis of 1929. It continued to adhere to the gold standard, resulting in Thai rice becoming expensive internationally. But, in the domestic market, the price dropped by two-thirds, which hit the peasants severely. They were unable to pay taxes and pay back loans as their income was much reduced. Prajadhipok undertook economic reforms for minimizing expenditures. He was unable to procure loans, and the revenue from the export of rice and teak had been reduced. The government officials suffered due to the cut down in expenditures. The budgetary allocation of ministries was curtailed, resulting in the scaling down of salaries and retrenchment of hundreds of officials. There was an exemption for the princes from the Civil Service Law of 1928. The royalty and aristocracy were being taxed lightly. The army was not happy as the Supreme Council had also cut the military budget, slashing the salaries of army officers. The prestige of the monarchy had suffered as Prajadhipok was not able to take swift decisions. His close advisors belonging to the royal family were looked down upon as incompetent. The government had become ineffective in the eyes of many officers in bureaucracy and the army. Although the king was not adverse to constitutional reforms, his coterie believed strongly that Thailand was not yet ready for democracy. Prajadhipok also did not do anything tangible toward this end and went along with the advice of his trusted lieutenants. A coup became inevitable as the economic woes were spiraling out of control.

END OF ABSOLUTE MONARCHY

While the king was relaxing in the royal summer residence in Hua Hin, the coup leaders began their operation in the early hours of June 24, 1932. The junior army officers, Western-educated intellectuals, and civil servants belonging to the *Khana Rasdr*, seized power without any bloodshed. Numbering around 114, they were led by Pridi Phanomyong, Phraya Phahol Pholphayuhasena (Phahon Phonphayuhasena, 1887–1947), Khuang Abhaiwongse (1902–1968), Prayoon Phamornmontri, and Luang Phibun Songkhram (1897–1964); all were destined to play a greater role in Thai politics and history afterward. Apart from Phahon, the inspector-general of military education, the military leaders taking part in the coup were Praya Songsuradet (1892–1944), superintendent of educational section of the army, and Praya Ritakhane (1890–1960), commander of the local artillery regiment. They had gathered along with soldiers of the military academy, a unit of the navy, and an infantry battalion. The Commander of the Royal guards was captured along with 40 high officials, who were interned in Ananlasanakan Hall of Bangkok. Prince Nakhon Sawan (1881–1944), who was the Interior Minister as well as the supreme advisor of the king, was also taken hostage by the coup leaders known as "Promoters." The two other prominent members of the royal family arrested were Prince Damrong (1862–1943) and Prince Narisa (1863–1947). An ultimatum of one hour was given to the king asking for his acquiescence in a constitutional monarchy. The king was "invited" to the capital to reign as a constitutional monarch. The king agreed to the demands, mentioning that he was considering such a proposal himself. He also made his intention clear that he wanted to avoid any violence. The king returned to Bangkok on June 25 and after two days met the leaders at the Sukhothai Palace. Prajadhipok, in a symbolic gesture, ordered the unfurling of the Thai national flag, replacing the traditional one of the Chakri dynasty. On the same day, the erstwhile ministers and heads of the department were made to retire and the Executive Committee of *Khana Rasdr* took over the reigns of a provisional government. The National Assembly, composed of 70 appointed members, was the legislative branch. Praya Manopakorn Nititada (1884–1948), the ex-president of the Court of Appeal, was the head of the Executive Committee. A committee was appointed by him to frame a constitution. Thailand was going to have rule of law within the framework of a democratic form of government. The leaders of the revolution sought to blend Western ideals of constitutionalism with the realties of Thailand. The country was just coming out of old order, although the wealth of the country was concentrated with only a few families.

On December 10, 1932, Prajadhipok signed Thailand's first constitution, ending the rule of absolute monarchy spanning 692 years from the Sukhothai period. In spite of promulgation of successive constitutions, the basic framework of the Thai constitution has remained unaltered. Despite the end of absolute monarchy, the prestige and deference to the crown were preserved. He had become the symbol of love, respect, hope, and aspiration of the Thais. In a moment of crisis, his advice was sought. His power was similar to that of the British constitutional monarch. He could veto legislation once only. It would become law with the approval of the assembly again. The king had the power to dissolve the assembly, but had to call for elections within three months. The royal princes were banned from holding any executive position. But they could become members of the diplomatic corps or function in an advisory capacity. The national assembly, a bicameral one, was composed of elected and nominated members in equal proportion. The king was to appoint the 78 members on the advice of the Cabinet to the Senate (the Upper House). Election was indirect through an electorate of local and district bodies to the House of Representatives (the Lower House). It was to be held every four years on the basis of universal suffrage. Within 10 years, it would be a fully elected body. The cabinet was responsible to the Assembly. Manopakorn remained as the first Premier of Thailand (August 28, 1932– June 20, 1933). Phahon was the commander-in-chief of the army with Songsuradet as his deputy.

The events of 1932 have been criticized for being elitist and not democratic. Rural folks were hardly affected by it. Instead of the royalty, it was the new caucus that governed the country. In addition to the remnants of nonroyal elements in bureaucracy, there was an influx of new persons belonging to the same upper-class society. Moreover, the constitution gave scope to instability in politics by tolerating some opposition. The army began to dominate, and instead of royalty it was the rule of the army in Thai politics many times. Although Thailand became a constitutional monarchy, the army began to have a prominent role. The democratic experiment was punctuated by the military coups. There was dominance of *Khana Rasdr* with excessive concentration of power. Formation of *khanathipatai* (cliques) became a feature of Thai politics henceforth. There was hardly any role for the people as such in the 1932 revolution. In spite of the validity of the criticism to an extent, the fact remained that 1932 was a watershed in the long history of Thailand. Democratic institutions had begun in rudimentary form. After all, a revolution was not an end in itself. It would take years to bring democracy in its true sense. Even after the French Revolution of 1789, there were revolutions of 1830 and 1848 to make France more democratic. The end of czarist Russia witnessed the one-party rule of the Bolsheviks and it took 73 years for democracy to arrive. The revolution of 1932 was the beginning of a process toward the democratization of Thailand. The absolute monarchy was over and the stage was set for alternate democratic and military regimes.

9

Wars and Coups

The history of Thailand after 1932 is a turbulent one. The experiment with democracy had many pitfalls. Political instability and military coups became the hallmark of Thai history and politics. Very soon Thailand became involved in the Second World War, with devastating consequences. In the subsequent Cold War, Thailand became one of the closest allies of the United States. It also joined the Vietnam War, which had a great deal of impact on its society, politics, and economy. The communist rebellions in northeastern Thailand threatened the security of the nation. Unrest in society and ideological polarization brought about rifts and acrimonious feelings among the votaries of different ideologies, which was also a threat to the very unity of the nation.

POST-1932 SCENARIO

The political system of Thailand was dominated by elite infighting, the dominance of bureaucracy, and the influence of the army. After the promulgation of the Constitution on December 10, 1932, the government of Monapahorn Nitithada was beset with several problems. The leaders of the coup were composed of both civilians and military personnel. Factionalism among the ruling elite soon became conspicuously divisive. The civilian movement led by Pridi Phanomyong was pitted against the military clique. The latter also had two factions, the senior group led by Phahon Phonphayuhasena and the junior army officers supported by the navy under Phibun Songkhram. But the two merged under the leadership of Phanon afterward and toppled the government of Nithiada on June 20, 1933. Another party called *Khana Chat* (Nationalist Party) had been established in January 1933 under the leadership of Luang Wichit (Luang Vichitr Vadakarn, 1896–1962), which was vocal in its criticism against dominance of the *Khana Rasdr*. The manifesto of the *Khana Rasdr* at the time of the revolution had become the guiding principles of the new government. It had envisaged the economic betterment for people, equal rights, liberty, educational opportunities, and preserving the independence of the country. On March 1, 1933, Pridi, who was in charge of finance, chalked out a revolutionary economic program for the entire country. It was accepted as one of the principles in the 1932 revolution. Bordering on a socialist agenda, it called for dividing the economy into cooperatives, the nationalization of natural resources, and imposing taxes on inheritance as well as income. Pridi's plan was opposed by the conservative faction of the party and it was denounced as being communist by Prime Minister Monapahorn Nitithada and Praya Siwisanwacha (Srivisar Vacha, 1897–1968), the foreign minister. The army leaders also were against the plan. Cracks began to appear in the government over the question of the registration of the new party, the *Khana Chat*.

Amid all the foregoing developments, the conservatives gained the upper hand. Prime Minister Monapahorn, along with the tacit support of the king, adjourned the National Assembly, the power base of *Khana Rasdr*, on April 1, 1933. A new cabinet was formed and Pridi fled into exile to France and his supporters were sidetracked. A jail term for 10 years was earmarked for anybody professing communism. Thailand was not yet ready for an overhaul in the social and economic structure of the country. The abolition of absolute monarchy with the rudiments of a democratic system was enough. The new cabinet ordered all officials to withdraw themselves from *Khana Rasdr* membership, and in Thai politics there was to be no legal party. On April 22, the *Khana Rasdr* called itself the People's Party Club, without any political objective. The move by the premier to induct top officers of the pre-1932 regime alarmed the military leaders of the coup such as Phahnon and Phibun, who had already resigned from the party. These disgruntled members staged a coup on June 20 and Phahnon became the new premier. The national assembly was reopened and the military faction of the erstwhile *Khana Rasdr* began to wield real power. Monapahorn went to the British colony of Penang Island, where he lived the last years of his life. In September Pridi came to Bangkok again with promised cooperation with the new government's economic measures. The anti-*Khana Rasdr* group was not sitting silently. It was planning to topple Phahnon's regime, accusing it of pro-communist tendencies. Prince Boworadet (1878–1953), grandson of Mngkut and the ex-defense minister under King Prajadhipok, led the pro-Royalist army officers marching from Korat to Bangkok intent on toppling the government. On October 12, the Air Force headquarters at Don Muang, north Bangkok, was captured and a one-hour ultimatum was given to the government to resign. The royal couple took refuge in Songkhla. The newly formed *Khana Ku Banmuang* (National Salvation Party) presented a list of demands, which were rejected by the prime minister. Fighting soon broke out and the army led by Phibun Songkram defeated the rebel forces by October 24. The sanctity of the constitution was proclaimed by the government, and on November 2 a law was passed by which persons suspected of anticonstitutional activities were to be punished. Elections were completed by November 28 for the 78 seats of the National Assembly. Only 10 percent of the voters participated in the elections, which confirmed the popularity of Pridi. However, Phibun also had become a major force in Thai politics, and he remained as the premier. The government was determined to preserve the constitution and helped in forming *Samakhom Khana Ratthathamanun* (Society for the Constitution) on December 14. The society had 27 members drawn from among civilians as well as army officers, and its task was the protection of the constitution and promotion of unity among the Thais. Pridi was the chairperson. The society also opened branch offices in the provinces, and provincial governors were kept in charge of these offices. Although the *Khana Rasdr* was not in existence as a political Party, members of the society had become influential in the politics of the country. The members of the *Khan Rasdr* had control over the government, as was evident from the appointment of second-category assembly members after the elections of November. Most of them were participants in the 1932 revolution.

The relationship between the king and government, which had been close, was now deteriorating. Prajadhipok did not give consent to the appointment of the second category of members. The king left for Europe in January 1934 on personal grounds to seek eye care. He charged the government with high-handed actions as it did not abide by the royal veto. The king had exercised his veto powers to reject bills passed by the National Assembly. He had vetoed drafts of the inheritance law and bills for the revision of criminal procedures as well as the military criminal code. All three were passed by the assembly, overriding the veto. The king announced his decision to abdicate, as reconciliation with the government was not feasible. On March 2, 1935, Prajadhipok abdicated without naming a successor. The National Assembly proclaimed Prince Ananda Mahidol (Rama VIII, 1935–1946), nephew of Prajadhipok, as the legal heir. As the prince was studying in Switzerland, the assembly appointed a Council of Regency to perform the functions of the monarchy as enshrined in the constitution. Thailand was without a resident monarch for the first time in its history. Prajadhipok died of heart attack on May 30, 1941, in Britain.

The premiership of Phahnon from June 21, 1933, to December 16, 1938, was marked by a struggle between the military and civilian forces for dominance in Thai politics. It became all the more intense after the abdication of the king. Phibun, who had proved his mettle in crushing the royalist counter-revolution of October 1933, was emerging as the spokesperson of the military force. The army was in an advantageous position with its dedicated cadre, strength, and discipline. Once it dabbled in politics, it would be difficult to challenge it. The share of the military in the budget was increased to 26 percent. One of the acts of Phibun was the pro-Japanese stance that became responsible for Thailand's abstaining from the censuring motion in the League of Nations. After the Japanese invasion of Manchuria (Dongbei or northeast), the League had passed a motion in 1933 branding the Japanese as the aggressors. The Thai military officers were sent to Japan for training in 1935. An Association of Friendship was established between the two countries. Thailand purchased 24 warships from Italy and Japan. Both the army and the air force were modernized and equipped with sophisticated weapons. Phibun's collaboration with the Axis powers was evident in the Second World War. The government also passed censorship legislation in 1934 to muzzle newspapers and radio broadcasts.

Pridi, the law professor and author of the 1932 revolution, also endeavored to consolidate the civilian base. He had the support of the Thai intelligentsia. Pridi had a genuine desire for the participation of people in democracy and wanted ordinary people to have an education. He was instrumental in setting up the University of Morals and Political Science in 1934, which came to be known as Thammasat University (University of Morals). There was a fourfold hike in expenditures on education, which increased the literacy rate. In primary schools, the student enrollment increased from 700,000 in 1931 to 1.7 million in 1939. A special school for dance and drama was started in January 1934. The government also initiated major reforms in various spheres. Trade recovered as the baht went off the gold standard. In 1937, direct elections were held for the National Assembly. Phahon once again became the premier. The local bodies were also empowered. The parental consent for marriage was abolished.

ADVENT OF MILITARY DICTATORSHIP

August 1938 brought increasing confrontation between the first and second category members in the national assembly. A proposal for an amendment was brought up, which would make it mandatory on the part of the government to submit the draft of the budget before the national assembly.

It was approved and on September 11, 1938, Phahnon dissolved the assembly by saying that the proposal would restrict the functioning of the government. He did not accept the post of prime minister again and Phibun became the new premier with the support of second category members on December 16, 1938. He took over the post of Minister of Defense as well as commander-in-chief of the army. He was the supreme leader of Thailand, and his policies went hardly unopposed. Thailand drifted toward military dictatorship. His political enemies were arrested. A special court sentenced 25 persons to life imprisonment and 18 were given capital punishment.

Phibun Songkram dominated Thai politics as the premier from 1938 to 1944 and again between 1948 and 1957. His concept of nationalism bordered on the concept of an extreme xenophobia, chauvinism, irredentism, the superiority of the Thai race, and a personality cult. He was an admirer of Nazism and fascism. Phibun made close alliances with Japanese militarism. Instead of an absolute monarch, Thailand now had a dictator and the Vajirbudh's "king" was replaced by *Phunam* (Leader). The ideological basis of Thai politics made a complete volte-face; from *prativad* (revolution) to *phadetkan* (dictatorship). Phibun wanted the Thais to emulate the doctrine of fascism; *credere, combattere, and obbedire* ("believe, fight, and obey"). Paramilitary youth organizations similar to Nazi Germany's brown-shirted SA, the *Sturmabteilung* (storm troopers), and black-uniformed S.S., the *Schutzstaffel* (security echelon), were established. The Thai militarism glorified the martial values and army recruitment increased with the military budget. A combination of traditional Thai cultural mores, Western practices, and discrimination against non-Thais were some of the parameters of Phibun's cultural nationalism. The *rathaniyom*, or state regulations, made Western style of dress mandatory. The Ministry of Culture insisted upon putting on Western clothing, gloves, and hats. The wearing of the *panung* (indigenous skirt) was discouraged. Chewing of the betel nut was prohibited. Around 1938, Phibun began to set up a national code of honor, the *wiratham*, in line with the Japanese *busido*. It stressed loyalty, economic self-sufficiency, and certain Buddhist doctrines. The people residing in outlying areas were identified with Thai connotations such as Thai Muslim and Thai Isan. The Chinese were targets of sustained racial campaigns undertaken by the state. The government closed down 271 Chinese schools. Chinese newspapers were suppressed. Luang Wichit Wathakan, the spokesperson of Phibun's regime, was the head (1934–1942) of the new Fine Arts Department established in January 1934. A number of plays, dance dramas, and writings came out, glorifying Thai history and its culture. He harped back on the cultural efflorescence of the Thais during the Sukhothai period. Wichit's play *Nanchao* (1939) was full of venom against the ethnic Chinese. The state-run schools received free copies of *Luat Suphan* (*Blood of Suphan*), which delineated the invasion of Myanmar during the Ayudhya period. The Thai language as well as Buddhism received official patronage that was unheard of in earlier regimes.

In the economic sphere, state enterprises in textile and oil were established under the auspices of the Ministry of Defense. By the year 1941, the Ministry was controlling the agricultural, transportation, and many industrial sectors. The underlined subtle motive was to oust the Chinese-controlled industries. The Thais received preference in government-sponsored programs. The code of nationality of 1939 made it obligatory to have Thai names and learn the Thai language. To top it all off, the official name of the country was changed from Siam to Thailand (after *Muang/Prathet Thai* or "land of the Thai") in 1939. Phibun was impressed by the expansionist policy of Germany, Italy, and Japan. The military strongman of Thailand was nurturing a desire to get back the lost territories of Thailand. His jingoism led to a pan-Thai movement aimed at recovering Thai territories of the extended empire. Phibun's assertive nationalism had resulted in the publication of maps showing Laos and parts of Cambodia along with Vietnam as part of Thailand. The onset of the Second World War was an opportunity that Phibun did not want to miss.

THAILAND AND THE SECOND WORLD WAR

When the German war machines marched into Poland in a blitzkrieg (lightning attack) on September 1, 1939, World War II began. At first, Thailand professed neutrality. The traditional Thai policy was to "bend with the wind" and join the winning side so that the country's interests would be best served. It had fought in the First World War on the side of the Allies in the belief that the unequal treaties would be revised and that Thailand would join the international community. When the Axis powers were on a winning spree in the initial years of the Second World War, Thailand decided to join with them. Over a period of about two years, the juggernaut of Hitler's Wehrmacht (armed forces) incorporated Poland, Norway, Denmark, the Netherlands, and Belgium. The fall of France on June 22, 1940, was another triumph for Hitler. Japan was also expanding over a large area in Southeast Asia. It was desperately struggling for new acquisitions in Southeast Asia in order to gain raw materials and oil. The Japanese forces were in Indochina and were ready to invade the Dutch East Indies. Phibun thought it was the right time to recover lost territories from the trans-Mekong region, Cambodia, Myanmar, and the Malay sultanates. After the surrender of France, the balance of power between Thailand and French Indochina altered drastically in favor of Thailand. Popular opinion claimed and clamored for retrieving lost territory acquired by France in 1893, 1904, and 1907.

Some of the nationalist leaders of Southeast Asia collaborated with the Japanese with a view to getting rid of Western domination. The Japanese slogans such as "Asia for Asiatic" and "Greater East Asia Co-Prosperity Sphere" appealed to the anti-Western sentiments of nationalist leaders. Phibun collaborated with the Japanese to spare the country devastation as well in an attempt to regain the lost territories. Thailand had sent a mission to Tokyo to purchase weapons. The increasing Thai-Japanese cooperation was evident. Japan was the second largest trading partner with Thailand after Britain. Japan had a full-fledged embassy in Bangkok with consulates in Chiang Mai and Singora. Moreover, the Axis was the winning side in 1940–1941. To be on the safe side, Phibun had signed provisional nonaggression pacts with France and Britain on June 12, 1940. On the same day, he had also signed a friendship treaty with Japan. But the situation changed after the triumphant Nazi army's entry to Paris on June 14 and the signing of the armistice at Compiègne eight days afterward. Marshal Henri Philippe Petain (1856–1951) was the premier of the puppet Vichy government. Bangkok took advantage of Vichy Indochina's weakness to secure the lost provinces in Laos and Cambodia. Thailand's demand in October for the return of territories was rejected by Vichy France. Phibun took recourse to an undeclared war from November, which continued for three months. The five divisions of the Thai army, numbering around 50,000, began to mobilize itself. It also had 100 modern fighter planes and its navy was superior to that of French Indochina. By the third week of November, there were border clashes and the Thai army crossed the Mekong River in December. In the first week of January 1941, the Thai army launched a full-scale invasion on Laos, Dangreks zone, and the Battambang province. Although the Thais were in advantageous positions in both the ground and air wars, they were defeated in the naval war of Koh Chnag by the Vichy forces on January 17, 1941. With Japanese mediation, an armistice was signed aboard the Japanese warship *Natori* and a treaty was signed on May 9, 1941. Thailand gained the disputed territories of Laos, the Battambang province, and a part of Siem Reap. But after the end of the Second World War, the territories once again reverted back to the possession of the French colonial government. In 1941, Phibun was the national hero of Thailand and was promoted to the rank of field marshal.

Japan was the real wielder of balance of power in mainland Southeast Asia. By skillful diplomacy, it aimed at increasing its dominance in Indochina. Afterward Japan would acquire the British possessions in the Malayan archipelago. For this, close relations with Thailand were not sufficient. December 7, 1941 (Japan Standard Time, December 8), was an important day in the history of the Second World War. The Japanese war machine moved deep into Southeast Asia, incorporating it with the Greater East Asian Co-prosperity Sphere. The Japanese Imperial army landed in Thailand from its bases in Indochina. The war had also become truly global after Japanese warplanes struck the military and naval installation of Pearl Harbor at 7:55 a.m., on December 7

(03:25 a.m., Japan Standard Time, December 8). The next day, the United States declared war on Japan. Germany and Italy declared war on the United States three days afterward. Fighting broke out between the Thai army and the Japanese 1st Infantry Battalion of the 143rd Infantry Regiment at Chumphon for a few hours during the morning hours of December 8. Singora (Songkla) port on the eastern coast of the Thai Malay Peninsula was the headquarters of the Sixth Army Division of Nakhon Sri Tammarat. The harbor along with its airfield was the ideal place to launch the Japanese invasion into Malay. On December 8, Lieutenant General Tomoyuki Yamashita, commander of the Japanese 25th Army, landed in Singora. There was hardly any fighting because of the order of Phibun. He also gave orders for an immediate cease-fire and consequently fighting in places like Patani, Hat Yai, Surat Thani, Samut Prakan, and Prachuap Khiri Khan also stopped. Thailand followed the pragmatic course of action and prudently spared Thailand the devastation that was experienced by Burma (Myanmar). The country maintained its sovereignty and the only price to be paid for was permission granted to the Japanese for using Thai territories and facilities. Right of passage was given to the Japanese army for marching into the British colonies of Myanmar and Malay. On December 21 Thailand and Japan signed a mutual defense pact in the Temple of the Emerald Buddha, by which the former would get back territories lost to Britain. The Anglo–Thai Convention of 1909 had stipulated renunciation of sovereign rights over the four southern states of the Malay Peninsula: Kedah, Perlis, Kelantan, and Trengganu. Thailand also would possess the areas of Myanmar, Mongpan, and Kengtung. Bangkok would assist Japan in its war with the Allied powers. On January 25, 1942, Thailand became a belligerent country in the Second World War and the Allied planes began raiding Bangkok.

   The pro-Japanese policy of Phibun was not liked in many quarters, and a clandestine organization against the Japanese was set up called *Khabuankarn Seri Thai* (Free Thai Movement). Apart from the stigma of siding with the fascist forces, the pro-Japanese policy was creating havoc with the Thai economy. There was a phenomenal increase in cost of living. The stationing of 150,000 Japanese soldiers created a burden on Thailand and shortages of essential goods and materials. The external trade of the country also declined. Some of the officials took recourse to shady dealings with the Japanese. The Chinese became targets of persecution at the behest of the Japanese and their assets were frozen. The bombing raids resulted in causalities and damage to properties. In the war front, Lieutenant General Tomoyuki Yamashita (1885–1946) was instrumental in conquering the British colonies of Malaya and Singapore in February 1942. Three months afterward, the American and Filipino troops surrendered in Manila Bay. The Japanese reached the borders of India after occupying Myanmar. In Thailand, the Free Thai movement centered around Pibun's rival, Pridi. He had resigned from the post of finance minister and was the regent for King Ananda. The United States Office of Strategic Services (OSS) and the British Force 136 based in Ceylon (Sri Lanka) were in touch with the agents in various places of Thailand. With the Allied assistance, about 50,000 Thais were resisting the Japanese. A plan to establish a parallel government in north Thailand was given up and instead a core group of Free Thai known as the X-O Group came up.

Seni Promoj (1905–1997), the Thai ambassador in Washington, organized the Free Thai movement in the United States. He did not deliver formally the government's declaration of war against the United States. Therefore, technically, Thailand was not at war with the United States and the latter did not declare war on Thailand. Seni had also met the U.S. Secretary of State, Cordell Hull (1871–1955), and discussed the matter with him. He also used the frozen Thai assets in the United States and organized the Free Thai movement with the help of Thai expatriates in the United States. Seni submitted to the American authorities a list of notable Thai nationals such as his brother Kukrit Promoj (1911–1995), Pridi, Khuang Aphaiwong, and Direk Chaiyanam, who were anti-Japanese and supporters of Free Thai. About 40 Thai students studying in various universities of the United States expressed their willingness to join the OSS and were sent as Free Thai officers to China in the middle of 1943. The military attaché, Colonel Luang Khunchon commissioned the volunteers as Free Thai officers. As the government of Britain received the letter of declaration of war from Thailand, it declared war against Thailand. But the Thai residents of Britain also had formed the *Seri Thai*. The important members were persons belonging to the royal family such as Queen Rambai Barni, widow of King Prajadhipok, her brother Prince Suphasawat Wongsanit, and Prince Chula Chakrabongse. The queen was the head of the *Seri Thai* in Britain and was one of the four women taking up nonmilitary tasks. The Thai students (numbering 36) of Britain like Snoh Tambuyen and Puey Ungphakorn became members of the Pioneer Corps. Prince Suphasawat joined as a major in the British army.

In July 1944, Phibun was forced to resign as Nazi Germany's defeat was imminent. Events were not going in favor of the Japanese either. Khuang Apaivongse, one of the leaders of the Free Thai, became the prime minister in August. The political prisoners were released and many of the projects of Phibun were done way with. Meanwhile, the Free Thai was gaining momentum during the last year of the war. The local representatives of the national assembly mobilized the common mass against the Japanese. They maintained regular contact with anticolonial groups of Indochina. One notable figure of the region was Tiang Sirikhanth (1909–1952), a member of Parliament of Sakon Nakhon, who had supported Pridi's social and economic programs. Peasants were given training in arms in the Phu Phan Mountain area. Tiang also was in touch with Lao leaders. By the end of Second World War, the Free Thai cadres had reached 3,000 in Isan. The volunteers of the Free Thai recruited from all over Thailand had been armed, and contact was maintained with the Allied High Command in Sri Lanka. The Thai 1st Army was in readiness against the Japanese troops stationed in Bangkok. The Allied bombing increased on Japanese installations and paratroopers landed on Thai soil. Pridi was very much active in recruiting Thai students from the Universities of Chulalongkorn and Thammasat for underground work. He was also in touch with the Allies for taking the best possible advantages for Thailand at the end of the war. At the behest of Pridi, Admiral Sangvara Suwannacheep launched a police training program and the Japanese commander General Akeo Nakamura was told that it was for resisting Allied invasion. The strategic ruse worked very well. Pridi also was careful not to antagonize the British as the Shan states of Myanmar had been occupied by the Thai Phayap army since May 1942. Meanwhile, the Allied bombings inflicted causalities and damaged buildings as they missed their targets. On March 5, 1945, 78 people were killed on the east bank of the Chao Praya River along with damage to Pridi's residence, hospitals, and Thammasat University. After 17 days, a train carrying Thai soldiers was hit near Paknampo. The indiscriminate bombing continued throughout April, damaging railway stations, airports, and power plants. Hundreds of civilians were killed.

The Free Thai units were ready for a coordinated attack on the Japanese installations, and Pridi was waiting for a green light from the Supreme Allied Commander of Southeast Asia, Lord Louis Mountbatten (1900–1979), for the Allied invasion. However, the dropping of atomic bombs on August 6 and 9 led to the Japanese surrender. Japan signed the instrument of surrender on the USS *Missouri* in Tokyo Harbor on September 2, 1945. Japan was placed under international control of the Allies and lost all its overseas possessions. The efforts of the Free Thai Movement spared Thailand the fate that befell the Axis powers. There were reports about Thailand being ceded to Britain, but the plan was scotched and Bangkok had to supply 3 million tons of rice to London as reparation. Thailand's diplomatic relations with the United States and Britain were restored on January 5, 1946. The reparation claim of the British and the French was reduced to a large extent due to the role of the United States, which honestly believed that many Thai people were not behind Phibun. The Thai leaders had also lobbied in the United States and Pridi had gone to meet the American president Harry S. Truman (1884–1972). Even the Free Thai had considerable support from police as well as the army. The Thai military did not come under control of the Allies after the war. It retained its strength and once again dominated Thai politics after three years. Thailand surrendered the territories annexed during the war from Myanmar, Malay, Cambodia, and Laos. Phibun was imprisoned in Japan as a war criminal and was allowed to return to Thailand in 1947. Many of the Free Thai members had distinguished careers in Thai politics, bureaucracy, and business. Pridi and Promoj became premiers. Puey Ungphakorn (1916–1999) was the chairperson of the Bank of Thailand and Rector of Thammasat University. Siddhi Savetsila (1919–) became the Air Chief Marshal and Foreign Minister.

STRUGGLE FOR POWER

After the war, Thai civilians and military personnel struggled for power. Politics was marked by factional infighting among elites. Sometimes there was a sharing of power, but at other times bitter rivalries led to the ousting of an enemy group. There were democratic experiments, and then the army would take over. Again civilian regimes would be installed only to be deposed by a military junta. The post-1945 period centered around two major civilian groups. There was a tussle between the liberal following of Pridi, comprising intellectuals as well as bureaucrats, and the traditionalists as well as royalists who joined hands with Khuang and Seni Promoj. All the while, the military was looking for an opportunity to seize power.

The elite infighting was evident from the fact that between 1944 and 1948 Khuang held the office of prime minister three times, while Seni and Pridi each enjoyed the post only once. Tawee Boonyaket (1904–1971) and Rear Admiral Thamrong Nawasawat (1901–1988) were premiers for short periods. Khuang resigned on August 31, 1945, and was replaced by Tawee, who remained in the post for only 18 days. Seni was called back from the United States and he assumed the office on September 17, 1945. Once again Thailand was known as Siam. Seni found that the political atmosphere in Bangkok was not suitable to his temperament. The Cabinet was full of Pridi loyalists. He resigned on January 31, 1946, and Khuang again became prime minister for three months. The political parties had become legalized and elections were held on January 6, 1946. In Thailand, parliamentary democracy had been fully restored with elections being held after 10 years. Khuang had formed the *Prachathipat* (Democratic Party), which did very well in the elections. He was against a bill for reducing public expenses and had to resign on March 24. Thereupon Pridi became prime minister and would continue in office until August 3. On May 10 he promulgated a new, liberal constitution providing for a bicameral legislature. For the first time, the members of the House of Representatives were fully elected, and they were to elect the members of the Senate for a tenure of six years. The right to organize political parties was established in the constitution. The active civil and military officials were barred from holding political posts in the Parliament or Cabinet. The majority in the Parliament facilitated the task of Pridi in enacting liberal measures. Censorship laws were relaxed and anti-communist laws were scrapped.

The civilian interregnum was marked by writings influenced by socialism. The anticolonial struggle going on in Indochina against the French gave rise to socialist and democratic ideas.

King Ananda Mahidol had returned to Thailand in December 1945 and the constitution had been drafted in his honor. He was shot dead on June 9, 1946, under mysterious circumstances. The persons responsible for the regicide have never been determined and Pridi was held morally responsible for the sad demise of the king. The king's younger brother Bhumibol Adulyadej (Rama IX, 1946–) ascended the throne. He returned to the country only in 1951 as he was studying in a Swiss school. Pridi resigned and one of his followers, Thamrong Nawasawat, became the prime minister, serving until November 8, 1947. He faced vehement criticism unleashed by the Democratic Party of Khunag. Thamrong faced problems relating to finance, corruption, and the inquiry of the murder of Ananda Mahidol. He tried his best to control the food prices. Treasury gold bonds were sold to raise state income. Barely did he survive a no-confidence movement against him in May 1947. Meanwhile, Thailand became the 55th member of the United Nations Organization (UNO) on December 16, 1946.

PHIBUN'S SECOND TENURE

The military force that had wielded power for so long was getting restless after its debacle in 1945. It was looking for an opportunity to step in once again. The cut down in troop strength did not go well with the top brass of the army. The general criticism of the army by the civilian ministers was not appreciated. The common soldiers also had faced hardships while withdrawing from Shan states, which were given back to the British. The army units facing the Chinese Guomindang (Kuomintang—KMT) in 1946 had suffered without essential supplies. There was general discontentment in the country due to economic woes related to the war, such as the reparation payments and high inflation. The corruption in bureaucracy and mismanagement by governmental agencies undermined civilian regimes. Even then, the advent of an army takeover would not have been feasible had the nonmilitary elite remained united. In a span of three years, there were nine administrations. A section of the society was looking for stability amid rampant corruption, bureaucratic inefficiency, and economic chaos. It seemed as if the elite of about 5,000 were after the spoils of office rather than doing something meaningful for the country. The political parties were striving to achieve power by hook or by crook. The conservative and liberal groups worked at loggerheads, which often created breaches that were filled by military resurgence. The prominent military leaders like Lieutenant General Phin Choonhawan (1891–1973), Colonel Sarit Thanarat (1908–1963), and Phao Sriyanond (1910–1960) staged a coup by deposing Nawasawat on November 8 and invited Khunag to take over the reigns of government. Nawasawat went into exile to Hong Kong. The next day, the 1946 constitution was abrogated and Prince Rangsit (1885–1951), the regent of the king, accepted the new charter of the coup leaders. An important feature of the charter was removal of the ban on military and civil officers to work in the Parliament and Cabinet. The Senate was recast as an appointed body having 100 members. Khunag joined as prime minister on November 10. In the general elections of January 29, 1948, the Democratic Party of Khuang and Seni Promoj won. The relations between the army and Khuang were deteriorating gradually as the latter did not become pliable to army demands. There was disagreement over the appointment to the Cabinet and Senate. Phibun, the strongman of Thai politics, was brought back by the military from exile and by an open coup Khuang was forced to resign on April 8, 1948. The development in Phibun's regime became the yardstick for events in coming decades. Close alliance with the United States during the Cold War period and a repressive state apparatus would become the hallmark of Thai politics. The state would not tolerate any dissent to the regime. The dominance of military power would continue. Thailand would get involved in the Vietnam War as the closest allies of the United States in Southeast Asia. Phibun took the reins of the government on April 8, 1948, and once again Thailand relapsed into the assertive nationalism of his earlier government.

The name Siam was replaced by Thailand again in 1949. In social behavior, conformity with Western standards became the norm. The military budget increased. Again, the Chinese were the targets of a discriminatory policy, which became more intense after Mao Zedong established the People's Republic of China on October 1, 1949. The victory of communism in China made the Thai ruling class panicky. The workings of Chinese business houses, schools, newspapers, and social organizations were curtailed. An assimilation policy of intermarriage between the Thai and the Chinese was encouraged. Phibun cut down the immigration quota of the Chinese from 10,000 to 200 only and imposed exorbitant alien registration charges. The Chinese were looked at as communist sympathizers and hence disloyal to Thailand. The spread of communism in Indochina, the onset of the Korean War, and unrest in the Isan region of the northeast generated a communist phobia among Thai elite. In 1952, the Communist Party of Thailand was banned. Phibun unleashed a reign of terror against the dissidents of the regime. Phao Sriyanond (1910–1960), the notorious police chief of Thailand and a close ally of Phibun, was the person responsible for crushing opponents of the regime through his clique, the "Knights of the Diamond Ring." In March 1949, three MPs from Isan were shot dead. The Free Thai leaders, including Tiang Sirikhanth, Thawin Udom, Thawi Thawethikul, and Chan Bunnak, were eliminated in an extrajudicial manner. Tiang, the most vocal opponent of Phibun's dictatorship, and his associates were arrested and murdered in December 1952. Phon Malithong, the MP from Samut Sakhon, was strangled to death as he had provided evidences of huge wealth amassed by the police chief through fraudulent means.

An abortive coup backed by supporters of Pridi was crushed on February 29, 1949. Pridi went to China as an exile. A new constitution was promulgated on January 23, 1949, replacing the charter of earlier years. The drafting committee under Seni Promoopj was dominated by the royal princes Rangsit and Dhanivat Vidyalabh (1885–1974). It elevated the monarchy by providing it with power to appoint members of the Senate and strengthening the veto power. The king could even call for a referendum for amending the constitution. This constitution also was abrogated in 1952 and Phibun became the regent for the king. In the single national assembly, 103 out of a total 123 members were either from the army or the police squad. Afterward, provisions for the election for half of the legislature were introduced in March. Naturally, Phibun won the elections and the other half appointed members from the military. The Thai dictators had used the royalty to buttress their own position and crush communist revolts in Isan. The king became the symbol of national unity. Although there was no absolute monarchy, the influence of the king remained in Thai society and politics. After his coronation on May 5, 1950, King Bhumibol and his Queen Sirikit (Mom Rajawongse Sirikit Kitiyakara, 1932–) had made an extensive tour of the country. The royal couple had a genuine love and respect for the common people. A learned man, the king also was involved in many developmental projects of the country. He did not refrain from interfering with politics as in the 1973 or 2006 crises for the good of the nation. For the Thais, he was revered as a semidivine figure in keeping with centuries-long Buddhist-Hindu tradition.

In external affairs, Thailand adapted itself to the post-1945 scenario. For the United States and the Soviet Union, who had recently defeated in the Axis powers a common enemy, a new form of struggle ensued. The world was now divided into two blocs. Apart from the communist regimes behind the Iron Curtain, communist parties proliferated in South Asia, Southeast Asia, the Far East, and Europe. For Thailand, the new enemy was communism. In addition to China, a second country neighboring Thailand, Vietnam, had become communist. In Laos and Cambodia, communism was spreading. In Thailand itself, there was danger of communism from within after the establishment of the CPT in 1942. Keeping in tune with the policies of Chakri rulers, Bangkok thought it judicious to align itself with the dominant power. It was Britain earlier. In the Second World War, for many, it was Japan. The sun had set in the British empire and the choice now was for the United States. Bangkok evolved a policy of close alliance with Washington, D.C., joining the American bloc in the Cold War. From the 1950s, gradually, for a quarter century, pro-U.S. and anti-communist policies guided Thai foreign policy. Thailand became

America's staunchest ally in the latter's policy of the containment of communism.

In 1950, Thailand signed educational, cultural, economic, and technical agreements with the United States. Thailand's security relationship with the United States had a foundation dating back to 1950, which was strengthened as the Cold War progressed. In October came the Thai–U.S. Military Assistance Agreement. In the Korean War, 6,500 Thai troops served under the United Nations Command and there were 1,250 causalities. In the Geneva Conference of 1954 pertaining to Indochina, Thailand supported the policy of the United States. While the peace-making process was going on in Geneva, the United States initiated the Southeast Asia Treaty Organization (SEATO), or the Manila Pact. The main architect of this pact was the American secretary of state John Foster Dulles (1888–1959), who wanted collective defense against communist aggression. On September 8, 1954, the United States, Great Britain, France, Australia, New Zealand, Pakistan, Thailand, and the Philippines became signatories of the SEATO. A special protocol added Cambodia, Laos, and South Vietnam to be protected by SEATO. Phibun agreed to the view of Dulles that if communism was not to be checked, the noncommunist states would fall like dominoes. Bangkok was the head-quarters of the civil and military organization of SEATO. The post of Secretary General was instituted in 1957 and Pote Sarasin of Thailand (1905–2000) was the first person to hold the post. The treaty was viewed as another attempt to bring the Cold War to South and Southeast Asia. The joining of Thailand invited criticism from the Afro-Asian bloc as it was seen as serving the designs of neocolonialism in the region. The Cold War conflict was intensified in Southeast Asia because of SEATO. The Soviet Union, China, and North Vietnam condemned the treaty. But SEATO was not helpful to the concerns of the United States and Thailand in stopping ongoing communist victories. In the Vietnam War, the treaty was not beneficial in the anti-communist drive of the United States. After the communist victory in the Indochinese states in 1975, SEATO was an anachronism in the region. The member nations decided to disband the treaty in a meeting in September 1975 held in New York. SEATO was formally dissolved two years later.

While Phibun was aligning with the United States, his own position was being eroded. The military had its own factions. In an abortive coup attempt by the navy in 1951 he was almost killed. Phibun could have retained his position because of the rivalry between Phao Siyanon and Sarit Thanarat (1909–1963), Commander of the First Division stationed in Bangkok. The trium-virate of Phibun, Phao, and Sarit was the most powerful in Thai politics. Sarit was at somewhat of a disadvantageous because of his close collaboration between the other two. Phibun was the chairperson and Phao was the secretary of the newly formed official party, the *Seri Manangasila* (Free Stone Seat Party), which was the largest party with enough funds to spend. Less than a month after the February 1957 elections, which were rigged according to the opposition, Phibun formed a new government with Phao as the interior minister. After Sarit criticized Phibun vehemently relations between the two became strained and cooled off. Phibun had ordered that military or civil officials should not have any dealings with business establishments. It hit Sarit hard as he had commercial interest in many companies. On September 17, Sarit, who had become commander-in-chief of the army, deposed Phibun and Phao in a bloodless coup. Phibun went to Japan as an exile. Phao fled to Switzerland, where he had deposited a huge amount of his ill-gotten money in Swiss banks.

SARIT–THANOM REGIMES

Pote Sarasin served as the caretaker prime minister between September 21 and December 26, 1957. After general elections, General Thanom Kittikachorn (1911–2004), a close aide of Sarit, became Prime Minister on January 1. Thanom handed over the power to Sarit after the latter's return to Thailand from the United States, where he had received medical treatment. Sarit became the Prime Minister of Thailand on February 9, 1959, as head of the Revolutionary Party. After his death on December 8, 1963, Thanom headed the government until October 14, 1973. The Sarit–Thanom regimes did not see any changes in domestic and foreign policy. Thailand became more closely aligned with the United States. The military elite became rich as their pockets swelled with large portions of the billions of dollars' worth of American aid that passed through their hands at the time of the Vietnam War. Relations with China and North Vietnam deteriorated. Sarit decided to rule the country with an iron fist by banning opposition parties and newspapers and suspending constitutional amendments, while simultaneously seeking to stamp out Thailand's opium trade, police corruption, and organized crime. He tried to build up traditional Thai values. The promotion of Buddhism and cultivation of the monarchy were important features of his policies. Sarit cleverly utilized the monarchy both to enhance his own legitimacy and to strengthen the institution of the monarchy itself. The components of nation in his concept were the *Phokhun* (Leader), *Kharatchakarn* (Bureaucracy), and *Prachachon* (People). The economic policies of Sarit encouraged huge U.S. and Japanese investment and gave rise to a new wealthy class due to land speculation and sustained economic growth of 5 percent per year. Major projects of electrification and irrigation were undertaken with assistance from international agencies. Thailand formed the Association of Southeast Asia (ASA). It was the first step toward regional integration of Southeast Asia, along with the Philippines and Malaya (since 1963, Malaysia). The legacy of Sarit after his death in 1963 was the Thai involvement in the Vietnam War and the establishment of development-oriented technocratic agencies. Thanom, who had become field marshal in 1964, faced communist revolts. International investment and American military expenditures in Thailand resulted in considerable economic growth for the country. It was primarily through the initiative of Thailand that a regional association was established to strive for peace and prosperity of the region. The Association of Southeast Asian Nations (ASEAN), with Indonesia, Malaysia, Singapore, Thailand, and the Philippines as original members, was established on August 8, 1967. In the February 1969 elections, Thanom's *Saha Prachathai* (United Thai People's Party) secured 75 seats out of 219 in the lower house, giving it the largest representation among the 13 parties. The Democratic Party, with 57 seats, came second. Popular discontent against Thanom was growing and on November 17, 1971, he staged a bloodless coup against himself. The constitution was abrogated and the National Assembly was dissolved. Thanom assumed dictatorial power and imposed martial law. The National Executive Council was formed. Thanom, Field Marshall Prapass Charusathiara (1917–2001) and son of Thanom, Narong Kittikachorn (who was also son-in-law of Prapass), were the three most powerful persons of Thailand. They were known as the "Three Tyrants." Protests arising out of consequences of the Vietnam War were increasing. The social discontent in north and south Thailand had given rise to communist insurgencies. The labor organizations, student unions, and intellectuals rose against Thanom. His rule was over after the October 14, 1973, revolution.

THE VIETNAM WAR

Thailand was the most trusted Southeast Asian ally of the United States in the war against communist forces in the Vietnams, Laos, and Cambodia. It sent troops to Indochinese countries, collaborated with the CIA, allowed the stationing of American troops on Thai soil, and permitted bombing raids against the Indochinese countries from its air bases. From the dispatching of a marine helicopter detachment to Thailand under the administration of President John F. Kennedy (1961–1963) in March 1961 to the withdrawal of the American military in July 1976, the Thai government as well as the army established a patron-client relationship with the United States. For maintaining its security, Bangkok joined the war efforts of the United States against communism. Even before the escalation of the Vietnam War, cooperation between the governments of the United States and Royal Lao government (RLG) was strong. American aid was passing through Thailand to landlocked Laos, and the United States had built new airfields in northeastern Thailand. Thailand was panicky as the leftist Pathet Lao's forces were gaining ground in the Lao civil war. Transport and communication facilities improved between Thailand and Laos, which was a part of the U.S.-sponsored communication network in Laos, Thailand, and South Vietnam.

Thailand was for a friendly regime in Laos and all the while it supported the rightist RLG. The failure of the Geneva Accords of 1962 saw Laos embroiled in the Vietnam War.

On March 6, 1962, the United States and Thailand signed the Rusk–Thanat agreement, which spelled out that obligations under SEATO were "individual as well as collective." The United States declared a unilateral defense guarantee, and military assistance to Thailand was doubled. American troops in Thailand were increased to 49,000 by 1972. Thailand became the sanctuary for the air war against Indochina. From air bases in Don Muang, Korat, Nakhon Phanom, Takhli, Utapo, Ubon, Udorn, and Khon Kaen, B-52 bombers delivered million of tons of bombs. The aircrafts used napalm and defoliants sometimes and bombing was characterized by heavy civilian toll and was responsible for creating a large number of refugees. The number of Thai troops increased in Laos; from 5,000 in 1965–1966 to 20,000 in 1972, and Thai pilots were flying the special planes called T-28s in bombing the Pathet Lao areas in Laos. In 1966, the first Thai contingent, called "The Queen's Cobra Regiment," was sent to Saigon (Ho Chi Minh City) and the number of Thai troops increased to 12,000 afterward. The Thai government also granted the United States the use of the large naval base at Sattahip.

Thailand's involvement in the Vietnam War witnessed infrastructural developments of the country. These included growth of Thai business and economy. But most of the benefits were enjoyed by the upper strata of the society. A culture developed, particularly among the middle and upper classes, with an emphasis on consumerism. This emphasis was there earlier, as noted, after Thailand's entry into the modern age, but it became more widespread with the coming of the Vietnam War. From the middle of the 1960s large segments of Thai society came into contact with Western fashions and styles of living. The cities of Thailand transformed their hotels, clubs, and massage parlors, and the sex industry grew in order to accommodate the American military personnel coming for rest and recreation (R&R) as mentioned earlier. Although it would be naive to say that prostitution came to Thailand with the Vietnam War, there was no doubt of its proliferation because of the war. Sex tourism was one of the reasons for the influx of tourists. Anti-American sentiments were expressed in some quarters of society. A feeling developed that the Thai culture was being threatened. A sense of resentment developed due to the presence of foreign troops on Thai soil and the alignment of Thai policy makers with U.S. interests.

10

Contemporary History
of Thailand

Thailand's history since the 1970s is full of momentous events that have placed the country in a unique position. The student revolution of October 1973, struggle for power between civilian and military regimes, social discontent, end of the Cold War, globalization, and Islamic insurgency have shaped the nation in various ways. Thailand was at the threshold of momentous developments when the new millennium arrived. In Southeast Asia it had become a major power. The economy had recovered after the Asian financial crisis, and the integrity as well as sovereignty of the nation were intact. In spite of political instability due to military coups and violence in the south, Thailand showed remarkable resilience while facing disturbances within and tackling problems at regional and international levels.

SOCIAL DISCONTENT AND THE STUDENT
REVOLUTION OF 1973

Beginning from the middle of the nineteenth century onward, Thailand had been modernized under the Chakri rulers. After the 1932 revolution, Thailand ushered in a new era. There were remarkable changes in Thai society. But the bulk of the masses did not receive many benefits, as the advantages did not percolate downward. In the countryside, the peasants had to toil as hard or harder than always. Gradually, discontent arose against elite dominance in Thai society. The infighting between different categories of the elite hardly affected the life of the masses, whose predicament was increasingly deplorable. In the northeastern region of Isan, the poverty index was more in comparison to many other areas of Thailand. Poverty was significant in rural areas and outlying regions. The inequality of income had been growing since 1960. Emphasis on nonagricultural manufacturing industries had augmented the gap between the living standards of core and outlying zones. The poverty incidence (head-count ratio) in 1962–1963 was 57 percent for whole of the country, but in rural areas it was 63 percent. The percentage of rural households living below the poverty line in the central plains was 34.9 percent in 1971–1972, but for Isan the figure was a staggering 74.7 percent. Isan had been a neglected region, and the ethno-regional consciousness of the people made it a breeding ground for insurgency. From the 1960s to 1980s, Isan became the strongest base for the Communist Party of Thailand (CPT). The ruling elite were apprehensive of communist domination in Thailand and a confrontation arose between the ideology of the left and that of the rightists, their counterparts.

The CPT had been established on December 1, 1942, and the Free Thai Movement had given it an opportunity to come in contact with rural regions. Apart from its strategic location, Isan had a long history of resistance against Bangkok. The violent anticommunist repression policy unleashed by the Sarit regime had driven the communists to the countryside. In 1961, the CPT had founded the Democratic Patriot Front for indoctrinating peasants in armed struggle. In March 1962, the CPT radio station, Voice of the People of Thailand (VPT), was established in southern China. On August 7, 1965, clashes occurred between government troops and insurgents. The revolt spread all over the country, including the northern and southern regions. A 13-year struggle continued from the August events in the Phupan range, with increasing clashes between communists and government troops. The opium war of July 1967 had enabled the CPT to recruit cadres from the refugees from Laos and other places who had been relocated by the government. The communist insurgency also received support from China, North Vietnam, and Pathet Lao from Laos. A communist commando unit made an attack against the air base of Udon on July 26, 1968. The number of clashes increased from 154 to 680 in 1972.

From the early 1970s different classes of the population were in discontent. The time was propitious for a revolution. The inflation of 1972 caused the price of rice to climb by almost one percent per month. The government was mismanaging the affair, as it had allowed the export of rice on a large scale. Thanom's son Narong was put in charge of price controls. His efforts were to no avail and led to further mismanagement. Hoardings, shortages, and long lines to buy rice in urban areas resulted. Wage earners were hard hit. The working class resorted to strikes beginning in January. Labor organizations organized as many as 40 strikes, including the Thai Steel Company strike, a month-long affair. The students, who had established the National Student Center of Thailand (NSCT) in 1968, came to the forefront. They held a major demonstration in October 1971. The manifestation of student movements continued throughout 1972. In November, the NSCT held a weeklong demonstration against Japanese imports. There was anti-Japanese sentiment and the demand for concessions to Thailand for its trade deficit with Japan. In December, the students, now having organized themselves into a political force, rose against the governmental control of the judiciary. The announcement of an interim constitution with an appointed legislative assembly provoked widespread protest. The students came into the streets in May 1973, demanding elections and a democratic constitution. The beating and expulsion of nine students from Ramkhamhaeng University in June for making a caricature of the regime led to widespread protests. (The students were reinstated afterward.)

The students had become frustrated due to the lack of job opportunities after graduation. They orchestrated protests against "The Three Tyrants" of the military government—Thanom, Prapass Charusathiara, and Narong Kittikachorn—by appealing to religion and monarchy. In the protest rallies several figures of Buddha, pictures of the king, and the national banner were waved. The antimilitary movement gathered momentum after it attracted the support of factory workers, intellectuals, and the middle-class population of Bangkok. Popular discontent was mounting against the government. Even the civilian political elite, sections of the business community, and rival military factions protested against the policies of the government. The civilians were aggrieved as they had been debarred from the sharing of power. The rising inflation as well as Japanese economic influence ran counter to indigenous commercial interest. There were also protests over the stationing of American troops and the military regime's strong support of Washington. The power wielded by Thanom's son Narong was not liked by a section of the army. The aggrandizement of wealth as well as concentration of power by Thanom, Narong, and Prapass was not to be tolerated by the majority of people. The venom against the triumvirate resulted in a massive demonstration of 250,000 people, who had gathered before the Democracy Monument, the symbol of the 1932 revolution. After 41 years, Thailand was witnessing another upsurge. In the violence that ensued, 400 persons died and thousands were wounded due to police gunfire. Four buildings were burned. October 14 was designated as *Wan Maha Wippasok* (The most tragic day). A memorial at the junction of Central Ratchadamnoen Avenue and Tanao Road was erected afterward in memory of those young students, who sacrificed their life for a noble cause. The king interfered and further violence was averted. Prime Minister Thanom resigned and left the country, along with his son and the Deputy Premier Prapass. The rule of the "Three Tyrants" was over. Thailand had witnessed two revolutions in a span of 41 years, each resulting in momentous changes. The critics had castigated the 1932 revolution as elite-initiated and the one in 1973 for leading to the dominance of the military after three years. The character and leadership of both had come under the scanner of critics. But the fact remained that injustice and inequality would not last long. When the boundary of tolerance reaches its optimum point, a revolution has to occur. The gains of it in the long run can be realized if one takes a long-term view of progress in the history of a country. In that sense, 1932 as well as 1973 were not lessons in failure but turning points in the hopes and aspirations of people toward democratization. Even under the military regimes, there was apprehension about another mass upsurge. A ruling clique, whether military or civilian, could not afford to drive the masses to a point where the clique would be obliterated in another mass upsurge. The ruling elite in the post-1973 era would be conscious of the needs of the common people.

Professor Sanya Thammasak (1907–2002), Rector of Thammasat University, was appointed as the prime minister of Thailand by a Royal Decree on October 14. He remained in the office until May 22, encountering the problems arising out of students and bringing normalcy after the revolution. The militant student faction was unhappy over the direction toward which the government was heading. The NSCT had been divided into moderate and radical factions. The former was composed of university students belonging to the middle class. The students from technical schools were radicals who were not averse to violence. However, in spite of different groups among students such as the People for Democracy of Thirayuth Boonmee (1950–) and the Federation of Independent Students led by Saeksan Prasertkul, the involvement of students in the affairs of the nation was increasing. They were in various committees of bureaucracy. The students developed contact with laborers and peasants, who became vocal in asserting their rights. Even some in the police and military service began to question the counterinsurgency policy. The membership of the CPT increased. Somkid Srisangkom's (1918–) Socialist Party of Thailand also became more active. The secretary of the party was Boonsanong Punyodyana (1936–1976), who, along with 13 other activists, had been arrested by Thaonom's regime. The Thai Party was organized by the former president of NSCT, Sombat Thamrongthanyawong, and the academic Pongpen Sakultpai. The ideological divide among students, intellectuals, and other sections of the society became conspicuous. The communist victories in neighboring Indochina and the withdrawal of American troops from Southeast Asia made the conservative section of society apprehensive of leftist dominance.

A new constitution was adopted in October 1974 providing for a bicameral national assembly. The members of the House of Representatives were to be elected by popular ballot and the senators to be appointed by the king. The stronghold of military and bureaucracy over Thai politics was loosened by abolishing the provision of financial secrecy, right of appointed members in a no-confidence vote, and holding both the office in assembly as well as military or administration. In the elections of January 1975, 44 parties participated with 22 gaining seats. On February 15, 1975, Seni Promoj, the leader of the *Pak Prachatipat* (Democratic Party), became the prime minister, leading a three-party coalition government. Within a month of assuming office, he did not get a vote of confidence and his brother Kukrit Promoj, leader of the *Pak Kit Sangkhom* (Social Action Party), was selected to head a coalition ministry on March 17. By April both Cambodia and Vietnam had communist governments, which worried the rightist forces in Thailand. Kukrit also visited China. There were strikes by farmers and students in May and July. The left was campaigning for U.S. withdrawal and the end of the support of the military. The U.S. military force, numbering 27,000, began to leave Thailand starting in March 1975 and the process was completed the next year. There were anti-American demonstrations after the *Mayaguez* incident of May 1975, when the United States used the airbase of Utapo without the consent of Bangkok. The anti-American rhetoric, along with a move toward the left in public opinion, goaded the rightists to retaliate. A witch hunt began with virulent criticism against the left. Rightist organizations such as *Nawa Phon* (New Force), Red Bulls, *Luk Sua Chaoban* (Village Tiger Cubs), and the Village Scout Organization were established in 1976 with the motive of confronting the left. Once again the ultranationalists, composed of conservative civilian elements and senior military officers, defended the Nation-Religion-King regime with the rallying cry of *Nawa Phon*. Political assassinations and attacks against student demonstrations became a regular affair. Right-wing militancy was steadily growing in 1976 and the government of Kukrit was helpless in checking the violence that had erupted. The April 4, 1976, election was one of the bloodiest in Thai political history, with 30 casualties including the Socialist Party leader Bunsanong. The *Pak Prachatipat*, with 114 of the 279 seats, became the largest Party. On April 21, 1976, Seni became the prime minister again, heading a coalition government of four parties.

STRUGGLE FOR POWER: CIVILIAN AND MILITARY REGIMES, 1976–2006

For 30 long years, Thailand witnessed a duel between civilians and the military to hold the reigns of the government. In spite of a tradition of a rudimentary democracy after 1932 and ascendancy of liberal forces after 1973, the military was constantly lurking behind the scenes, ready to seize power. This was due to weakening of the civilian forces, changing regional as well as international scenarios, and economic travails. The military seized upon the opportunity when the whole of Indochina went red. The communist insurgency within the country was also increasing. The bogey of communism provided the military an opportunity to crush the civilians after unleashing a reign of terror. It led to the downfall of Seni's government on October 6, 1976.

There began stage-managed crises of which the left bore the brunt. Facing violent retaliations by the rightists, they were branded as communists and antinationals. In August Prapass, one of the "Three Tyrants," appeared in Thailand, but he had to make a hurried departure to Taiwan after widespread demonstrations against him. Thanom returned after a month, donning a monk's robe. He was well protected by rightist organizations like *Nawa Phon* and *Luk Sua Chaoban*. Students who protested against his stay in Thailand were accused of being communists because of their opposition to a Buddhist monk, and two protestors were hung in Nakhon Pathom. The government was demoralized and there were conflicts between the liberals and rightists after a reshuffling of the cabinet. Emotions ran high, leading to a volatile atmosphere. The students had gathered in Thammasat University and staged a play enacting the hanging of the two student protestors. On October 5, the right-wing newspapers published manipulated images of a student actor resembling the crown prince. A pretext was made to attack the rally of the students as they had indulged in the act of lèse-majesté. On October 6, hundreds of right wingers followed by the police as well as the military stormed the campus of Thammasat University, killing hundreds of students and arresting 3,000. Violence and mayhem were perpetrated against some students as they tried to escape. The army seized power and established the National Administrative Reform Council (NARC). The civilian government of Seni was ousted, the constitution abrogated, and martial law proclaimed. The experiment with democracy was over and Admiral Sangad Chaloryu (1915–1980) became chairperson of the National Administrative Reform Council (NARC). He continued in this post until November 23, 1980. A new government under Thanin Kraivichien, an ex-judge of the Supreme Court, was formed with the support of the king and NARC. A diehard conservative and an avowed anticommunist, he remained in the office from October 8, 1976, to November 12, 1977.

The Thanin government was one of the most repressive regimes that Thailand had witnessed. It enforced strict censorship of media, tight control of trade union activities, and the expulsion of communists from bureaucracy as well as from universities. The leadership among communist cadres swelled after the Thammasat massacre as intellectuals along with students and farm and labor leaders fled to the jungles to escape secret punishment from the coup leaders. On March 26, 1977, General Chalard Hiranyasiri made an abortive coup and was summarily executed. The oppressive rule was too much even for the military and Thanin was replaced by General Kriangsak Chomanand (1917–2003), who became prime minister on November 12, 1977. Sangad Chaloryu became the defense minister.

The government of Kriangsak showed comparative political stability. Thailand and its communist neighbors followed a policy of rapprochement. In 1978, Thailand signed agreements on trade with Laos as well as China. It also restored diplomatic relations with Vietnam. China declared in 1979 that it would no longer help the CPT. This was the period when the communist states fought against one another. Vietnam's invasion of Cambodia in December 1978 was followed by the Chinese attack against Vietnam in February 1979. The events in Cambodia had great repercussions on Thailand's security and economy. The Thai and Vietnamese forces confronted each other after the proclamation of the pro-Vietnamese People's Republic of Kampuchea. Thailand, members of ASEAN, the United States, and China demanded the withdrawal of Vietnamese forces from Cambodia. Thailand provided logistical and financial support to different factions operating against the Phnom Penh regime. The influx of a large number of refugees placed a great strain on the Thai economy, resulting in inflation, which greatly affected country's industry and agriculture. On the domestic front, the CPT was weakened due to the new direction of foreign policy of the government, the rift among communist nations, and the reconciliatory policy of Kriangsak. He had raised the minimum daily wage for workers in Bangkok and surrounding areas. The 18 dissidents arrested in the wake of the October 1976 events were pardoned in September 1978. The general amnesty program resulted in the surrender of 8,000 insurgents. The constitution of 1978 established a bicameral national assembly. The 225 members of the Senate were to be appointed by the prime minister. It was powerful as it could block important measures concerning national security and economy, which were already passed by the House of Representatives. The members of the House of Representatives, numbering 310, were to be elected. The military and civil servants received a stay of five years for appointment to ministerial posts. The April 1979 elections resulted in the victory of moderate rightist parties. A coalition government was formed with Kriangsak remaining as the prime minister. The opposition to his government was increasing as Thailand was witnessing deteriorating economic conditions due to the international oil crisis. The prime minister announced a hike in the prices of oil, gas, and electricity. He was forced to resign on March 3, 1980, due to the large scale opposition to his policy, and General Prem Tinsulanonda (1920–), the commander-in-chief of the army, became the prime minister.

   Prem's administration, with its five successive coalition cabinets, witnessed an emphasis on exports and industrialization, leading to a rapid development of the Thai economy from the middle of the 1980s onwards. The policy toward Vietnam became tough and there were border skirmishes between the two countries. The danger to the stability of Thailand due to insurgency was reduced to a considerable extent with the surrender of rebels. Popularly known as Papa Prem (although a bachelor), he had a clean professional record and he enjoyed the support of the monarchy. In Thailand, the political system was becoming accommodative of various groups. The different components of the ruling elite like military, business, political parties, and technocrats had never wavered from the commitment to democracy. Narrow interests of each group appeared to have the only motive of being in government by hook or by crook. They were compelled to tolerate each other, as there was no other option left for them. The military also knew that it was impossible to rule as it was doing in the 1950s. The time had changed and there were different factions in the army. The Young Turks had been instrumental in ousting the two prime ministers in 1977 and 1980 successively. General Arthit Kamlangek made abortive attempts in 1981 and 1985 to oust Prem, who, with great dexterity, had built his power base. He played one group against the other and maintained a balancing act between political parties and military-civil officers. With support from the king and regional military commanders, Prem was able to crush the rebellion of the Young Turks on April 3, 1981. The rebels, led by General San Chipatima, fled from the country and the rest of the participants were granted royal clemency. Another attempt by the Young Turks on September 9, 1985, also failed and General Chavalit Yongchaiyuth (1932–) took a leading part in suppressing it. Prem was successful in driving Khun Sa, the mastermind behind the narcotics trade, from his base at Baan Hin Taek in the Chiang Rai Province. He fled to Myanmar along with his Shan United Army in January 1982. On the 40th anniversary of CPT's establishment, about 1,000 communists surrendered themselves to General Arthit on December 1, 1942. China also closed down the radio station of the party. The ruling class was relieved after the end of the communist menace. Prem received support from the Democrat Party and the Social Action Party in the House of Representatives and in the cabinet the majority of members were civilians. In the Parliamentary elections of April 1983, none of the political parties were able to enjoy majority in the House of Representatives. Prem formed another government. He made structural changes to the Thai economy. The Thai business associations were successful in persuading the government for a Joint Public and Private Sector Consultative Committee. There was demand from students and the middle class of cities that the prime minister be an elected member. Prem, in spite of support from monarchy, business groups, and major political parties wanted to avert a political crisis.

He resigned on August 4, 1988, after the elections, as he was never an elected member of the Parliament. Prem became a member of the Privy Council. The new prime minster, Chatichai Choonhavan (1920–1998) of the *Pak Chart Thai* (Thai Nation Party), continued in the office until February 23, 1991.

As the first fully elected prime minister after 12 years, Chatichai reasserted the role of Thailand as a major economic power in Southeast Asia. It pursued an active role in the ASEAN and followed a dynamic foreign policy with neighboring Indochinese countries. But the urban middle class as well as military charged the government with corruption, as it was using its power for personal gains. On February 23, 1991, the coup leaders, known as the National Peace Keeping Council, seized power. The commander-in-chief of the Royal Thai army, Suchinda Kraprayoon (1933–), was the coup leader. General Sunthorn Kongsompong (1931–1999) remained as the chairperson of the council from February 23 to March 7. The public had welcomed the coup as military leaders had mentioned that they were ousting the government only with a view to eradicate corruption. Anand Panyarachun (1932–), a diplomat and businessman, was appointed as prime minister pro term by the military clique. The drafting of a new constitution witnessed confrontation between the military and its opponents. It was clear that the military was in no mood to give up political control. There was a large scale protest of 50,000 people on November 19, 1991. A new party of retired army officers, called *Samakkhi Tham*, began to project Suchinda as the next prime minister. The 1992 elections were rigged with utter corruption and free play for rampant vote-buying. Suchinda took office on April 7, which led to a popular uprising. Once again, the military, which was at the receiving end, took recourse to violence in suppressing the outburst. The various groups such as the urban middle class, trade unions, and students thronged in Bangkok and in these four days of violence about a 1,000 people were killed. The international opinion showed concern at the developments in Thailand. Professional groups and the business community were showing apprehension over the impact of military rule on the Thai economy. A wider section of people had joined the antimilitary movement. Public awareness was much more prominent than it was during the earlier movements in the 1930s or 1970s. The mass media and political commentary by intellectuals had made many groups of people aware of the true nature of military rule. On May 24, 1992, Suchinda had to resign after being forced to by King Bhumibol, who granted amnesty to demonstrators. Anand headed an interim government, bringing out major reforms which led to economic growth. Chuan Leekpai (1938–) of the Democratic Party won the elections and a coalition government of pro-democracy parties took office on September 23.

The government of Chuan came under much criticism due to its policy toward Myanmar, failure of a reforestation program, and corruption. In fact,

Chuan had faced criticism in 1987, when he was the Speaker. His brother had fled from the country after embezzling U.S. $10 million. Chuan's cabinet ministers were accused of large-scale corruption. Banharn Silparcha (1932–) of the *Pak Chart Thai* (Thai Nation Party) became the prime minister on July 13, 1995, after winning the elections. Banharn's government also was plagued with corruption. He was compelled to conduct elections soon and thereby General Chavalit Yongchaiyudh, leader of the *Pak Kwam Wang Mai* (New Aspiration Party), took office on December 1, 1996. The Asian financial crisis of 1997 doomed his fate and he had to resign, paving the way for Chuan's second term from November 9 onward. Meanwhile a new constitution had been promulgated on October 11. This was hailed as the most democratic Constitution that Thailand ever had. The Constitution was, to a considerable extent, in conformity with the meaning of the word "constitution" in the Thai language. It was governance as per *dharma* or *ratha thama noon*. The drafting assembly had been elected by popular election. The party system was strengthened and the various articles enshrined in the constitution were democratic. Both of the houses of the Parliament were to be elected. The 1997 constitution made several innovations as compared to previous constitutions. Voting became compulsory and there was a provision for an independent election commission. A system of checks and balances was introduced with the creation of new agencies including the Office of the Auditor General, the National Counter Corruption Commission, the National Human Rights Commission, and others. Perhaps the most laudable feature of the constitution was the section on human rights, which truly made the constitution a democratic one like any other document of a modern democratic state. There were as many as 40 rights provided in it compared to only 9 rights in the constitution of 1932. The Thais had rights to free education, freedom of information, public health, and protests.

Chuan's government of seven party coalitions came under bitter criticism because of corruption, violations of human rights, the nomination of Thanom as an honorary royal guard to the king, and favor shown to large financial institutions. The ministers holding key positions were found guilty of embezzling millions of dollars. The villagers protesting against the Pak Mun dam had to bear police brutality. The editor of the newspaper *Pak Nua* faced an assassination attempt. Chuan's decision to honor Thanom was dropped due to protests. The social activists, intellectuals, and business entrepreneurs criticized the neo-liberal policy of government and launched a self-sufficiency campaign. The victory of the *Thai Rak Thai* (TRT, Thai Loves Thai) party of telecommunications billionaire Thaksin Shinawatra (1949–) in the January 2001 elections was on a nationalist platform. He had a program of popular scheme of economic distribution campaigning against corruption, organized crime, and drugs. Thaksin's popular mandate was larger than that of any other prime minister and he took office on February 9, 2001. Thaksin endeared himself to the royal family, business class, and military personnel to consolidate his position. In the Asian financial crisis of 1997, Thailand had borrowed heavily from the International Monetary Fund (IMF). It was paid back well before time. The economy was once again booming. The country became the leading exporter of rice by 2004 and world's seventh-leading exporter of automobiles in 2005. The sophisticated manufacturing units produced goods for the domestic market as well as for exporting.

Thaksin also became the first elected prime minister in Thai history to complete a full term in office and get reelected. His policies pertaining to health, education, foreign relations, finance, drugs, and energy got him a landslide victory. Poverty had gone down remarkably by half in a span of five years. The healthcare system improved. His populist measures included medical facilities, housing plans, and credits at a subsidized rate. There was a revamping of the school curriculum. For the less affluent students, loans were given for education. Thaksin's drug policy became highly controversial. His all out campaign for drug eradication resulted in the killing of about 2,700 people. The provincial governors had a more active role to play as they became chief executive officers. He vehemently criticized the old order and outmoded institutions with the slogan, *Think new, act new*. The new slogan, *The heart of TRT is the people*, became very popular in 2003. Thaksin's measures became universal and people in general felt the presence of a benevolent government. The popularity rating of the prime minister rose from 30 to 70 percent. On December 26, 2004, a tsunami hit Thailand's southern coast; particularly the holiday resort islands of Phuket and Phi Phi as well as the province of Phang Nga. The consequence was devastating with 5,400 causalities and 2,800 missing persons. The emergency response and relief operations undertaken by the government were praised by the international community. Utapao air base and Sattahip naval base became centers of international relief efforts for the entire region. Thaksin won a spectacular victory in the 2005 election by getting 61 percent of the vote and winning 377 out of 500 seats. But within a year he was no longer in power. The opponents of Thaksin did not appreciate his aggressive mode of functioning, abuse of power, and undermining of institutions, and they alleged corruption against him. The court's ruling absolving the prime minister over shares in the Shin Corporation was not accepted by the opposition. His detractors argued that his personal and authoritarian style ran counter to development of a healthy democracy. Thaksin publicly expressed his disdain for old institutions, academicians, rule of law, and human rights, all of which he claimed were quite often hindrances in working for the benefit of people. From December 2005 onward, the anti-Thaksin campaign became intense. In an ever present tussle between military and democracy, he was ousted in a coup on September 19, 2006, led by General Sonthi Boonyaratglin (1946–).

11

Thailand Today

In recent years, the focus of attention in Thailand has been on Islamic insurgency, the economy, foreign policy, and the workings of the present military government. Islamic insurgency has a historical background and there is no sign of any meaningful solution. In the last few decades, Thailand has become a major economic power in Southeast Asia, and its economy had been revived after the Asian financial crisis. Coming out of the compulsions of the Cold War, Thai policy makers had reformulated their foreign policy so as to cope with changing circumstances.

ISLAMIC INSURGENCY

Religion has been an important factor in shaping the destinies of the people of Southeast Asia. Brunei, Indonesia, and Malaysia are predominantly Islamic countries. In the Philippines and Thailand, there are sizable numbers of Muslims. At the time of the decline of the Indianized Kingdoms of Southeast Asia, Islam began to penetrate the region. Islam had arrived at Thailand from various regions like India, China, the Malay-Indonesian archipelago, Myanmar, and Cambodia. The Arab and Indian traders were pioneers in bringing Islam. The spread of Islam accelerated after the founding of Melaka. The Persian traders, who were frequent visitors to Ayudhya, also brought Islam. There was also an influx of Sulawesi Muslims, who fled from the Dutch persecution in southern Celebes around 1666 and 1667. In the central plains, there are Muslims of Persian, Pakistani, Indian, and Indonesian and Cham descent. In the northern provinces of Lampang, Chiangmai, and Chiang Rai, the Muslims were from Myanmar and southern China. The insurgency in southern Thailand's Muslim-dominated regions has escalated in recent years. Secessionist tendencies were not new in the region. There were alternate phases of independence and subjugation from Thai central rule in the three southern provinces of Patani, Narathiwat, and Yala. As noted earlier, the Malay-speaking Muslims constitute about 6 million or nearly 10 percent of the country's total population. The economic disparities between Bangkok and rural areas has resulted in the economic underdevelopment of the south. There seems to be an imagined as well as a real perception that the region is neglected by Bangkok.

The Patani region remained as a vassal state, but there were revolts against the Thai rule. In 1786, Patani was annexed by the Thai kings of the Chakri dynasty. It was divided into seven zones under a centralized bureaucracy. By the Anglo-Thai Convention of 1909, Thai control over Patani was recognized and the four states of Kedah, Perlis, Kelantan, and Trengganu were given to the British. The convention thus fixed the present existing boundary between Malaysia and Thailand. The Muslims of the Malay states were freed from the Buddhist rule of Thailand, but those of Patani hoped that they would be united with their counterparts of the Malay states. Thus the separatist movement in southern Thailand had a historic legacy, which was aggravated afterward in the modern period.

Thailand followed a policy of noninterference in the first three decades of the twentieth century. But under the military dictatorship of Phibun, the policy of forcible assimilation alienated the Thai Muslims. The government wanted to bring minority groups into mainstream Buddhist Thai culture. The introduction of Buddhist laws in place of the *shariyat* (Islamic laws), discrimination against the Malay language, and the banning of sarongs and of carrying loads on one's head (Malay-style) created bitterness among the Thai Muslims. The latter did not have soft feelings toward the influx of poor Buddhist cultivators to the south with governmental support. The installation of a massive statue of Buddha outside Narathiwat, cancelation of Friday as a holiday, looking down upon the Malay language as *pasar khaek* (language of strangers), and the visit of Thai officials to mosques without removing their shoes angered the Muslim population of southern Thailand. The attitude and behavior of the Thai bureaucracy had not helped in solving the minority problem. It had hampered progress toward a climate of understanding. The rural areas of the south are underdeveloped. Even though Thailand belongs to the middle-income group of countries with a rank of 73 in the Human Development Index, the regional imbalances persist. The deprivation and inequalities of opportunities among the underprivileged classes in the northeast and south have resulted in discontent. In northeastern Thailand, a communist insurgency movement accompanied the era of the Cold War. The southern provinces are the least developed, with people taking recourse to agriculture, fishing, and working as laborers in rubber plantations. The household income in the south was one-fifth and gross domestic product one-fourth, respectively, of the national average.

A feeling of social alienation and cultural subordination has added to the growth of separatism. The government is taking some steps to solve the problem. The Thai constitution gives equal rights and opportunities to the Muslims. Freedom of worship exists. There are about 5,000 mosques and several thousand *madrasas* (religious schools) across Thailand. The Thai Muslims have taken part in politics. There are many examples of Muslims becoming successful politicians and government officials. Both Wan Muhammad Noor Matha and Surin Pitsuwan had remained as the President of the National Assembly and Foreign Minister of Thailand, respectively. The Thai Muslims also express their voice through the Democratic Party of Thailand, which has remained a popular party of southern Thailand. In 1988, a political faction called *wahdah* (unity) was formed.

But the ethnic minority residing in remote areas far from the capital feels politically slighted as well as economically exploited. The communal interaction between the Thai Muslims and the Thais is rather scant. Barriers of language and strict adherence to the *shariyat* prevent Thai Muslims from having any meaningful interaction with other communities. The educational opportunities for the community are few, and this lack of proper education has been another factor in aggravating their problem. The religious schools manned by the ulema do not help the Muslim youths to get jobs in today's competitive market. The famous *pondok* system of education continues imparting religious education. However, there is integration through a comprehensive program in Islamic private schools, which prepares Muslim youths for a professional life. The Ministry of Education has recruited qualified teachers from Indonesia, Malaysia, Egypt, Saudi Arabia, India, Pakistan, and Turkey. In schools and colleges of southern Thailand the percentage of Muslim teachers is very low. The introduction of Thai as the national language was resented. The schools and Buddhist teachers are targeted by militant youths. The presence of a civil society is not strong in southern Thailand. The region also has been marked by lawlessness, high crime rates, and a proliferation of illegal business. The latent dissatisfaction has been channeled into a path of confrontation between the government and Thai Muslims. Violence as a method to realize the objective of independence persisted.

The insurgency movement that began in the 1940s continued until 1980s. But again it has flared up in the twenty-first century with unabated violence. The rise of Islamic fundamentalism and free flow of money from the Middle East has intensified the separatist movement.

Separatist movements advocating for an independent Patani have emerged since the 1940s in its first phase and remained until 1980. The four main actors in the irredentist movements were as follows: the minority group (Thai Muslims), host government (Thailand), mother government (Malaysia), and the sympathizers in the mother government. When the government of Phibun undertook the policy of the assimilation of Thai Muslims, a leader of the Thai Muslims, Haji Sulong, demanded recognition of Islamic laws, 80 percent reservation in government jobs for Muslim youths, and that locals remain in charge of the administration of Muslim-dominated provinces. Haji was arrested and about 2,000 Thai Muslims fled to Malaysia. There was even a demand for the incorporation of southern Thailand into the newly formed Federation of Malay. The Patani National Liberation Front (*Barisan National Pemberbasan Patani*, or BNPP), which can trace its roots to the year 1947, was led by Yala Nasir, a descendent of the Patani sultanate. Badri Hamdan led the movement after Nasir's death. Its army wing, the Patani People's National Liberation Army (*Tantera Nasional Pemberbasan Patani*, or TNPP), was led by Bapa Idris. It was known for the kidnapping of Chinese businessmen for ransom. In 1969, the Patani United Liberation Organization (PULO) was formed under the leadership of Tunku Bira, a Patani aristocrat, who used to travel frequently to Middle Eastern countries and Malaysia. The problems of Thai Muslims are voiced in international Islamic conferences. It made a daring attack on the life of the royal couple when they visited the province of Yala in September 1977. Another organization known as the Organization of Warriors of Allah (*Perrubuhan Agkatan Sabilullah*) was urban based and came to the surface in 1975 after the killing of 11 Thai Muslims. It advocated for a militant Islamic state.

The left-leaning and rural-based National Revolutionary Front (*Barisan Revolusi Nassional*, or BRN) was formed in 1960. Led by Ustad Karim, it advocated for an Islamic state on socialist lines. It was closely aligned with the Malay Communist Party (MCP). The MCP appealed to Muslims on both sides of the border and set up the *Partai Persaudaraan Islam* (Islamic Fraternal Party). The CPT joined and formed the Muslim Liberation Army of Thailand (MLAT). It called for autonomy in southern Thailand. The secessionist movements in its first phase were characterized by sporadic attacks against police forces, throwing a bomb sporadically, and demonstrations. It received external assistance. The secessionist leaders like Suolng and Yala had their strategic operations from the territory of Malaysia. Arms and money from private quarters poured into southern Thailand. The leaders went to Middle

Eastern countries to garner support for the cause of Thai Muslims. The Thai government contained the secessionist movement by intensified police operations. From 1980 onward, the Thai government changed its policy. It stopped the assimilation policy, declared a general amnesty, and brought out a development plan. But the relatively quiet period was soon over and in its second phase the separatist movement was intensified with terrorist activities.

The belief that terrorism was waning was short-lived. After the September 11, 2001, terrorist attacks on the United States, the country saw a recrudescence of terrorist violence. It flared up with a series of raids, attacks, and murders. The secessionist organizations had regrouped themselves. At the time, when the secessionist organizations remained low-key and had almost stopped violent activities, attention was diverted toward organizational matters. Talks were held to coordinate different factions. The United Front for the Independence of Patani or *Bersatu* (United) was formed for pooling resources from different organizations. The leaders from PULO and the newly formed Mai PULO (New PULO), BRN, BNPP, and *Mujahadden Patani* met on August 31, 1989, and established the *Payong* organization. It was decided that there would be a unity of purpose for the struggle. Apart from getting help from the fellow ethnic Malay Muslims of the provinces of Kenantan and Kedah of Malaysia, the secessionist organizations were provided with money and arms by Osama bin Laden's (1957–) Al Qaida, formed on August 11, 1988. The Patani Islamic Mujahideen Movement (*Mujahideen Islam Patani*) established in 1995 is believed to be affiliated with Al Qaida. With the motive of setting up the Islamic state, terror groups like *Al-Maunah* (Malaysia), *Laskar Jihad* (Indonesia), the Moro Islamic Liberation Front (the Philippines), and BRN, along with the *Mujahideen Islam Patani* (Thailand), stepped up terrorist activities. Transnational Islamic fundamentalism was active in southern Thailand with the help of persons educated in religious schools abroad. The growth of Islamic identity among Thai Muslims had been increasing. The donations from the Middle East had fostered fundamentalism in the religious schools that dotted southern Thailand. These had become breeding grounds for radical Muslims. The Thai Muslim students, who had graduated from schools in Saudi Arabia and Pakistan, returned home and became votaries of Islamic fundamentalism.

The latest outburst of violence that began in 2001 witnessed the murder of 19 police personnel and about 50 terrorist activities in the three southern provinces of Thailand. The following year, there was an upsurge in violence with 75 incidents and the killing of 50 police officers. Since January 2004, about a 1,000 people have met violent deaths due to rebellion. Martial law was imposed in several districts of the Narathiwat province after rebels stormed an arms depot and burned 18 schools on January 4, 2004. On February 15 a village official and telecommunications workers were shot dead.

Thirty-six government buildings were torched on March 18. On April 28, 108 Muslim rebels were killed in a clash with Thai security forces. The Thai Muslim demonstrators, numbering around 84, were suffocated to death after they were dumped in trucks by security forces in October. In the year 2005, the same pattern of violence continued. On January 23, 2005, two Buddhist monks were shot dead by Islamic militants. In the February elections, the candidates of Thaksin lost. The government declared emergency rule in the three provinces on July 15. General Sonthi became the first Muslim to occupy the post of army chief in a major reshuffle in August. The move was aimed at placating the Thai Muslims of the southern border provinces, where 30,000 soldiers were engaged in combating insurgency. There was report of talk between PULO and Thai authorities in Switzerland, which was denied by the government. The beginning of the New Year was marked by the killing of two police officers in Yala in January 2006. The arbitrary detention and torture of suspected militants by the police at the time has been criticized by international human rights groups. In September, motorcycle bombs killed three people and wounded about 60 in the southern town of Hat Yai.

There was no perceptible change under the new military regime, with relations between ethnic Malay/religious Islamic vis-á-vis Thai/Buddhist identities remaining strained. The violent incidents and killings related to the insurgency went on. Even the royal family was not spared. Princess Sirindhorn (1955–) came under attack when a bomb was placed on the landing pad of her helicopter. In March 2007, the convoy of Crown Prince Vajiralongkorn (1957–) was targeted. Busy commercial areas, schools, and hotels were also under the insurgent's target many times till present day. A negotiated settlement to the problem of Thai Muslim insurgents is the need of the hour. The formation of an independent state for Thai Muslims is not feasible in the near future, though it is hoped that this group can work with the government to negotiate legitimate demands in order to end the violations of human rights.

FOREIGN POLICY

Thailand today has strayed a long way from the close military alliance it had with the United States during the Vietnam War period. The Thai foreign policy aimed to mend relations with the communist countries and increase regional integration. In spite of different political ideologies, Thailand established full diplomatic relations with China in 1975. An attempt was made to improve relations with Indochinese countries. But the special relationship with the United States continued. It was the largest trading partner of Thailand in the beginning of the new millennium. Thailand, the "major non-NATO ally," had allowed the air base of Utapao and a naval base in Sattahip to be used for logistical support for the U.S. military in Afghanistan and Iraq. After the September 11, 2001, attacks, the Thai government established the Counter Terrorism Intelligence Center (CTIC) for intelligence sharing between Thai intelligence agencies and the CIA. In August 2003, the dreaded terrorist Riduan Isamuddin of the *Jemaah Islamiyah* (1993–) outfit of Indonesia was arrested in Ayudhya. Thailand had committed itself to fight international terrorism in Southeast Asia. It was assumed that if violence in southern Thailand escalated with the involvement of international Islamic networks, Bangkok might expand its cooperation with the United States at an increased level of commitment. Thailand, the United States, Japan, and Singapore participated in the joint military exercise in Thailand known as Cobra Gold 2005. In 2006, a security alliance was formed including, in addition to the United States and Thailand, Japan, South Korea, Australia, and the Philippines. In case things should get out of hand, the alliance might come to the rescue of Bangkok. It had also sent around 450 troops to Iraq in the "reconstruction" effort of that country, despite criticism from many quarters in Thailand. It withdrew its troops in September 2004.

Regionalism played a significant role in Thai foreign policy after the end of the Cold War. The spirit of ASEAN aimed at pacific settlement of disputes among members. With the inclusion of the three communist states of Indochina, it became broad based and created a space for it in international relations. The member countries like Thailand, Indonesia, Malaysia, the Philippines, Singapore, Brunei, Laos, Cambodia, Myanmar, and Vietnam had bilateral as well as multilateral agreements on trade, tourism, industry, energy, education, science, banking, and culture. The development of Southeast Asia as a whole had been an undergoing process and Thailand was contributing substantially to it. Thailand, along with the rest of the members of ASEAN, had endeavored to tackle problems such as drug trafficking, trafficking in women, money laundering, terrorism, and other transnational crimes. In December 1997, the leaders of the ASEAN countries envisaged the ASEAN Vision through organizations like the ASEAN Regional Forum (ARF), Special ASEAN Ministerial Meetings, ASEAN Chiefs of Police (ASEANAPOL), ASEAN Centre for Combating Transnational Crime (ACTC), Senior Officials Meeting on Transnational Crime (SOMTC), and ASEAN Ministerial Meeting on Transnational Crime (AMMTC). Steps were taken to combat various forms of crimes affecting Southeast Asia in particular and the world in general. On October 30, 2005, Thailand hosted the ASEANPOL conference, where cooperation in matters relating to drug trafficking, cybercrime, terrorism, and credit card fraud were discussed.

The ASEAN group looked beyond Southeast Asia for political and economic cooperation. Thailand had been an active participant in the endeavor of ASEAN. The member countries attended the meetings and participated in deliberations of the Asia-Pacific Economic Cooperation (APEC), the Asia-Europe Meeting (ASEM), and the East Asia-Latin America Forum (EALAF). In 1994, the ARF was established with non-ASEAN countries including the United States, Russia, China, and India to discuss security issues and take steps in confidence building. An agenda was developed for an enhanced role of the ARF in matters of security dialogue and cooperation. Meetings were held in the Cambodian capital and Potsdam, Germany, in 2004 and 2005 respectively. The Fourth ASEAN Summit, held in Singapore in January 1992, called for annual consultation between ASEAN and its dialogue partners like Australia, China, the European Union, India, Japan, the Republic of Korea, Russia, and the United States. The December 2005 ASEAN Summit, held in Kuala Lumpur, noted with satisfaction progress toward creation of a Free Trade Area with Australia, China, Japan, New Zealand, India, and the Republic of Korea. ASEAN cooperated with the East Asian nations of China, Japan, and the Republic of Korea, and they were accorded a special status of ASEAN Plus Three. They will have a free trade agreement by the year 2010.

Thailand has taken major steps in improving relations with its Asian neighbors on a bilateral level. A business-oriented approach was the hallmark of Thai policy. In spite of different political ideologies, Thailand established full diplomatic relations with China in 1975. China exported military equipment to Thailand, when Beijing and Bangkok supported the resistance groups against the Vietnamese-installed regime. Both had also promoted the Greater Mekong Sub-region (GMS) Economic Zone. In 2005, there was a major agreement between the two countries concerning investment and trade. Bangkok was also going to open four new consulates in China. There was an attempt at improving relations with Indochinese countries. Border clashes between Thailand and Laos had become things of the past and border crossing became easier. The Thai–Lao cooperation had been strengthened by mutual visits of leaders, officials, media personalities, and cultural delegations. The foreign minister of Thailand, Nitya Phibun Songramm (1941–), welcomed in August 16, 2007, a delegation from the Lao foreign ministry. Both countries had active cooperation in bodies like the GMS and Ayeyawady-Chao Phraya-Mekong Economic Cooperation Strategy (ACMECS). Thailand also joined with organizations involving South Asian countries. The BIMSTEC (Bangladesh, India, Myanmar, Sri Lanka, and Thailand Economic Cooperation) aimed at close cooperation among member countries. The Mekong–Ganga Cooperation (MGC) was founded in November 2000 for better understanding and close relations among member countries like India, Myanmar, Thailand, Cambodia, Laos, and Vietnam. A Mekong–Ganga Tourism Investment Guide would facilitate travel in the region and promote package tours and developing transport networks such as the East–West Corridor and the Trans-Asian Highway. There would be greater linkage between the two after the completion of the third Friendship Bridge, connecting the Nakhon Phanom province of Thailand and the Khammouane district of Laos.

In spite of clashes between Thai and Cambodian troops in 2002, relations between the two countries have been fairly good. The Thaksin government had placed special emphasis on maintaining a cordial relationship with Myanmar for the past few years. In 2004–2005, the Shin Corporation had been granted a profitable contract for providing communication networks in Myanmar. In December 2004, Thaksin went to the extent of calling the detention of Aung Sun Su Kyi (1945–) reasonable. The dispute over the maritime boundary with Vietnam was resolved. Thailand had used the expanding market of Vietnam for its consumer goods. Relations with Malaysia were a bit complex due to the Islamic insurgency in southern Thailand. The matter had been complicated by militant camps along the Thai–Malaysian border and a shared ethnic bond between Thai and Malay Muslims. However, the relations had remained fairly good. Malaysia hosted the meeting of the Organization of Islamic Countries (OIC) in December 2005 and there was no support given to the Islamic insurgency of Thailand.

Throughout its history, Thailand has followed a flexible and dynamic foreign policy. It has allowed itself to bend with the wind and yet has retained its freedom of action as well as national sovereignty. The close identification with American interest was long over. After the end of the Cold War, Thailand devoted its energy to bringing stability to Southeast Asia as well as contributing to the solution of transnational problems in the present-day world. It had diplomatic relations with major governments, membership in many international bodies, and served as the headquarters of several international organizations.

THAI ECONOMICS

The economic growth of Thailand was remarkable from the middle of the 1980s. From a regional agrarian economy, the country became a globalized industrial economy. Thailand became one of the Asian tigers along with Singapore, Taiwan, South Korea, and Hong Kong by 1991. It was the new member of the "newly industrializing countries." With the fad for a socialist economy on the wane worldwide, many countries took recourse to a market-oriented economy. Thailand became entrenched within the global economy. With the new mantra of liberalization and globalization, the world had become a huge market for investments and sales of commodities. Thailand did not lag behind in the race. The shift from rural to urban areas led to the consequent growth of urbanization. Social mobility became common, and the employment boom especially within the 10 years after 1985 resulted in people flocking from rural to urban areas.

There was ample foreign investment in Thailand. As the baht had been attached to the U.S. dollar, it became cheaper for the Japanese to invest, as the value of the dollar went down against the yen. Thailand had increased exports as well as trade with Japan. The Stock Exchange of Thailand (SET) reached a high figure of 1753.73 in the beginning of 1994. The financial institutions and banks were flooded with foreign funds. Private capital inflows surged the financial market of Thailand. The offshore banks began to arrive from Japan and the West. But from late 1996 cracks began to appear and bubbles began to burst. Thailand, which was a model for economic development, was going to be hit by a crisis resulting in foreign debts, currency depreciation, unemployment, and inflation. What started in 1997 as a regional economic crisis beginning in Thailand developed into a worldwide economic crisis within a year. The Asian economic crisis commenced from July 2, 1997, when the Bank of Thailand decided to float the baht. The repercussion was swift with great impact over the money market of Southeast Asia. The value of the Philippine peso, Malaysian ringgit, and Indonesian rupiah went down. The fixed exchange rate of the baht, the plunge in price of the property market, and decline in exports became responsible for the Thai economic predicament. The baht, which was pegged at 24.3 to the U.S. dollar in June 1997, went down as low as 44 by the end of December. In January 1998, it made a slide to 52.5. The situation in the financial sector became critical and 56 finance companies were shut down by the end of 1997. The SET reached its lowest point in 1999 with an index of 481.92. Thailand faced recession and its economic growth rate was 5.9, −1.7, −10.2, and 4.2 for the years 1996, 1997, 1998, and 1999. The halt in high-rise construction projects resulted in massive amounts of defaulted loans. The ambitious sky train project linking different areas of Bangkok also was shelved. The country's credit rating went down and investments decreased considerably, with a capital outflow from private sectors amounting to a staggering sum of 645,096 billion baht. In August the IMF gave a credit of U.S. $17.2 billion to Thailand with the condition that it maintain a budget surplus. The Thai government would have to cut down expenditures and increase its revenues so that the surplus would amount to 60 billion baht. The government had to initiate major reforms in financial sectors. It increased the value-added tax (VAT) from 7 to 10 percent. Consumer spending went down. About 2 million people lost their jobs, leading to a lowering in the standard of living. The Thai economic crisis also witnessed a major change in the ownership of companies and financial institutions. Foreign firms went for joint ventures with local business houses, and their share in banks also increased.

The government initiated a series of economic reforms such as making changes in lending practices, encouraging incentives, and making corporate governance strong. There was gradual economic recovery. In the middle of

1998, the IMF also loosened its hold over the government in the face of criticism. The measures initiated by Chuan's government resulted in bitter social protest, and there was a perception that the government was averse to the plight of the common people. The prime minister cooperated with the IMF. Globalization was attacked from many quarters because there was bankruptcy. Unemployed people flocked to their ancestral villages to earn their livelihood. The emphasis became more focused on local communities and welfare plans. The community-based plans were mooted by governmental departments to ward off the economic crisis. By the year 2000, the country had weathered well the economic consequences of the crisis and limped back to economic recovery. The Thaksin government launched an ambitious program of reforms by which domestic demand would be stimulated. Support was accorded to domestic firms. But at the same time, there was a promotion of open markets as well as foreign investments. The agenda of Thaksinomics were: distribution of 1 million baht to each village, a three-year moratorium on small-scale debts of farmers, disbursement of loans to poorer sections, and the creation of the National Asset Management Corporation (NAMC). The NAMC took over bad debts from banks at a discount. The customers again received new credits from the banks. By 2001 Thailand had recovered from the crisis, and its GDP was 5.2 percent the next year.

Thailand witnessed an economic boom again. In 2004, 55 percent of the labor force was employed in the industrial and service sectors. Educational opportunities increased manifold. Avenues of opportunities opened along with foreign investments, industrialization, and the growth of technology. Women's empowerment was marked as a vast majority of women were employed in different sectors. In human development, Thailand showed tremendous progress. There was a rise in the per capita income from U.S. $7,010 to $7,595. The average life span also increased from 69 to 70 years. With a Human Poverty Index Rate of 28, the population below poverty line came down to 10 percent only, although poverty was still significant in poorer regions and villages. The Gross Domestic Product (GDP) grew by 5 percent in 2006. The manufacturing share of GDP increased from 22 percent in 1980 to 35 percent after about 25 years. The foreign reserve of Thailand was U.S. $67 billion. The import growth fell from 9.3 percent in 2005 to 1.6 in 2006. The main items of imports were capital and intermediate goods, raw materials, and fuels. Thailand was exporting rice, textiles, fishery products, jewelry, automobiles, and electrical appliances. The volume of exports increased steadily from 4.3 percent for the year 2005 to 8.5 in 2006. Increases in exports and falls in imports were major factors behind the GDP growth. The inflow of foreign capital had increased and the exports accounted for about 70 percent of the GDP. The Thai economy was strong enough to weather any storm. Its future seemed to be bright.

THE COUP AND ITS AFTERMATH

The coup of September 19, 2006, once again demonstrated the dominance of the military in Thai politics. Thaksin had ruled with an iron fist, overriding all opposition. His populist measures had made him prime minster twice, both times with a big mandate. But there was increasing dissent against misuse of power. A leading critic in the beginning was media moghul Sondhi Limthongkul (1947–). A rally was organized on February, 4, 2006, against a huge deal concerning the Thaksin family's 49.6 stake in the Shin Corporation. The share, amounting to U.S. $1.9 billion, was sold to Singapore's Temasek Holdings. No tax was paid to the government as the transaction was done through a company registered in the British Virgin Islands. Although the court verdict made it legal, Thaksin came under criticism. An organization known as the People's Alliance for Democracy (PAD) was established on February 8, drawing support from middle and upper-class Bangkok residents, academics, students, socialites, and some Buddhist monks. The five-member central committee included Sondhi Limthongkul, politician Major General Chamlong Srimuang (1935), University Professor Somkiat Pongpaibun, labor leader Somsak Kosaisuuk, and social activist Phiphob Thongchai. Mass rallies and television shows were organized by the PAD clamoring for the prime minister's resignation. Thaksin dissolved the Parliament and called for elections.

In the elections held on April 2, 2006, Thaksin secured 460 out of 500 seats in the House of Representative. The opposition parties such as the Democratic Party, Thai Nation Party, and Great People's Party boycotted the election and Thaksin resigned two days afterward. Chidchai Vanasatidya acted as prime minister on behalf of Thaksin from April 5 to May 23. The Constitutional Court afterward invalidated the elections and in May the cabinet decided to hold new ones in October. The protest led by Sondhi against Thaksin also went against parliamentary norms as the latter was being criticized abusively. The chairperson of Amnesty International's Thailand branch condemned the manner in which Thaksin was being criticized. Sondhi's *Manager Daily* wrote a series of articles mentioning that Thaksin was planning a republic against the royalty. Sondhi's involvement in the PAD and talk shows had garnered profit for his media companies to the tune of U.S. $6 million in late 2005 and early 2006. While the PAD was planning for a massive rally on September 20, Sonthi Boonyaratkalin (1946–), a Muslim and commander-in-chief of the Royal Thai army, backed by retired army commander General Surayud Chulanont (1943–) and Privy Council president Prem Tinsulanonda (1920–), staged a coup one day before the rally was to take place. Thaksin was in New York for a meeting of the United Nations General Assembly and he declared a state of emergency. Sonthi, who was the chairperson of the newly formed Council for Democratic Reform, dissolved the Parliament and abrogated the constitution. The PAD announced its dissolution on September 21. Remaining as prime minister for 11 days, Sonthi handed over charge to Surayud on October 1.

As the coup was backed by the king, the large majority of people did not oppose it. There was no shedding of tears generally at the removal of Thaksin. Speculations and different interpretations emerged for his ouster. In the white paper issued by the junta, factors like corruption, abuse of power, and the destruction of Thai unity were cited. Conflict with royalty as well as class conflict between the rural poor and urban elite also led to Thaksin's removal. It seemed that the combination of many factors inherent in Thai politics were responsible for the seizure of power by the military. There had been cycles of Parliamentary elections, coming of democratic governments, corruption in civilian regimes along with factionalism, military coups, and elections. It was arrogance of power that ultimately destroyed Thaksin. The question remained as to how many months or years it would take for the military regime to hand over power. After the September coup, the first public protest was staged on September 22, with less than 100 demonstrators at Siam Square. Three days afterward, 30 demonstrators and 100 journalists organized a rally at Thammast University. In September and October there were sporadic protests at Chulalongkorn University, Thammasat University, near Democracy Monument, and in front of the Arm Headquarters. On October 10, Constitution Day, 2,000 demonstrated in front of the Democracy Monument. There were also online petitions. However, the military regime was quite safe as there was no coordinated movement against it. The coup leaders went on a witch hunt against Thaksin and his supporters. Chidchai Vanasatidya and Defense Minister Thammarak Isaragura were soon arrested. The Thaksin loyalists in the military were purged. The diplomatic passport of Thaksin was revoked on December 31. Committees were set up to look into irregularities committed by the earlier government.

In January 2007 the Constitutional Drafting Council was appointed with the military having control over the membership. On April 26, the Drafting Committee prepared a draft constitution, which would go for a referendum. The draft provided for a bicameral legislature with an elected House of Representatives consisting of 400 members. The 160 members of the Senate would be an appointed body by a royal order after the selection by the Senator Selection Commission. The draft envisaged fundamental rights for the Thais such as equality before the law, the right to liberty, and freedom of expression, among others. The draft charter would be approved by the public referendum on August 19. The constitution would be the 18th one since Thailand became a constitutional monarchy. The main criticism against it was that unlike the 1997 Constitution it included a provision for an appointed Senate. The number of elected members of the House of Representatives had been slashed from 500 to 400. The persons who had drafted the charter were not elected members. The draft charter also undermined the party system. However, it had retained the fundamental rights of the citizens, raised the profile of the judiciary, and empowered voters to launch impeachment proceedings against elected representatives. In a landmark judgment on May 30, 2007, the Constitutional Tribunal dissolved the *Thai Rak Thai* and banned Thaksin along with 110 senior officials of the party for five years from politics. It acquitted the Democrat Party. After six days, the military junta lifted the ban on political activity. In a future election, the Democratic Party would hold the sway. The military clique was coming under mounting criticism and the United Front of Democracy against Dictatorship (UDD) staged hourlong demonstrations on July 22 by 6,000 protestors. It was also reported that the junta had disbursed 1.5 billion baht to military officers for joining the coup. Sonthi was accused of having two wives, which was in violation of Thai criminal code. The prime minister had also been accused of shady land deals.

While attending the meeting of ASEAN in Manila, Foreign Minister Nitya said that general elections would be held in December. He also was a party to the draft charter of ASEAN for banning the coups and respecting human rights. Indications of a return to democracy were in the cards. After a referendum for the constitution was over, there was a strong feeling that process of normalization would take place along with a realignment of political parties. The TRT had been dissolved and its members formed a new party called the People's Power Party (PPP) with a non-TRT politician, Samak Sundaravej (1935–), as its leader. An archrival of Prem, he had been instrumental in Prem's quitting politics in 1988. Samak's *Prachakorn Thai* was in the coalition led by Chatichai's ministry. The Democratic Party remained one of the strongest parties after coming out unscathed from the May court ruling. The newly formed *Rak Chart* (Love the Nation) had the blessings of the military and the ability to develop candidates from among the corps of retired army officers.

The PPP leader Samak Sundaravej (1935–) formed a coalition government in January 2008 with five smaller political parties, after his party emerged victorious in the elections held the previous month. Thailand limped back to democracy after 15 months' military rule. But the country witnessed a political duel between the PPP and PAD that was marked by demonstrations and strikes. In February, the former premier Thaksin returned to Thailand. The PAD launched widespread protests in August and September. A state of emergency was declared in the capital. After Samak's resignation in September 2008, Somchai Wongsawat (1947–), brother-in-law of Thaksin, became the premier. He could barely hold the office for three months. The political turmoil of Thailand became unprecedented with the seizure of Bangkok's two airports on November 25 and blockading of Parliament by the PAD. On December 2, 2008, the Constitutional Court banned the PPP and dissolved the government. On December 15, 2008, Abhisit Vejjajiva (1964–) of the Democratic Party was elected the new prime minister and was endorsed by the king two days later.

The government of Abhisit had faced a lot of opposition and demonstration. Sometimes it was marked by violence. The ghost of Thaksin loomed large over the premier. Unlike Thaksin, Abhisit was not elected and lacked a popular mandate. The supporters of Thaksin called "Red Shirts" were drawn mainly form the rural areas of northeastern Thailand as well as some poor people from cities. The capital city of Bangkok witnessed demonstrations by the protestors. A clash with the army led to the death of 27 persons on April 10, 2010. Abhisit would be facing a lot of problems if he would not dissolve Parliament. Central Bangkok was burning for the last two months. The Premier had announced plans for holding elections on November 14 on the condition that the Red Shirts would end their protest. The protestors wanted sincerity of the government in holding elections. In this situation, the King would play a decisive role. The city of Bangkok had been turned into an urban war zone due to a bloody conflagration between the army and protestors. About a dozen more people had been killed after April 10 due to firing by Thai troops. The total death tally was about 39 and the injured figure was about 300. The crisis would be intensified if there was no definite solution. The situation continued to be tense in spite of withdrawal of demonstrations on May 19. A civil war-like situation would emerge threatening the country's political and economic stability. The clash, which was a tangled web of different interest groups, had to be contained. The best way was to go for a negotiated solution. The political pundits would watch the coming events with interest.

Notable People
in the History of Thailand

Buddha (563–483 B.C.E.). Although Buddha was not born in Thailand, his life and teachings have had considerable influence on Thai history, culture, and society. The Buddhist Era in Thailand is calculated taking the year 543 B.C.E. as the base year. The year 2010 is 2553 the Buddhist Era. Lord Buddha was born in Kapilavastu, Nepal, and began his spiritual journey in 543 B.C.E. He preached the first sermon at Sarnath, India, called turning the Wheel of Law. After his death, Buddhism spread to different parts of Asia. Buddhism had taken roots in Thailand from the lifetime of Buddha himself, as per traditions. Under King Ashoka (273–236 B.C.E.), the Buddhist Theras Sona and Uttara came to Suvarnabhumi, with its capital at Nakon Pathom, to propagate Buddhism, and a huge stupa, Pathom Chedi was built to commemorate the event. The majority of the people (about 90 percent) profess Buddhism in Thailand. The genius of Thai artists can be discerned in the Buddhist Wats, stupas, and icons of Buddha.

Mangrai (r. 1259–1317). Mangrai was the founder of the Lan Na Kingdom in northern Thailand, contemporary with that of Sukhothai. He belonged to the Yuan Tai family ruling over the Chiang Saen region. Various warring tribes from different principalities were unified under his leadership. The capital city of Chiang Rai was established in 1262. He had a close alliance with Sukhothai as well as another autonomous Thai state called Phayao. Mangrai, Rama Khamheng, and Ngam Muang of Phayo never fought against each other. Mangrai subjugated the Mon Kingdom of Haripunchai (Lamphun) in south. He kept his capital changing and in 1296 established the city of Chiang Mai, which became the center of a unique Isan culture. The Kingdom of Mangrai was subject to frequent raids from the Mongols, who were repulsed with the help of Sukhothai's army. Mangrai compiled law codes known as *Mangraisart*. After his death, 17 kings and queens ruled over Lan Na.

Rama Khamheng (r. 1277–1298). Rama Khamheng, or Rama the Great, was born in 1239. He was the son of the founder of the Sukhothai dynasty, Sri Indraditya (r. 1238–1270). One of the greatest monarchs of Thailand, Rama the Great left a vast Kingdom in the south at the time of his death in 1298. His domain included Luang Prabang and Nakhorn Sri Thammarat, as well as parts of the lower Chao Praya, the upper Mekong, and the lower Salween Valleys. He made friendship with China, assuring the stability of his Kingdom. The king also developed friendly relations with the Lan Na ruler Mangrai (r. 1259–1317). Rama Khamheng visited Beijing in 1282, bringing Chinese potters back with him. The ceramic industry became important economically for a long time. A true *dharmaraja*, he looked after the welfare of his subjects. Rama Khamheng was the originator of Thai script, and many facets of Thai culture originated during his reign period.

Rama Tibodi I (r. 1350–1369). The founder of the Ayudhya Kingdom, General U Thong, assumed the title of Rama Tibodi at the time of his coronation in 1350. The capital city was named Ayudhya after the capital of the Kingdom of Rama, hero of the *Ramayana*. He expanded the Kingdom at the cost of the declining powers of Sukhothai and Angkor. Administrators, artisans, and Brahmans came to Ayudhya from Angkor. His Kingdom penetrated to the lower Chao Praya River, the Gulf of Martaban, and the Malay Peninsula. He followed the practice of the Hindu kings and styled himself as the *devaraja*, or divine king. Thus his legitimacy was established. He was also a lawgiver. His decrees were added to the legal code written in Pali and remained in force until the last decade of the nineteenth century. Tibodi embraced Theravada Buddhism in 1360, and it became the state religion of Ayudhya.

Trailoknath (r. 1448–1488). The son of Boromaraja II (r. 1424–1448), Prince Ramesuen was at one point the governor of the Phitsanulok province. Ayudhya and Lan Na fought indecisive wars in the 1470s. Trailoknath came into conflict with Melaka ruler Muzaffar Shah (r.1445–1459). Ayudhya's dominance over the whole of the Malay peninsula did not materialize and the Thai troops were repulsed. An innovator in administration, he brought all the Thai principalities together under centralized control. The Kingdom was divided into provinces, each headed by a *Chao Phraya*, or governor. In the central administration, there were five important *krams* (departments). The nobility had varying amounts of *sakdina* (honor marks) and were categorized into seven grades. The king codified the Kot Montien Ban (Palace Law) pertaining to royal families and tributary states in 1450. A post of heir-apparent, *brah maha uparaja* (vice king) was created for peaceful succession. The Vanaratnavong or the Pa-Kaeo sect of Buddhism became popular during his reign. He died as a Buddhist monk at Wat Chulamanee in Phitsanulok in 1488.

Queen Suryothai (d. 1548). Suryothai was the Queen of the Ayudhya ruler Maha Chakraphat (r.1548–1568). The ruler of the Toungoo dynasty of Myanmar, Tabinshweti (r.1531–1550) attacked Ayudhya in 1548 and both the rulers fought on elephants. Donning the uniform of a male soldier, Suryothai joined the battle mounting an elephant. The queen fought bravely and put herself between the two rulers as her husband was losing the combat. Tabinshweti killed Suryothai and retreated afterward. As per legend, the valor and sacrifice of the queen shamed the Toungoo ruler. Suryothai is famous in Thai history, culture, and popular imagination for her bravery. She is a revered figure in Thailand. Her saga of bravery has been immortalized in the Hollywood movie *The Legend of Suryothai* (2003). The Thai version released in 2001 became one of the biggest box-office hits. The ashes of Suryothai are preserved in a *chedi* (reliquary) at the Suan Luang Sobsawan temple.

Patani Queens (r. 1584–1688). Under the rulers of the Ayudhya dynasty, the Patani region enjoyed alternate phases of independence and subjugation. Patani was a prosperous Kingdom because of international trade. The Queens of Patani were looking after the subjects well. They tried their best to maintain independence, but were not always successful. After the death of Sultan Bahadur (r. 1573–1584), his daughters Raja Hijau (Green Princess r. 1584–1616), Raja Biru (blue Princess r. 1616–1624), and Raja Ungu (Purple Princess r. 1624–1635) became successive queens. They were named after the colors of the rainbow. Hijau was quite well known in the Chancelleries of Europe, Ayudhya, and Japan. Under Biru and Ungu, the Thai attacks were repulsed. Simultaneously, there were also exchanges of friendship missions between the two Kingdoms. Raja Kuning (r. 1635–1688), daughter of Raja Ungu, was the last queen of Patani. Known as the "Yellow Queen", her reign was marked by the decline of Patani. She visited Ayudhya in 1641 and was welcomed by King Prasat Thong (r. 1630–1656). She accepted nominal suzerainty of Ayudhya and sent *bunga mas* (gold leaves) as a sign of tribute.

Naresuan Maharaj (r. 1590–1605). After the plunder of Ayudhya, the Toungoo ruler Bayinnaung (r. 1551–1581) installed Maha Thamraja (r. 1569–1590) as a vassal ruler, and his son Naresuan, a boy of nine years was taken as a hostage. He was allowed to return in 1576. Naresuan organized an army and made Ayudhya independent in 1584. He became the king of Ayudhya after the death of his father Thamaraja. There were trade agreements with European powers during his reign. In 1593, the invading troops of Myanmar were defeated again. He erected a pagoda at Don Chedi in Suphanburi to commemorate the event. A fair is organized every January in honor of Naresuan, and it is also Thailand's National Armed Forces Day. The king then took initiative of attacking Myanmar. For maritime commerce, Thailand needed ports in the Indian Ocean and in 1593 troops were dispatched to southern Myanmar. The southeast frontier was secure after a successful invasion against Cambodia. In 1595, Lan Na came under his suzerainty. He died after falling sick with a carbuncle on his face, while on a march against Myanmar.

Narai, the Great (r. 1656–1688). Narai was the son of Ayudhya king Prasat Thong. He became preoccupied with rebellion in the northern states and signing treaties with European powers. Narai established diplomatic missions with Asian and European countries. His reign witnessed the beginning of influences from the West. The newly constructed palace in Lopburi had contributions from Jesuit architects. Determined to have a trade monopoly, the Dutch blockaded the mouth of the Chao Praya River. Narai signed a treaty in 1664, which gave the Dutch a monopoly of trade in hides and extraterritorial rights of jurisdiction. The king took the help of French engineers to build forts in Thonburi, Nonthaburi, and Ayudhya. The French were allowed to open a trading station in Songkhla. In spite of efforts of the French Jesuits, Narai did not change the religion. The king made the Greek adventurer Constantine Phaulkon (1647–1688) his confidant. The relations between Ayudhya and France became close due to efforts of Phaulkon. Narai became very sick with dropsy in 1688 and died afterward.

Phya Taksin (r. 1767–1782). The half-Chinese general Phya Taksin, the governor of Tak province, restored the pride of Thailand after the devastation of Ayudhya in 1767. Known as the "Liberator of Siam", he became the leader of the resistance against Myanmar. He established himself as king of Thailand in the town of Thonburi. A new capital was built with help from his paternal home in Chaozhu. The Chinese supplied labor force and building materials. Finally Ayudhya came under his sway. He had complete control over central Thailand. The Vietnamese influence over Cambodia diminished temporarily and was replaced by Thai influence in 1771. Luang Prabang became an ally in 1774. Vientiane was occupied in 1778 as it had defied Taksin by maintaining an alliance with Thailand's traditional enemy Myanmar. The famous Emerald Buddha that had been in Vientiane's possession since 1564 was brought to Bangkok. He began to show signs of insanity. The hostility of Buddhist monks led to his downfall and imprisonment. A remarkable king of Thailand, he also had rallied the Thais against alien occupation. He was not only a warrior, but also a lover of arts and literature. The equestrian statue of Taksin adorns the large circular ground of Thonburi.

Rama I (r. 1782–1809). Born on March 20, 1737, to a noble of the Ayudhya Kingdom, Phra Aksorn Sundara Smiantra, Chao Phraya Chakri had a distinguished career in the army of Phya Taksin. After becoming the king as Rama I, he shifted the capital from Thonburi. The attacks from Myanmar were successfully repulsed in 1785 and 1787. The Sultans of Malay Peninsula such as Kedah, Kelantan, and Trenggannu acknowledged the suzerainty of the Thai monarch. They used to send *bunga mas* (gold leaves) as a mark of insubordination to the Thai court. Rama I annexed provinces of Battambang and Siem Reap of Cambodia. The Sultan Muhammad II of Patani acknowledged the suzerainty of Rama I. He made changes in the administration and introduced a new code in 1804. He initiated the royal writings known as Phra Rajanibondh. He was the author of the Thai version of the Indian epic, the *Ramayana*. Rama I died on September 7, 1809, in Bangkok and was succeeded by his son Prince Isarasundorn as King Rama II (r. 1806–1809). He left his mark in Thai history as patron of literature, law giver, and empire builder.

Sunthorn Phu (1786–1855). One of the great Thai literary figures, Sunthorn was born in Bangkok. He led a colorful life in the royal court. Even his childhood was spent there as his mother was working as a wet-nurse. He had a love affair with a woman of the court and married her later. He became a court poet and Rama II (1809–1824) bestowed on him the title Khun Sunthorn Wohan. Sunthorn was jailed in 1821 due to his involvement in a brawl. After Rama II's reign, he lost royal patronage and became a monk. His poetic romances were in the *sepha* (a type of ballad) style. His magnum opus, the *Phra Aphai Mani,* narrated the romantic adventurers of Prince Aphai in ancient Thailand. It began while he was a prisoner and was finished after 20 years. Sunthorn also penned nine *nirats* (travelogues), records of his visits to different places. He wrote in a simple language for the common people, describing everyday life. Thailand celebrates Sunthorn Phu Day June 26.

Sri Suriyawongse (Chuang Bunnag, 1808–1883). Sri Suriyawongse was born on December 23, 1808, to Prayoonrawongse (Dis Bannag) and Tan Poo Ying Chan. His ancestors come from the Persian Gulf region and officiated in high positions in finance and the military. An educated person, he had progressive ideas. He was in charge of military affairs. An experienced administrator, Suriyawongse was appointed as regent when Chulalongkorn was a minor. After the king assumed charge, he had differences of opinion with Suriya-wong. The latter was not opposed to reforms *per se*, but wanted a slower pace. Suriyawongse supported the king regarding the abolition of slavery, but opposed financial centralization. When foreign companies started life insurance in Thailand, he was the first to have a policy. He died on January 19, 1883, in Ratchaburi. The Bansomdejchaopraya Rajabhat University was built at the site of his residence afterward.

Mongkut (r. 1851–1868). Mongkut, the grandson of Rama I was born in 1804 to Rama II (r. 1809–1824) and Queen Sri Suriyendra (1767–1836). He became a Buddhist monk at the age of 19. Well-versed in European affairs, he learned Latin and English. He ascended the throne in 1851 as Rama IV. In 1855, he signed an unequal treaty of friendship and commerce with Britain, followed by similar treaties with the United States and major European countries. The advantage was with the foreign countries, as they received the status of most-favored nation, extraterritorial jurisdiction, and tariff control. He also initiated reforms in education and health, encouraging medical work of missionaries, teaching his sons English and liberal arts, establishing a royal mint, and relaxing court rituals. Anna Leonowens (1834–1914) was the English governess of his children whose influence on the king has been exaggerated in novels and movies. Mongkut also established a Buddhist sect called *dhammayutika*. An avid astronomer, Mongkut invited the courtiers and foreign community to Thailand to observe the solar eclipse in 1868 in malaria-infested Sam Roi Yod. Stricken with the disease, he died soon afterward. He is remembered for his policies of modernization and preserving his country's independence.

Damrong Rajanubhab (1862–1943). Prince Damrong Rajanubhab, born on June 21, 1862, was the fifty-seventh son of Mongkut from a lesser wife named Choom. In 1880, he became commander of the Royal Pages' Bodyguard Regiment and after seven years was elevated to deputy commander-in-chief of the army. He was also the education minister of King Chulalongkorn and brought about major reforms in the Thai education system. As Minister of Interior from 1894, he revamped the provincial administration. After leaving the ministry in 1915, he indulged himself in writing books on Thai history, literature, and culture. He initiated the practice of distributing books at funeral ceremonies. Damrong lived many years in the British colony of Penang, where he died on December 1, 1943. He was the first Thai to be honored by UNESCO as one of the world's distinguished personalities.

Chulalongkorn (r. 1868–1910). Rama V, commonly known as Chulalongkorn, was one of the greatest Thai monarchs, noted for his foreign policy and modernization program. The fifth king of the Chakri dynasty was born to King Mongkut and Queen Debsirinda (1834–1861) on September 20, 1853, in Bangkok. He was a widely traveled person to neighboring countries, India, and Europe. The liberal rule of Chulalongkorn, which lasted a very long 42 years, witnessed reforms with far reaching consequences for Thai society and economy. The archaic feudal administration in provinces was changed with the division of the Kingdom into *changwat* (provinces) and *amphoe* (districts). In 1874, any person born during his reign was a free man, which was the first step toward the abolition of slavery. He gave away territory to the French and British, keeping Thailand as a buffer state between the two. In exchange for a 25 kilometer neutral zone along the Mekong's west bank, Thailand ceded the Champassak and Sayaboury provinces to the French in 1904 and 1907, respectively. By the Anglo–Thai Convention of 1909, Thailand surrendered suzerain rights over the four southern states of the Malay Peninsula: Kedah, Perlis, Kelantan, and Trengganu. Britain recognized the Thai control over the Patani sultanate. When Chulalongkorn died on October 23, 1910, in Bangkok, he left a modern state to his successors. October 23 is observed as a national holiday.

Phraya Manopakorn Nititada (1884–1948). The first prime minister of Thailand after the end of absolute monarchy was born on July 15, 1884, as Thongkon Hutasingha in Bangkok. The son of a cobbler, he attended Suan Kulap school, law school, and completed his education in London. He was a Minister of Justice, Privy Councilor, Finance Minister, and professor of law. He was the choice of the *Khana Rasdr* (People's Party) to head the government. He remained as Premier from August 28, 1932, to June 20, 1933. He continued in the post after the promulgation of the Constitution on December 10, 1932. His government was beset with problems, as factionalism among the ruling elite was becoming conspicuous. Manopakorn dismissed the Assembly on April 1, 1933, on the ground that members were floating communist ideas. The Economic Development Program of Pridi Banomyong had come under lots of criticism. In June, he was ousted by a coup and went into exile in Penang. He died there on October 1, 1948.

Phahon Phonphayuhasena (1887–1947). Phahon Phonphayuhasena, son of General Phahon Phonpayuhasena and Jub Bahalayodhin, was born in Bangkok on March 29, 1887. After finishing military education in Demark and Germany, he returned to Thailand in 1913. He became the inspector-general of military education. Phahon was one of the important leaders of the 1932 revolution. He, along with Phibun Songkhram toppled the government of Manopakorn

Nititada, and Phahon became the second prime minister of Thailand. His premiership from June 21, 1933, to December 16, 1938, was marked by struggles between the military and civilian forces for dominance in Thai politics. A military coup under the leadership of Prince Boworadet (1878–1953) was suppressed by Phibun in October. Phanon dissolved the national assembly in September 1938. He did not accept the post of prime minister again. He retired from public life and died of a stroke on February 14, 1947. A highway joining Bangkok and the border of Myanmar in the north is named after him.

Phibun Songkhram (1897–1964). Born into the farmer family of Keed and Sam-Ang Keetasangka in Nonthabui on July 14, 1897, Phibun received his education in Bangkok and at the Fontainebleau Military Academy, France. In Paris, he came into contact with the leaders of *Khana Rasdr* and one of the coup leaders in 1932. He was the army chief and defense minister before becoming prime minister on December 16, 1938. He dominated Thai politics as the premier from 1938 to 1944 and again between 1948 and 1957. An ardent admirer of Nazism and fascism, his concept of nationalism bordered on an extreme xenophobia, chauvinism, irredentism, superiority of Thai race, and personality cult. He allowed the Japanese troops passage through Thailand in the Second World War. Phibun made Thailand an aggressive nation on January 25, 1942, a move that was opposed by many. Close alliance with the United States in the Cold War period and a repressive state apparatus became the hallmark of his second tenure. On September 17, 1957, he was overthrown. Phibun went to Japan as an exile and died on June 11, 1964.

Pridi Phanomyong (1900–1983). The Thai political leader, prime minister, and author was born on May 11, 1900, in the Ayudhya province to a rich Chinese rice merchant and Thai mother. A bright student, he studied in Thailand and France. He organized the Thai Student's Association in France and afterward was mainly instrumental in forming the *Khana Rasdr*. In the governments formed after 1932, he held positions of the Interior, Foreign, and Finance. He was instrumental in setting up the University of Morals and Political Science in 1934, which came to be known as Thammasat University. He was the leader of the Free Thai movement in the Second World War. Pridi was prime minister between March 24 and August 23, 1946, and resigned after the mysterious death of the King Ananda Mahidol. He remained in China until 1970 and moved to Paris until his death on May 2, 1983. *The Impermanence of Society* (1957) and *What Is Philosophy?* were his two major works of Pridi, who had believed in "Democratic Scientific Socialism."

Khuang Apaivongse (1902–1968). The three time Premier of Thailand was born on May 17, 1902, in Battambang, which was a Thai province at the time.

His father, Chao Praya Abhayahubet, was the governor of the Battambang province. Khuang studied engineering at the Ecole Centrale de Lyon in France. He was the Director of the Telegraph department and later joined the Royal Guard. He was one of the free leaders of the Free Thai movement and became prime minister on August 1, 1944. He released political prisoners. In the elite political infighting, he resigned on August 31, 1945. His second term was for three months. Khuang had formed the *Pak Prachathipat* (Democratic Party), which dominated Thai politics many times. He became prime minister for the third time on November 10, 1947, but was forced to resign on April 8, 1948, after a disagreement with the military. He remained in the opposition as leader of the Democratic Party. Khuang died on March 15, 1968.

Queen Rambai Barni (1904–1984). The only wife of King Prajadhipok, Queen Rambai Barni was born on December 20, 1904. When the king abdicated the throne on March 2, 1935, she accompanied him to Britain. The royal couple lived in Surrey. As they had no children, the couple had adopted an infant son from one of Prajadhipok's deceased brothers, who became a fighter pilot in the Royal Air Force. The queen became the leader of the *Seri Thai* (Free Thai) movement of Britain, organized by Thai residents. The important members were the queen's brother Prince Suphasawat Wongsanit and Prince Chula Chakrabongse. She was one of the four women taking up non-military tasks in the Second World War. The queen returned to Thailand in 1949 with the ashes of her dead husband. She died on May 22, 1984.

Kulap Saipradit (1905–1974). Kulap Saipradit, born on March 31, 1905, was a political activist, journalist, and novelist. He was jailed between 1942 and 1944. Kulap was the president of the Thai Newspaper Association in 1944 and 1945. The activities of his Peace Foundation of Thailand invited the wrath of the dictator Phibun. He was imprisoned from 1952 and 1957. He went to China to attend the Afro-Asian Writer's meeting. Apprehensive of a jail term again, he remained in China for rest of his life and died of pleurisy on June 16, 1974. *Manutsayatham* or humanism characterized his novels. Writing under the pen name Siburapha, he wrote *Khang Lang Phap* (*Behind the Painting*, 1936) depicting a tragic love affair between a student and unhappy female Thai aristocrat. It became a classic in Thai literature. His other works were *Luuk Phuu Chai* (*A Real Man*, 1928), *Songkhram Chiwit* (*Life Struggle*, 1931) and *Phajon Barb* (*Facing Sin*, 1934).

Seni Promoj (1905–1997). A great-grandson of Rama II and son of Prince Khamrop and Mom Daeng, Seni was born on May 20, 1905, in the Nakho Sawann province. After finishing his education in Britain, he joined the legal service and later worked in the Foreign Ministry. He was the Thai ambassador in Washington. Seni organized the Free Thai movement in the United States and did not formally deliver the government's declaration of war against the United States. He became prime minister on September 17, 1945, and found that the political atmosphere in Bangkok was not suitable to his temperament. He negotiated hard for avoiding the British protectorate over Thailand. He resigned on January 31, 1946. Seni became the leader of the Democratic Party in 1968. On February 15, 1975, he became the prime minister, leading a three party coalition government. After a month in office, he did not get the vote of confidence and resigned. On April 21, 1976, Seni became the prime minister again, heading a coalition government of four parties. There was a rightist backlash headed by the military, unleashing a reign of terror, which led to the downfall of Seni's government on October 6, 1976. Seni left politics and turned to legal practice. He died on July 28, 1997.

Sarit Thanarat (1909–1963). Son of Major Luang Detanan, Sarit was born in Bangkok on June 16, 1909. He graduated from the military academy of Chula Chom Klao in 1929. An efficient and ambitious army officer, Sarit became commander of the First Division and commander-in-chief. He engineered a nonviolent coup overthrowing the government of Phibun. He proceeded to rule the country with an iron fist after becoming premier on February 9, 1959. He banned opposition parties and newspapers. Constitutional amendments were suspended. Simultaneously he sought to stamp out Thailand's opium trade, end police corruption, and battle organized crime. Bilateral relations between Thailand and the United States were further strengthened by the Rusk–Thanat Agreement of 1962, which represented an American guarantee of Thai security. Sarit supported the rightists in Laos in their fight against the communist-oriented leftist organization Pathet Lao. His economic policies resulted in U.S. and Japanese investment, rise of a new wealthy class due to land speculation, and sustained economic growth of 5 percent per year. He died on December 8, 1963. His legacy was the Thai involvement in the Vietnam War and the establishment of development-oriented technocratic agencies.

Vajiravudh (r.1910–1925). Born on January 1, 1881, to Chulalongkorn and Queen Sri Bajarindra (1864–1919), Vajiravudh (Rama VI) was educated at the Royal Military College, Sandhurst, and Christchurch College, Oxford. The king emphasized three parameters of nationalism: *Chat, Sasana*, and *Phramahakasat* (Nation, Religion, and Monarch). He created a paramilitary organization, Sua *Pa* or Wild Tiger Corps, to protect the throne. The king introduced monogamy and asked women to adopt Western styles of dress. Western medicine became popular because of his efforts. He also ordered the use of the term "Buddhist Era (B.E.)" for the official records in 1912. Vajiravudh ordered the creation of surnames for every Thai family. The Chulalongkorn University was established in March 1917 under his reign. He had a great love for traditional Thai drama and acted in plays as well. The king had some of the works of Shakespeare translated. His notable works were *Phra non Kham Luang* and nationalist articles entitled, *Muang Thai Chong Tun Thoet* (*Wake up all Thais*). He was considered to be an extravagant person. There were rumors and gossip about the king's fondness for men and dislike for the opposite sex. He was married late at the age of 38 to Queen Suvadhana (1905–1985). He died on November 25, 1925.

Kukrit Pramoj (1911–1995). The younger brother of Seni Promoj, Kukrit Promoj was born on April 20, 1911, in Bangkok. Educated in Oxford, he was with the Ministry of Finance. He joined politics and founded the Progressive Party in 1945. It merged with the Democratic Party the following year. In 1946, he became a member of Parliament. A prolific author, translator, journalist, and banker, he founded the newspaper *Siamrath* in 1950. He authored novels including *Four Reigns* (1953), *Many Lives* (1954), and *Red Bamboo* (1961). He emerged as a key figure in politics after the Student Revolution of October 1973. He was the Speaker of the National Assembly in 1973–1974. In 1974, he founded the *Pak Kit Sangkhom* (Social Action Party). He was the prime minister of a coalition government between March 17, 1975, and April 21, 1976. The American troop withdrawal and recognition of China were his major achievements. Right wing militancy was steadily growing in 1976 and Kukrit was helpless in checking violence. He was the recipient of the Fukuoka Asian Culture Prize in 1990. Kukrit died on October 9, 1995.

Thanom Kittikachorn (1912–2004). Born in the Ban Nhong Ploung, Tak province to Amphan and Linchee Kittikachorn on August 11, 1912, Field Marshal Thanom Kittikachorn was a military dictator, ruling Thailand from January 1, 1958, to October 20, 1958, and again between December 9, 1963, and October 14, 1973. He had graduated from the royal military academy of Chula Chom Klao in 1931. His second term witnessed major developments in Thai history. Thailand became more closely aligned with the United States. Relations with China and North Vietnam deteriorated. The Association of Southeast Asian Nations (ASEAN) was established on August 8, 1967. Military rule was imposed in 1971. Thanom, Field Marshall Prapass Charusathiara (1917–2001), and son of Thanom, Narong Kittikachorn, who was also the son-in-law of Prapass, were called the "Three Tyrants." Student unrest and mass demonstrations led to the end of the regime on October 14, 1973. Thanom fled to the United States. The government's decision to honor Thanom in 1999 for his service to the Royal Guard was dropped due to protests. He died on June 16, 2004.

Prem Tinsulanonda (1920–). Son of Luang Winithantakarma and Ord Tinsulanonda, Prem Tinsulanonda was born on August 26, 1920, in the province of Songkhla. He became a career army officer after studying at the Army College and National Defense College. He became commander-in-chief of the Royal Thai Army in 1968. In the 1970s his political career began and he was named a member of Parliament, deputy Interior Minister, and Minister of Defense. He was the prime minister of Thailand from March 3, 1980, to August 4, 1988. His administration, with five successive coalition cabinets, witnessed rapid development of the Thai economy. With support from the king and regional military commanders, Prem was able to crush the rebellion of the Young Turks in 1981 and 1985. He resigned after the 1988 elections, as he was not an elected member of Parliament. Enjoying the confidence of the king, Prem became a member of the Privy Council and backed the coup of September 2006.

Prajadhipok (r. 1925–1935). Born on November 8, 1893, Prajadhipok (Rama VII), the younger brother of Vajiravudh, was educated in Eton, Woolwich Military Academy of Britain and afterward at the Ecole Superieure de Guerre, France. The king was a liberal and intelligent man. He was inclined toward political reforms. The king was aware of the fact the reforms were necessary and an absolute monarch could not last long. He had brought about some notable changes in the country before he was ousted from power in 1932. The expenditure of the royalty was slashed by 40 percent under his rule. The Civil and Commercial Code was promulgated in 1925. He believed in monogamy, having one wife only, Queen Rambai Barni (1904–1984). The king took special care to improve libraries, promote the publication of Buddhist textbooks, and preserve ancient monuments. On December 10, 1932, he signed Thailand's first constitution, ending the rule of absolute monarchy. His relations with the new government were deteriorating and he abdicated on March 2, 1935. His last days were spent in Britain. He died of heart failure on May 30, 1941, in Surrey.

King Bhumibol Adulyadej (1927–). The longest-living monarch of the world, Bhumibol Adulyadej (Rama IX), was born on December 5, 1927, in Cambridge, Massachusetts, to Prince and Princess Mahidol of Songkla. He was educated at Lausanne University. He became the king on June 9, 1946. While he was hospitalized in Lausanne after an accident, Sirikit, the daughter of the Thai ambassador visited him frequently. They got engaged in July 1949 and married in April 1950. The royal couple have one son and three daughters. The king is engaged in the social welfare and economic development of Thailand. He is the most venerated figure in Thailand. At times of national crisis, the king plays an important role in defusing the crisis. The king, who is immensely popular, is a painter, photographer, and author.

Queen Sirikit (1932–). Queen Sirikit, wife of King Bhumibol, was born on August 12, 1932, to Colonel Mangkala Kitiyakara and Bua Kitiyakara. She was educated abroad in countries such as France, Denmark, and Britain, where her father was the Thai ambassador. While studying in Switzerland, she met King Bhumibol. In July 1949, they got engaged in Lausanne and were married in April 1950 at Pathumwan Palace, Thailand. She was the regent, when the king was a monk in 1956. A respected figure, her birthday is observed as the country's official Mother's Day. The queen devotes her time to charitable work and is revered throughout the country. She has been the president of the Thai Red Cross since 1956. The queen promotes Thai culture and because of her initiative the movie *The Legend of Suriyothai* was produced. The royal couple have four children.

Ananda Mahidol (r. 1935–1946). Ananda Mahidol (Rama VIII), grandson of Chulalongkorn and son of Prince Mahidol Adulyadej, was born in Heidelberg on September 30, 1925. He received his education in Switzerland. After the abdication of his uncle Prajadhipok, he was appointed as king in 1935 by the national assembly. As he was a minor studying abroad, the Council of Regency performed the functions of the monarchy in his place. For the first time in its history, Thailand was without a resident monarch. He returned to Thailand in December 1945 but was found shot to death in his bedroom on June 9, 1946, under mysterious circumstances. Pridi Banomyong, the prime minister, was held morally responsible for the act and resigned shortly afterward. Investigations continued for six years without any conclusive findings. Some of the king's bodyguards were executed in 1954. It is generally believed that the king's .45-caliber automatic pistol might have been discharged accidentally.

Surayud Chulanont (1943–). Surayud Chulanont came from a family of military officers and his father was Lieutenant Colonel Phayom Chulanont, who joined the Communist Party of Thailand. After graduating from the Royal Military Academy, Surayud joined the army. He was close to Prem Tinsulanonda. Surayud became commander-in-chief in 2003 and later became a member of the Privy Council. While Premier Thaksin was in New York, commander-in-chief Sonthi Boonyaratkalin staged a coup on September 19, 2006, which was backed by Surayud and Prem. On October 1, Surayud became the prime minister of the interim government. He increased the military budget by 35 percent. There was an allegation against his government for the violation of human rights. The Islamic insurgency escalated in southern Thailand. There were protests against the government of Surayud quite often.

Sonthi Boonyaratkalin (1946–). Born on October 2, 1946, Sonthi Boonyaratkalin graduated from Chula Chom Klao Royal Military Academy in 1969. He was made the commander-in-chief of the Royal Thai army in October 2005, becoming the first Muslim to hold the post. Sonthi was backed by retired commander-in-chief of the Royal Thai army Surayud Chulanont and Prem Tinsulanonda for the coveted post. He had denied that the army would not be involved in a coup. Meanwhile, relations with Premier Thaksin Shinawatra were cooling off. He wanted more power for the army to deal with insurgency in southern Thailand. On September 19, 2006, he led a coup with the support of Surayud and Prem. He became the chairperson of the newly formed Council for Democratic Reform. He dissolved the Parliament, abrogated the constitution, and became prime minister for 11 days before handing over control to Surayud on October 1. There were public protests against the regime of Sonthi, but it was quite safe, as there was no coordinated movement against it. In January 2007 the Constitutional Drafting Council was appointed, with the military having control over the membership. On a referendum held on August 19, 2007, the draft constitution was approved by 58.24 percent of voters.

Sondhi Limthongkul (1947–). Media mogul Sondhi Limthongkul was born in Bangkok to an immigrant family from Hainan. He was educated at the University of California, Los Angeles. Sondhi began to publish a daily newspaper, *Phoojatkarn Rai Wan*, and later set up a publishing house called the Manager Group. He expanded his businesses and by 1996 had assets worth U.S. $600 million. Sondhi was bankrupt for three years after the Asian financial crisis. His companies were investigated for illegal transactions. His *Manager Daily* praised Thaksin initially, but the relations between Sondhi and Thaksin began to deteriorate and the former took leadership in anti-Thaksin campaigns by organizing public rallies and criticizing Thaksin on talk shows. Sondhi was instrumental in establishing the People's Alliance for Democracy (PAD) in February 2006. The Central Committee of PAD had five members: Sondhi, Major General Chamlong Srimuang (1935), university professor Somkiat Pongpaibun, labor leader Somsak Kosaisuuk, and social activist Phiphob Thongchai. Sondhi had also profited a lot—to the tune of U.S. $6 million by 2005. He was planning for a massive rally on September 20, 2006, but Thaksin was removed in a coup the day before. The PAD announced its dissolution on September 21.

Thaksin Shinawatra (1949–). Thaksin Shinawatra was born to a well-known business family of Chiang Mai. He joined the police academy and afterward received a doctoral degree in criminal justice from Sam Houston State University, in the United States. He entered into the telecommunications business, becoming one of the wealthiest people of Asia. He joined politics in 1994, holding different cabinet posts. He founded the *Thai Rak Thai* (Thai loves Thai)

Party, leading it to victory in the 2001 elections. He took office on February 9, 2001. Thaksin began a populist program, becoming an iconic figure in rural Thailand. Poverty levels had gone down remarkably, by half, in a span of five years. The economy also was once again booming. He was praised by the international community for his post-tsunami relief measures of December 2004. Thaksin won a spectacular victory in the 2005 election again. However, the opponents of Thaksin did not take kindly to his aggressive mode of functioning, abuse of power, and alleged corruption. He was removed in a military coup in September 2006. A constitutional tribunal dissolved the *Thai Rak Thai* in May 2007 for election fraud and banned Thaksin from politics for five years. He now lives in Britain with an uncertain political future.

Thirayuth Boonmi (1950–). A political activist and academic, Thirayuth Boonmi was born in 1950 in Nakhon Pathom. He studied engineering at Chulalongkorn University and became the leader of the National Student Center of Thailand (NSCT). On October 6, 1973, he, along with 12 other students, was arrested by the government for sedition as they demanded a new constitution. After the October 14 happenings, the NSCT was divided. Thirayuth had formed the "People for Democracy." He fled to the jungles in Nan after the military coup of October 1976 and joined the Communist Party of Thailand. In 1981, he returned and went to the Netherlands on a fellowship program. He later joined the Faculty of Sociology of Thammasat University. He was vocal in criticizing the policies of the government in his public speeches and writings. Thirayuth has written two books, *Strong Society* and *Turning Point of the Era*.

Maha Vajiralongkorn (1952–). Crown Prince Vajiralongkorn was born on July 28, 1952, to King Bhumibol Adulyadej and Queen Sirikit. A product of the Royal Military College of Duntroon, Australia, the heir apparent took part against communist insurgencies in 1970s in Isan. He is an officer in the Royal Thai army and took part in Thai–Cambodia border skirmishes. Vajiralongkorn participates in royal functions and makes frequent public appearances. He was married to Princess Soamsavali Kitiyakara (1957–) in January 1977 and divorced her in July 1993. The crown prince married again in 1994 to Sucharinee Polpraserth, who later left for Britain. Vajiralongkorn was married a third time in February 2001, to Srirasmi Akharaphongpreecha (1971–), who has no royal background. Known as Mom Srirasmi Mahidol na Ayudhya, she began a campaign for breast-feeding in June 2005 after the birth of a son.

Maha Chakri Sirindhorn (1955–). Born on April 2, 1955, to King Bhumibol and Queen Sirikit, Maha Chakri Sirindhorn was a very bright student, at the top of her class in school and on university examinations. She had obtained a doctoral degree from Srinakharinwirot University in 1986. An accomplished musician and master of many languages, the princess also teaches in the history department of Chula Chom Klao Military Academy. A goodwill ambassador of the UNESCO, she is the recipient of many awards including the Ramon Magsaysay Award for Public Service (1991), the Chinese Language and Culture Friendship Award (2000), and the Indira Gandhi Prize for Peace, Disarmament, and Development (2004). The princess takes an avid interest in the country's developmental projects. Sirindhorn is an admired and beloved figure in Thailand and is often referred to as *Phra Thep* (Princess Angel). Not currently married, she is third in line to the throne.

Abhisit Vejjajiva (1964–). Abhisit Vejjajiva, the current prime minister of Thailand, was born on August 3, 1964, to Dr. Athasit Vejjajiva and Dr. Sodsai Vejjajiva. He is married to Dr. Pimpen Sakuntabhai. Educated in Great Britain, he taught in the Thammasat University and Ramkhamhaeng University. He opted for a career in politics and became the Democrat Party MP from Bangkok 1992. Abhisit rose steadily in the party hierachy and became its leader in 2005. He was the opposition leader twice: from April 2005 to September 2006 and again in between February 2008 and December 2008. He assumed office as premier of Thailand on December 17, 2008. Abhisit had faced opposition from Thaksin's supporters, the Red Shirts. Abhisit is in a difficult situation due to mounting pressure on him to hold the elections.

Glossary of Selected Terms

ACARIYA/AJAHN — teacher

BAHT — basic unit of currency

BODHI — Enlightenment

BORIPHOK NIYOM — consumerism

BOT — hall

BRAH MAHA UPARAJA — vice king

BUNGA MAS — gold leaves

CHAKRAVATIN — the World Emperor as per Hindu–Buddhist cosmology

CHANGWAT — provinces

CHAOPHRAYA — One of the highest nonroyal titles in the traditional ranking system

CHAT — race/nation

CHATPRATHET — nation-state

CHEDI/STUPA — reliquary temple. A domed edifice containing relics of the Buddha

DHAMMA/THAMMA — doctrines of faith, teachings of Buddha regarding righteous conduct

DHAMMARAJA/THAMMARACHA — a king adhering to Buddhist precepts

EKKALAK THAI — Thai identity

FARANG — foreigner, generally a Westerner

ISAN — northeastern region of Thailand

ISUAN — god

JATAKA — a collection of stories from the past life of Lord Buddha

KAH — madam

KALAHOM — head of military affairs

KAM — karma, the law of cause and effect in Buddhism

KAMNAN — village chief

KAMSUAN — a poem dealing with the pathos of departed lovers

KAWII — All different forms and genres of poetry song

KHANA/PAK — party

KHARATCHAKARN — bureaucracy

KHRUNG THEP — city of angels

KHUN KLAHNG — minister of finance

KHUN MUAN — minister of local government

KLONG — canal

KOT MONTIEN BAN — palace law

KRAM — department

KRAPH — sir

LUANG — title of a person in royal employment

MAANA — mother water, denoting a river

MANUTSAYATHAM — humanism

MOKSHA — liberation

MUANG — a political unit

MUAY THAI — Thai kickboxing

NAI — master. Lowest rank in the traditional nobility system

NAROK — Hell

NÍPPHAAN — Nirvana, final enlightenment

NIRAT — a poetic form depicting the travel experience/journey of separated lovers

PHADETKAN — dictatorship

PHATHUNG — tube skirts

PHI — spirits having power over humans

PHRA — honorific title for Buddhist monks

PHRAI — a commoner or serf in the traditional order

PHRAYA/PHAYA — traditional princely title given to viceroys and those of second-highest rank in a bureaucracy

PHUNAM — leader

PRACHACHON — people

PRATHET — country

PRATIVAD — revolution

PUSSA — worship

RACHA — raja, king

RAD NA — rice noodles

RATHA SAPHA — national assembly

RATHA THAMA NOON — constitution

RUAN PHAE — houseboat

SAKDINA — traditional ranking system of nobility

SANGH — community/order of Buddhist monks

SAVAN — paradise

SAWADI — greeting

SEPHA — a type of ballad

SERI THAI — Free Thai movement against the Japanese in Second World War

SIN SAWT — bride money

SUA — tiger

TAI — family of languages spoken in Southeast Asia and south China, including Thai, Lao etc. Also, people speaking the particular language.

TAMBON — district

THERAVADA — Orthodox branch of Buddhism,also known as hinyayan

THEWADA — devata, god, deity

TRAIPIDOK — Tripitaka, "Three Baskets." Canon including sacred texts of Buddhism

VIHARA — monastery

WAT — Buddhist temple

Bibliography

Abuza, Zachary. *Conspiracy of Silence: the Insurgency in Southern Thailand*. Washington, DC: United States Institute of Peace Press, 2009.

———. *Militant Islam in Southeast Asia: Crucible of Terror*. Boulder, CO: Lynne Reinner, 2003.

Akin Rabiphadana. *The Organization of Thai Society in the Early Bangkok Period, 1782–1873*. Ithaca, NY: Cornell University Press, 1969.

Albritton, Robert B. "Thailand in 2005," *Asian Survey* 46, no. 1 (2006): 140–47.

Anderson, Benedict. *The Spectre of Comparisons: Nationalism, Southeast Asia and the World*. London: Verso, 1998.

Asian Development Bank. *Asian Recovery Report 2000*. Manila: Asia Recovery Information Center, 2000.

Aymonier, Etienne. *Khmer Heritage in Thailand*. Bangkok: White Lotus, 1999.

Baker, Chris, and Pasuk Phongpaichit. *A History of Thailand*. Cambridge, UK: Cambridge University Press, 2005.

Ball, Desmond, and David S. Mathieson. *Militia Redux: Or Sor and the Revival of Paramilitarism in Thailand*. Bangkok: White Lotus, 2007.

Bank of Thailand. *Economic Review*. Bangkok: Bank of Thailand, 1997.

———. *Economic Review*. Bangkok: Bank of Thailand, 1999.

Beer, Patrice de. "History and Policy of the Communist Party of Thailand," *Journal of Contemporary Asia* 8, no. 1 (1978): 143–57.

Cady, John F. *Southeast Asia: Its Historical Development*. New Delhi: Tata McGraw-Hill, 1976.

———. *Thailand, Burma, Laos, & Cambodia*. Englewood Cliffs, NJ: Prentice-Hall, 1966.

Chaloemtiarana, Thak. *Thailand: the politics of despotic paternalism*. Chiang Mai: Silworm Books, 2007.

Che Man, W. K. *Muslim Separatism: The Moros of Southern Philippines and the Malays of Southern Thailand*. Singapore: Oxford University Press, 1990.

Coedes, George. *The Indianized States of Southeast Asia*. Honolulu: East–West Center Press, 1968.

Connors, M. K. *Democracy and National Identity in Thailand*. New York: Routledge, 2003.

Corrine Phuangkasem. *Thailand and Seato*. Bangkok: Thai Watana Panich Co, 1973.

Dawee Daweewarn. *Brahmanism in South-East Asia*. New Delhi: Sterling, 1982.

Desai, Santosh N. *Hinduism in Thai Life*. Mumbai: Popular Prakashan, 1994.

Devi, Gauri. *Hindu Deities in Thai Art*. New Delhi: Aditya Prakashan, 1988.

Dhida Saraya. (*Sri*) *Dvaravati: The Initial Phase of Siam's History*. tran Abhassara Charubha. Bangkok: Muang Boran Publishing House, 1999.

Doner, Richard F. *The Politics of Uneven Development: Thailand's Economic Growth in Comparative Perspective*. New York: Cambridge University Press, 2009.

Englehart, Neil A. *Culture and Power in Traditional Siamese Government*. Ithaca, NY: Cornell Southeast Program, 2001.

Falvey, Lindsay. *Thai Agriculture, Golden Cradle of Millennia*. Bangkok: Kasetsart University Press, 2000.

Forbes Andrew D. W., ed. *The Muslims of Thailand*, 2 volumes. Gaya: Centre for South East Asian Studies, 1989.

Funston, N. J. *Divided over Thaksin: Thailand's Coup and Problematic Transition*. Singapore: Institute of Southeast Asian Studies, 2009.

Ghosh, Lipi, ed. *Connectivity and Beyond: Indo-Thai Relations through Ages*. Kolkata: The Asiatic Society, 2009.

Giles Ji Ungpakorn. *A Coup for the Rich: Thailand's Political Crisis*. Bangkok: Workers Democracy Publishing, 2007.

———. *Thailand: Class Struggle in an Era of Economic Crisis*. Bangkok: Workers Democracy Book Club, 1999.

Girling, John. *The Bureaucratic Polity in Modernising Societies: Similarities, Differences, and Prospects in the ASEAN Region*. Singapore: Institute of Southeast Asian Studies, 1981.

———. *Thailand: Society and Politics*. Ithaca, NY: Cornell University Press, 1981.

Glover, Ian, Pornchai Suchitta, and John Villiers, eds. *Early Metallurgy, Trade and Urban Centres in Thailand and Southeast Asia: Thirteen Archaeological Essays*. Bangkok: White Lotus, 1992.

Hall, D. G. E. *A History of South-East Asia*. London: Macmillan, 1968.

Haseman, J. B. *The Thai Resistance Movement during World War II*. Chiang Mai: Silkwork books, 2002.

Hewison, Kevined, ed. *Political Change in Thailand: Democracy and Participation*. London: Routledge, 1997.

Higham, Charles. 1996. *The Bronze Age of Southeast Asia*. Cambridge, UK: Cambridge University Press.

Higham, Charles, and Rachanie Thosarat. *Prehistoric Thailand: From Early Settlement to Sukothai*. London: River Books/Thames & Hudson Ltd., 1998.

Hoare, Timothy D. *Thailand: A Global Studies Handbook*. Santa Barbara, CA: ABC-CLIO, 2004.

Islam, Syed Serajul "The Islamic Independence Movements in Patani of Thailand and Mindanao of the Philippines," *Asian Survey* 38, no. 5 (May 1998): 441–56.

Keyes, Charles F. *Thailand: Buddhist Kingdom as Modern Nation-State*. Boulder, CO: Westview Press Inc., 1987.

Kirsch, A. T. "Complexity in the Thai Religious System: An Interpretation," *Journal of Asian Studies* 36, no. 2 (1977).

Kobkua Suwannathat-Pian. *Kings, Country and Constitutions: Thailand Political Development 1932–2000*. New York: Routledge Curzon, 2004.

Leonowens, Anna. *An English Governess at the Court of Siam*. New York: Roy Publishers, 1954.

Lieberman, Victor. *Strange Parallels: Southeast Asia in Global Context, c. 800–1830*. Vol. 1. Cambridge, UK: Cambridge University Press, 2003.

Lochan, A. "India and Thailand: A Study in Acculturation." Ph.D. diss., University of Delhi, Delhi, 1989.

Mabbet, I. W. "The 'Indianization' of Southeast Asia: Reflections on the Prehistoric Sources," *Journal of Southeast Asian Studies* 8, no. 1 (1977).

Manich, M. L. *History of Laos (Including the History of Lannathai, Chiengmai)*. Bangkok: Chalermnit, 1967.

Marr, David G., and A. C. Milner, eds. *Southeast Asia in the Ninth to Fourteenth Centuries*. Singapore: ANU, 1986.

McCargo, Duncan. *Tearing Apart the Land: Islam and Legitimacy in Southern Thailand*. Ithaca, NY: Cornell University Press, 2008

McCargo, Duncan, and Ukrist Pathmanand. *The Thaksinization of Thailand*. Copenhagen: NIAS Press, 2005.

Mead, Kullada K. *The Rise and Decline of Thai Absolutism*. London: Routledge Curzon, 2004.

Melvin, Neil J. *Conflict in Southern Thailand: Islamism, Violence and the State in the Patani Insurgency.* Solna: Stockholm International Peace Research Institute, 2007.

Mishra, Patit P. *A Contemporary History of Laos.* New Delhi: National Book Organization, 1999.

———. "A Discourse on Indo-Southeast Asian Relations: Prejudices, Problems and Perception," *Presidential Address of Indian History Congress,* 65th Session, Bareilly, December 28–30, 2004, Section, IV (Delhi, 2005–2006), pp. 912–45.

———. *Cultural Rapprochement between India and Southeast Asia.* New Delhi: NBO, 2005.

———. "Contact between Orissa and Southeast Asia in Ancient Times," *The Journal of Orissan History* 1, no. 2 (1980).

———. *Cultural Rapprochement between India and Southeast Asia.* New Delhi: National Book Organization, 2005.

———. "Islam in Southeast Asia: A Case Study of Southern Thailand," *Asian Studies* 5, no. 1 (January–March 1987): 1–9.

———. "Orissan Culture in Transit: Indo-Thai Relations" in S. Pradhan, ed. *Orissan History, Culture, Archaeology.* New Delhi: D. K. Printworld, 1999.

———. "Orissa's Cultural Contribution to Southeast Asia" in P. K. Mishra, ed., *Comprehensive History of Orissa,* Vol. 1, Part 3, New Delhi: Kaveri Books, 1997.

———. "Orissa in Trans-national Migration: A Study of Culture in Transit." D. Litt. thesis, Rabindra Bharati University, Calcutta, 1998.

———. "Hinduism in Thailand," in David Levinson and Karen Christensen, eds., *Encyclopedia of Modern Asia.* New York: Charles Scribner's Sons, 2002, Vol. 2, pp. 526–27.

———. "King Mongkut," in David Levinson and Karen Christensen, eds., *Encyclopedia of Modern Asia.* New York: Charles Scribner's Sons, 2002, Vol, 4, pp. 16–62.

———. "Laos in the Vietnam War: The Politics of Escalation, 1960–1973," *The Journal of Diplomacy and International Relations,* Kuala Lumpur. Volume, 4, 2008.

———. "Phya Thaksin," in David Levinson and Karen Christensen, eds., *Encyclopedia of Modern Asia.* New York: Charles Scribner's Sons, 2002, Vol. 4, p. 521.

———. "Rama Khamheng," in David Levinson and Karen Christensen, eds., *Encyclopedia of Modern Asia.* New York: Charles Scribner's Sons, 2002, Vol. 5, p. 49.

———. "Rama Tibodi I," in David Levinson and Karen Christensen, eds., *Encyclopedia of Modern Asia.* New York: Charles Scribner's Sons, 2002, Vol. 5, p. 49.

———. "Sarit Thanarat," in David Levinson and Karen Christensen, eds., *Encyclopedia of Modern Asia*. New York: Charles Scribner's Sons, 2002, Vol. 5, pp. 132–33.

———. "Thanom Kittikachorn," in David Levinson and Karen Christensen, eds., *Encyclopedia of Modern Asia*. New York: Charles Scribner's Sons, 2002, Vol., 5, p. 472.

———. "Trailok," in David Levinson and Karen Christensen, eds., *Encyclopedia of Modern Asia*. New York: Charles Scribner's Sons, 2002, Vol., 5, p. 525.

———. "Rapprochement between Thai Buddhism and Indian Traditions," *Tai Culture* (Berlin) 4 (1999).

———. "Thailand and the Philippines: A Discourse on Islamization and Insurgency," A. Komsuoglu and Gul. M, ed, *Siyasal Islam in Farkli Yuzleri*, Istanbul: Profil, 2009,

———, and J. Cement. "Thailand: Muslim Rebellion," *Encyclopedia of Conflicts since the Second World War*, Vol. 3. New York: Sharpe, 2007, pp. 664–66.

Moffat, Abbot Low. *Mongkut, the King of Siam*. Ithaca, NY: Cornell University Press, 1961.

Nelson, Michael H., ed. *Thai Politics: Global and Local Perspectives*. Nonthaburi: King Prajadhipok's Institute, 2004.

Ockey, James. "Change and Continuity in the Thai Political Party System," *Asian Survey* 43, no. 4 (2003).

Pansak Vinyaratn. *Facing the Challenge: Economic Policy and Strategy*. Hong Kong: CLSA Books, 2004.

Pasuk Phongpaichit and Chris Baker. *Thailand: Economy and Politics*. 2nd ed. Kuala Lampur: Oxford University Press, 2002.

———. *Thaksin: The Business of Politics in Thailand*. Chiang Mai: Silkworm Books, 2004.

Piriya Krairiksh. *The History of Thai Art*. Bangkok: River Books, 2007.

Praagh, David van. *Thailand's Struggle for Democracy: The Life and Times of M. R. Seni Pramoj*. Teaneck, NJ: Holmes & Meier, 1996.

Promsak Jermsawatdi. *Thai Art with Indian Influences*. New Delhi: Abhinav Publishers, 1979.

Prudhisan Jumbala. *Nation-building and Democratization in Thailand: A Political History*. Bangkok: Chulalongkorn University, 1992.

Reynolds, Craig J. *National Identity and Its Defenders: Thailand Today*. 2nd ed. Chiang Mai: Silkworm Books, 2002.

Rubenstein, Colin, ed. *Islam in Asia. Changing Political Realities*. New Brunswick, NJ: Transaction Publishers, 2001.

Samudavanija. *Chai-Anan. The Thai Young Turks*. Singapore: Institute of Southeast Asian Studies, 1982.

Sardesai, D. R. *Southeast Asia: Past and Present*. 4th ed. New Delhi: Vikas, 1997.

Shalgosky, Charlotte, and Charles Agar. *Thailand*. Hoboken, NJ: Wiley, 2008.

Silpa Bhirasri. *An Appreciation of Sukhothai Art*. Bangkok: Thai Culture, New Series No. 17, 1962.

Somchai Phatharathananunth, "Political Resistance in Isan," *Tai Culture 7*, no. 1 (June 2002): 106–33.

Stock Exchange of Thailand. *Fact Book 1998*. Bangkok: Stock Exchange of Thailand, 1998.

———. *Fact Book 1999*. Bangkok: Stock Exchange of Thailand, 1999.

Syamananda Rong, *A History of Thailand*. Bangkok: Chulalongkorn University and Thai Watana Panich, 1977.

Tarling, Nicholas, ed. *The Cambridge History of Southeast Asia*. Vols. 1 and 2. Cambridge, UK: Cambridge University Press, 1992.

Terwiel, B. J. 2005. *Thailand's Political History: From the Fall of Ayutthaya to Recent Times*. Bangkok: River Books, 2005.

Thongchai Winichakul. *Siam Mapped: A History of the Geo-body of a Nation*. Honolulu: University of Hawaii Press, 1994.

Warr, Peter, ed. *Thailand Beyond the Crisis*. London: Routledge, 2005.

Wattana Sugunnasil, ed. *Dynamic Diversity in Southern Thailand*. Chiang Mai: Silkworm Books, 2005.

Wenk, Klaus. *The Restoration of Thailand under Rama I*. Tucson: University of Arizona press, 1968.

Wood, William A. *A History of Siam, from the Earliest Times to the Year A.D. 1781*. Bangkok: Chalermnit Bookshop, 1959.

Wyatt, David K. *Thailand: A Short History*. 2nd ed., New Haven, CT: Yale University Press, 2004.

Yunanto, S., et al., eds. *Militant Islamic Movements in Indonesia and Southeast Asia*. Jakarta: FES and The RIDEP Institute, 2003.

Index

About the Author

PATIT PABAN MISHRA is Professor of History at Sambalpur University, India, where he specializes in World History with particular reference to South Asian and Southeast Asian History. He obtained his M.A. in History at Delhi University, and his M.Phil. (1974) and Ph.D. (1979) at JNU New Delhi in the Centre for South, Southeast and Central Asian Studies. In 1998 Professor Mishra was awarded the D.Litt. degree from Rabindra Bharati University, Calcutta. He has taught History for 30 years and supervised M.Phil., Ph.D., and D. Litt. scholars. In 2004, he was the President of Indian History Congress (Sect. IV). He is the author of over 35 research articles and has written about 900 articles in more than 65 encyclopedias, all published in the United States. Professor Mishra has an outstanding scholarly reputation as an encyclopedia editor, chairperson/participant of 24 international conferences, three dozen national conferences, visiting professor/fellow, and author or coauthor of numerous books. Currently he is engaged in coediting the *Encyclopedia of the Middle East and South Asia* (ME Sharpe) and *Native Peoples of the World: South Asia and Middle East Tribes* (ME Sharpe).

Other Titles in the Greenwood Histories of the Modern Nations
Frank W. Thackeray and John E. Findling, Series Editors